AF349288

I've Got the Shakes

I've Got the Shakes

Performing Richard Foreman

Shauna Kelly

BLOOMSBURY ACADEMIC

NEW YORK • LONDON • OXFORD • NEW DELHI • SYDNEY

BLOOMSBURY ACADEMIC
Bloomsbury Publishing Inc, 1359 Broadway, 12th Floor, New York, NY 10018, USA
Bloomsbury Publishing Plc, 50 Bedford Square, London, WC1B 3DP, UK
Bloomsbury Publishing Ireland, 29 Earlsfort Terrace, Dublin 2, D02 AY28, Ireland

BLOOMSBURY, BLOOMSBURY ACADEMIC and the Diana logo are
trademarks of Bloomsbury Publishing Plc

First published in the United States of America 2026

For legal purposes the Acknowledgments on p. vii constitute an extension of this
copyright page.

The photographs on pages 7, 15, 106, 117, 182, and 242 are reproduced with
the kind permission of the Fales Library and Special Collections, New York
University, Richard Foreman and Kate Manheim Papers, MSS 152, Box 31-4.

Cover design: Sally Rinehart
Cover image © T. Ryder Smith

Library of Congress Cataloging-in-Publication Data Available

ISBN: HB: 9781493090242
ePDF: 9798765160718
eBook: 9781493090259

Typeset and indexed by Deanta Global, Chennai, India
Printed and bound in the United States of America

For product safety related questions contact productsafety@bloomsbury.com.

To find out more about our authors and books visit www.bloomsbury.com and
sign up for our newsletters.

Dedicated to those who make art to their
own standard of excellence

Contents

Foreword

Jay Sanders

This book is both unlikely and astonishing in the history of modern theater: assembling a multitude of voices—those of the animating gears and bearings, the attention centers, and line deliverers, that is, the actors—who once personified Richard Foreman's enigmatic staged visions. They now speak from outside the intricate, fractured worlds Foreman created for them to inhabit, offering precious insights into their own experiences. In recounting, they reveal remarkable new perspectives typically obscured by the veneer of theatrical presentation and its outward analysis.

Richard Foreman's work was a revolutionary force in the theater. Emerging in the watershed late 1960s milieu of downtown New York's lofts and avant-garde, his stage became a makeshift laboratory for fundamentally reorienting the tenets of subjective experience. His artistic beginnings affiliate him with the starkly minimalist paintings of Frank Stella, the raw sculptural forms of Richard Serra, the repetitive task-like dances of Yvonne Rainer, the static conceptual music of La Monte Young, and the fever dream films of Jack Smith. Like these formidable contemporaries, Foreman sought not to innovate but to dismantle and reconstitute his medium, enacting a radical deconstruction that exhumed and reanimated the essences of theatrical form.

Foreman's work confronted viewers with an acute and dialectical exploration of transcendence built from the lowly impulses that comprise everyday life. His total creative autonomy was evident in his hands-on approach—designing and constructing his own sets and meticulously orchestrating every theatrical element over the course of extensive months-long rehearsals. His manifestos and essays, also dense and diagrammatic, offer deep insights into these artistic investigations. Foreman's philosophy was clear: his works were not simply plays but a form of embodied criticism, dissecting the conditions and needs of their own creation as they staged the materiality of human impulse. As he put it, "The art . . . must be isomorphic with the feeling aroused by itself."[1]

While Foreman's scripts provide the linguistic backbone of his works, they are only fragments of the total experience. His theater was just as much composed of sounds, lights, objects, and, as we see here, the glances and gestures, actions and reactions, entrances and exits of these very people, all precise nodes within reverberating overall structures. The actors, initially untrained and unconventionally deployed, were crucial in bringing Foreman's vision to life; their roles were not mere parts to be played but the living manifestations of Foreman's abstract ideas and dramatic experiments.

Despite Foreman's reputation for treating performers as objects within his art, the reality was far more nuanced. As his muse and most profound collaborator, actor Kate Manheim remarked, she felt more authentically herself in Foreman's plays than in any other context.[2] Over time, Foreman's work evolved to demand a new kind of actor—one who could match the unique requirements of his visionary direction: "I started out disliking actors. I was interested in placing on stage awkward, untrained people, to call attention to raw 'presence' rather than efficient emotional manipulation. If Kate had not appeared, I don't know what would have happened. Because after a number of years, Kate developed her own virtuosity, not exactly that of a normal actor but so intense and special that the interaction with other performers stranded her with no viable collaborators on stage. So I needed actors to be able to continue in the direction that she seemed to be enabling me to go as a director."[3]

Foreman retired from public view in 2013, and, despite the seismic echoes within us who experienced them, his original productions are no longer part of New York's artistic landscape. This illuminating book revives and preserves the essence of his work through the myriad accounts of those who lived within it. Full of revelations of how it all happened, Shauna Kelly's heroic and comprehensive social history provides invaluable insights, as if cracking through the surface of a mirror, to offer new understanding of the human experiences that shaped Foreman's extraordinary artistic world.

May 17th, 2025

Preface
Helen Shaw

There was a time in New York when being confounded by a Richard Foreman production was our annual rite. Starting in January, there would be another Foreman spectacular, perhaps at the Ontological-Hysteric Theater at St. Marks Church in-the-Bowery, or, in the last years—Foreman kept waggishly announcing his retirement and then reneging—at the Public. Each time, I would go in trying to make "sense" of what I saw, and every time the show's baroque superfluity would overwhelm me. Standing in the lobby before the production, I'd watch about a hundred relatively sober-seeming people troop into the auditorium. Afterwards, we'd all reel out, either in ecstatic transcendence or in mental disarray, eyes pinwheeling, our hair clutched into spikes, as if we'd just been released from seven years' imprisonment under the fairy hill.

"Writing," Richard Foreman said in "14 Things I Tell Myself," invokes "the gap, the mis-matching, which is where we *are* as consciousness, and which is a force." His dream-language scripts, his "The Cabinet of Dr. Caligari"-style sets, and his sound designs that rattled our limbic systems, he said, were not illustrations of that force but were rather conduits meant to allow that mysterious force through. ("The staging is such that it *allows* the force to come.") Foreman's fifty years of work did such a good job of letting that sensation of force through—he said the force was "disassociation, consciousness, displacement"—that it powered other movements downstream. Often his collaborators went on to form their own companies, and his shows certainly created a whole field of critics, all of us trying desperately just to describe what we had seen, let alone grasp it.

In the decade since his 2013 retirement—and now in the wake of his death—the subsequent generation of theater-makers hasn't enjoyed that same healthy exposure. (Perhaps inevitably in the aftermath of a pandemic, I have come to think of my annual Foreman adventures as existential booster shots which inoculated me against the conventional, as well as my own mental complacency.) We're now divided into an Ontological Era and a Post-Ontological Era, with thinkers from one period unable to explain themselves to thinkers from the other. What can bridge that gap? Those who saw the work can try to evoke it, but most Foreman scholars and critics are limited to the secondary remove of audience-ship and observation, which means we now rely on our memories of shows seen once or twice or, sometimes, videos. But there does still exist a whole bevy of people who worked most closely with Richard Foreman, whose understanding—is understanding the right word?—came through daily repetition, via experience itself.

What did it feel like to be *in* the Foreman universe? To be one of its constituent planets, obeying its gravity? Actors, technicians, designers, and the staff of the Ontological are experts in Foreman's work in a way totally different from those who watched it only from the bleachers. Often, their knowledge is demystifying and practical, although, threaded through the accounts in Shauna Kelly's book, you will sometimes also hear the heightened, hieratic language of some other world.

Foreman's collaborators and actors are describing here a kind of intense DIY visionary auteurship—Foreman painting the strings himself, his overnight overhauls of a production, the *months* of six-days-a-week rehearsals—which has, for a variety of reasons, vanished. Seeing it remembered in these pages can sometimes be painful, often inspiring. Certainly the Ontological's heyday was in a New York that has swiftly become unrecognizable. (The 1990s were like "Paris in the 1920s," says Bob Cucuzza, wistfully.) But it seems like such a little thing to make the world that kind of paradise again—just put a theater in the middle of a neighborhood where your artists live and where they can gather to make work together. Over Foreman's long, long career, he worked with hundreds of brilliant minds, who were observing him even as they moved like pieces across his odd, fascinating chessboard sets. Here, in a rare collection of thirty-six such voices, we get a sense of their backstage reality, of the challenge, and of the absorption of working with Richard Foreman. It is bizarre, but not unfamiliar. Here is another crucial facet of that much-missed, discombobulating, mysterious plane of existence—the same one that used to collide with ours every January.

May 22, 2025

Part I
Richard Foreman
An Introduction

Foreman 101

Through his unwavering, extraordinary commitment, Richard Foreman impacted the lives of countless artists and audiences and indeed the art of theater itself. Foreman wrote and directed new plays for his own Ontological-Hysteric Theater (OHT) from 1968 to 2013. Foreman's theater-making attracted adventurous audiences and talented collaborators. His theater thrived for half a century in New York City, one of the world's most competitive markets, and beyond. *I've Got the Shakes: Performing Richard Foreman* addresses how this was possible.

Exposure to mainstream theater and schooling ironically did not result in Foreman making traditional theater. Having been born and raised near New York City, Foreman saw professional theater performances throughout his childhood, but seeing what one doesn't like can be as formative as seeing what one does like. He pursued an education in theater at Brown University and the Yale Drama Graduate Program, graduating in 1959 and 1962, respectively. After all this, Foreman sought to make theater by his own standards.

On its own official website, the OHT is described as follows:

The OHT was founded in 1968 by Richard Foreman with the aim of stripping the theater bare of everything but the singular and essential impulse to stage the static tension of interpersonal relations in space. The OHT seeks to produce works that balance a primitive and minimal style with extremely complex and theatrical themes.[1]

But this simple explanation hardly captures what made Foreman's work so revolutionary and influential.

Foreman was among experimental theater artists of the sixties and seventies who, in the words of David Savran, " . . . rejected the commercial theater . . . redefined the performer's responsibilities and altered the traditional relationship between actor and role . . . produced a kind of anti-theater . . . questioned the notion that the *mise en scène* must be subordinate to a previously written script."[2] Foreman devised a distinctive theater world for which he won many prestigious awards.[3]

I've Got the Shakes is a collection of reflections on our[4] theater experiences with Foreman during his long career of making original work. The majority of this book is written memories and oral histories I solicited from thirty-six cast and crew members individually. The contributions from Foreman's closest collaborators detail our experiences working with this iconoclastic man, from the unorthodox casting and the surprises on the first day of rehearsal to the many uncanny challenges we encountered over rehearsal and performance periods of up to nine months at a time.

Commentary by people on the technical side of the house, production staff, and performers comes together in this book. The "Contributors and Interviewees" section provides credits and background for these individuals. Their contributions vary stylistically because many were submitted in written form, but others were derived from interviews I conducted and transcribed: Brendan Regimbal, David Herskovits, Jan Leslie Harding, and Willem Dafoe.

I also conducted four interviews with Foreman between 2015 and 2022 (from ages seventy-eight to eighty-five), face-to-face in his library-like apartment in SoHo, New York. One big takeaway from these conversations was that Foreman is always creating. After working in theater, he started making films and editing them for years at a time. Later he returned to writing by way of revisiting and editing his texts. Even at the age of eighty-seven, just months before his death on January 4, 2025, he was performing behind the microphone, recording recitations of some of his texts for future performances[5].

In our interviews, he philosophized about theater versus filmmaking, his instinctual approach, and how theater has been corrupted. We discussed the ways in which his theater was gritty and what he expected from performers, the legacy of his work, and more. These interviews comprise the first section of this book. I chose some of Foreman's quotes from these interviews to appear in other parts of the book, intertwined with thematic content. In this way, we can hear from the cast, crew, *and* director talking about similar subject matter.

This work is a tribute to the person many consider the father of downtown theater in New York. It is an attempt to capture why we value Foreman's contributions to the theater and our participation in it. By design, it captures the essence but not all the facts, given that we worked with him some time ago. But the experience of working with Foreman was undeniably memorable, so we have no trouble recalling the specifics. Foreman's theater-making process was consistent over the years, so there is some degree of uniformity in our experiences and recollections regardless of when we worked with him. Our distinct personalities and differing opinions make this a versatile tale of the artistry in Richard Foreman's experimental theater.

FOREMAN'S THEATER: AN OBJECTIVE SNAPSHOT

For those who have never seen a Foreman show, I will try to give you a taste of the experience: an "objective snapshot" from the perspective of an audience member watching real-time events unfold (on video) at the beginning of Foreman's 1996–7 theatrical production *Permanent Brain Damage*. Video of the full production is available at the University of Pennsylvania's PennSound and Electronic Poetry Center.[6]

The room is adorned with lanterns, eye charts, and a bed with white sheets. The foot of the stage is lined with 5-foot poles, each topped with a single lightbulb. White paper is strewn across the floor. There is loud chatter heard in voiceover, but it's in a foreign language, or many languages, or if it's English then it's incoherent. There is one man in a white suit, with a shaved head and full beard (let's call him "man").

Four others (let's call them "they") watch him and interact with him. They are dressed in a combination of only black, red, and white. One wears sunglasses, another a tie, and two wear aprons. One fluffs a pillow on a bed for the man and invites him to lay on it. Without much delay, the man runs away, and they chase him off stage right and return upstage center. The man crouches and grips the wall. With neutral facial expressions, they hold mirrors around the man. They hold two white eggs above his head and simultaneously in front of his crotch. One woman stuffs the eggs into the underside of a stuffed duck while holding it up high, facing the audience, over some strings that cross downstage. While facing upstage, the man steps into a body-sized bag, and someone ties it at the top. They open the back zipper, and he steps out. They crack an egg onto a silver serving tray above the man's head. In voiceover, we hear Richard Foreman say:

> Well, maybe there are things to be afraid of after all. He says I can't imagine being anywhere different from where I am right now. And then the other one said you should be ashamed of such a lack of imagination. And then he says what you see is what you get. And the other one says going backwards in time disproves any such belief system. And he says what I believe is certainly nothing I call believable because I'm ravished by all contradictory possibilities.

All the while, action on stage continues. The performers are unfazed by the voiceover, but sometimes their heads snap sharply and simultaneously in response to a piercing ping and flash of light. A knocking noise causes them to each hold their face with one hand. We hear Foreman in voiceover again:

> He said, nothing that ever frightened me turned into anything but a passing fancy. The other one says emotional miscalculation. And he says my mistakes are very productive and so I will ignore all warning signs and signals of disaster, thank you very much.

From left to right: Stephen Jordan, Claude Wampler, Robert Cucuzza, and D.J. Mendel (bottom) in *Permanent Brain Damage*, 1997. Photo by Paula Court.

Foreman's Theater: Subjective Descriptions

Contrary to my brief, mechanical snapshot of what is happening in a given play above, it is nearly impossible to describe the plot because there is no linear storyline of a Foreman show. Below are attempts by theater critics and writers to subjectively or even hermetically interpret the "plots" or concepts of select productions:

Rhoda in Potatoland

> "In *Rhoda in Potatoland*, the title character takes a trip: at times a dream voyage, at times a science fiction odyssey, at times a quest for fame, at times a mythical (and occasionally not so mythical) journey into the past."
>
> —Steven Simmons, *Artforum*[7]

I've Got the Shakes

> "The heroine is Madeline X, a woman who knows she's a teacher but has no idea what she's supposed to teach. Faced with this predicament, she decides to make herself 'available' to whatever presents itself. This plunges her into a paradoxical 'mental dance,' as Foreman's program notes put it, hungering for meaning."
>
> —David Sterritt, *The Christian Science Monitor*[8]

Miss Universal Happiness

> "An expedition into a third world located somewhere in the proximity of Central America. This is a territory that juxtaposes revolution and tourism, either of which can take place at a sidewalk cafe . . . Miss Universal Happiness herself could be anything from a Dragon Lady to a Miss Universe contestant spreading wealth and happiness to those less advantaged."
>
> —Mel Gussow, *The New York Times*[9]

Film Is Evil/Radio Is Good

"This is a cryptographic mystery about the encroachment of visual imagery into the world of sound. The heroic forces of broadcasting are represented by the proprietors of a small, unidentified radio station that suddenly finds itself besieged and undermined by a chorus of threatening cineastes."

—Mel Gussow, *The New York Times*[10]

Symphony of Rats

"Concerns the 'mental unease' of an American President who hears apocalyptic messages from outer space."

—Diane Solway, *The New York Times*[11]

Eddie Goes to Poetry City

"Eddie, a sweet, open-faced naïf, was a poet-Christ figure, wandering through a corrupt metropolis where a series of hardboiled female characters tried to lure him down the slippery, sexy path to wisdom. And yet he remained largely incorruptible."

—Hilton Als, *The New Yorker*[12]

Paradise Hotel

"Mr. Foreman's sex seekers think that life would be dandy if they could only arrive at that hotel, a palace of carnal delights. But they never get there, or if they do, they don't know it. . . . A chorus of hard-bitten, black-clad flapper types dance to the repeated phrase 'I'm happy, you're happy.' A mysterious, exquisite naked woman, her head wrapped in cloth, briefly materializes, though none of the fellows dare touch her. . . . People fall down a lot, commit suicide, come back to life and employ measuring tapes in vain hopes of quantifying the chaos around them."

—Ben Brantley, *The New York Times*[13]

Bad Boy Nietzsche

"The new work focuses on an encounter between the philosopher and a dray horse being beaten—a moment that, according to production notes, sent Nietzsche hurdling into madness."

—Robert Simonson, *Playbill*[14]

King Cowboy Rufus Rules the Universe

"A manic, carnivalesque projection of [George W. Bush's] mental interior . . . an old-world English gentleman who dreams of becoming a 'real American cowboy hero.' [King Cowboy Rufus] is variously described as a man to whom 'words don't come easily,' 'a man who works like a horse and then—sleeps like a big, fat, dirty log,' and 'a man who claims he has no desire to leave his own neighborhood.'"

—Jonathan Kalb, Hot Reviews[15]

The Gods Are Pounding My Head (AKA Lumberjack Messiah)

"At the heart of Foreman's carefully choreographed chaos are the wry Frenchie (T. Ryder Smith) and the melancholy Dutch (Jay Smith), a pair of lumberjacks drifting aimlessly through the shadowy junkyard of civilization. Too weary to wield their axes, our anti-heroes, played with stylistic deliberation, voice Foreman's nausea at the decay of intellectual and artistic complexity."

—Stella Gorlin, *The Village Voice*[16]

Zomboid!

"Henceforth, [Foreman's] work will consist of filmed tableaux in front of which he will position live performers. What intrigues Foreman most, however, seems to be neither what appears onscreen nor what appears onstage, but rather that which exists between the two, in what he chooses to call a 'staging arena' . . . every action onstage becomes tethered inexorably to the forward motion of the filmed images and sound . . . the live actors seem to take a cue from the screen actors, blindfolding and un-blindfolding each other. What Foreman wants to suggest, as his program notes detail, is that humans construct their own consciousness by editing what we let in."

—Les Gutman, CurtainUp[17]

Notes on Interviews and Terminology

I chose to preserve contributors' use of past versus present tense, rather than retroactively going back to rephrase their testimonials even when referencing Foreman before his passing (the work was completed just prior to Richard Foreman's death).

I solicited contributions and conducted interviews primarily between 2018 and 2021. Occasionally, current events such as Covid 19 are referenced, and I chose to retain them. The Ontological-Hysteric Theater is sometimes abbreviated as "the Ontological," "OHT," and even "the Onto," or referred to as "St. Mark's Church," "St. Mark's Church in-the-Bowery," "St. Mark's," or simply "the church." St. Mark's Church in New York's East Village housed the OHT from 1992 to 2009. It is architecturally a church but was converted into three performance spaces, including a black box theater, and had no religious affiliation or funding.

The commentary includes references to Richard Foreman as "Richard," and other times "Foreman," and occasionally "RF." This is not made uniform so that each contributor can maintain their voice and how they address and relate to him. Many contributors mention his wife and renowned lead actress for years, Kate Manheim (already introduced in Jay Sanders's Foreword), sometimes noted as "Kate," "the great Kate," "the sublime Kate," or "Richard's Muse." They lived and worked mainly in New York and Paris and still lived together in New York at the time of Foreman's death. For stage pictures of Kate Manheim, see Foreman's book, *Unbalancing Acts: Foundations for a Theater.*[18]

Organizations mentioned include the Public Theater, which is sometimes abbreviated as "the Public," the Brooklyn Academy of Music (BAM), Performance Space 122 (PS 122), and the National Endowment for the Arts (NEA).

"Dwarf" is a non-speaking role in Foreman's plays. It was common parlance within Foreman's theatrical world at the time and never meant to be derogatory, so I opted to retain it in the few instances in which contributors refer to it.

Often contributors abbreviate the titles of Foreman's plays. For instance, *Gods* refers to *The Gods Are Pounding My Head (AKA Lumberjack Messiah)*. Appendix A lists the full and abbreviated titles with dates.

Interviews with Foreman

Richard stopped making theater in 2013, but he did not stop making himself available to the curious, like myself. I did a series of interviews with Richard several years apart in order to see how his thoughts and reflections about the theater and being an artist changed over time.

2015

SHAUNA KELLY: Why did you open shows at the same time [January] every year?

RICHARD FOREMAN: My theater was not air conditioned so I wanted the plays to be performed at a time when everybody wouldn't be destroyed by the heat. When I was younger and stronger, I used to do more than one [show] a year, not only in my theater but I was doing other, somewhat more commercial plays for other theaters at the same time so I was keeping myself busy. Then it became a little much so I stopped and was only doing my plays.

SHAUNA KELLY: I'd imagined you were producing shows every year to meet the demand of your audiences.

RICHARD FOREMAN: No. Certainly not to fulfill the expectations of any audience or anything like that. Because you know I have always claimed that I made these plays for myself. The audience's reaction was something I couldn't deal with. I mean once the plays would open and I would sit there working the sound or sitting back and watching and I'd be in agony if I saw someone obviously not liking it but that's different you know. I wasn't making any decisions when I made the play that I thought "Oh, this will appeal to the audience." I liked the idea that people were interested in coming but that had nothing to do with the creative process.

SHAUNA KELLY: When I was in your show *King Cowboy Rules the Universe*, I invited agents to see me perform because I think your plays feature actors quite well. One agent jumped at the opportunity to see your show because your shows were a New York institution.

RICHARD FOREMAN: I think my plays, and some people have told me, feature actors quite well. I'm sure other people disagree, but I think that they are often better in my plays than most other things.

SHAUNA KELLY: How and why?

RICHARD FOREMAN: They are just able to be realer in a funny way as the object they are as opposed to straining to be somebody else. Like when I was doing normal classical plays at the Public or someplace, I always felt that people auditioning made a mistake to think, "Okay. I'm auditioning for Hedda Gabler so what would Hedda be like and how can I imitate her?" A couple of times I've had someone come in, audition, and just be themselves—off the wall—"That's Hedda Gabler?" But they were so unique and so fresh that you saw the thing in a totally different way and you cast someone who you never thought you would cast. The person you cast is the person you want to work with. I think actors don't have enough courage to say I'm not going to get most of the parts I audition for anyway so I'm just gonna go in and do what I want to do and then somebody, maybe one day, is going to fall in love and take me. I think that's a much better way to approach it.

From left to right: Brenda Hattingh, Shauna Kelly, and Michelle Diaz in *King Cowboy Rufus Rules the Universe*, 2004. Photo by Paula Court.

SHAUNA KELLY: Sometimes your plays have androgenous or gender-neutral characters. Why is that?

RICHARD FOREMAN: I pay attention to density and a certain kind of ambiguity. The ambiguity would carry over sometimes into gender just as it would be present in the language, music, and other things. Music sometimes makes a scene ambiguous. Say you had a scene (not in one of my plays) but say you had a scene where a man came in with a knife and said, "I'm angry at you and I'm going to kill you," and if there is typical Hollywood music, it makes it more intense. You feel his rage in that music. But let's say when he says that you had an innocent, tinkly tune that sounds like spring as he said, "I'm going to kill you," well, that renders that activity a little more ambiguous. What's really going on there? Gender is like that to a certain extent I suppose. I also like having doubles in the play—two people that sort of seem to be almost the same—twins or something. That too creates a kind of ambiguity and since I'm interested in what the play as a whole is saying, I suppose to have gender ambiguity at times is to say it's all part of this same common discourse. Is a man saying it or a woman?

SHAUNA KELLY: The performers, costumes, lights, set design, soundscape, and film used in performance are all integral and all have equal importance in your work. How do you think about them separately? Has the balance of those elements changed over time?

RICHARD FOREMAN: Of course I would have to think about them separately when I was changing the set or a costume or the lights but it was all controlled by some sort of intuitive feeling of what I wanted the experience to be like. So in that sense, I never thought of them separately really. I knew that the music for instance, which was pretty continual throughout the plays at a very low level, was sort of lifting the scenes—making them have a different color than they might have without that music. And I would always change the music because I thought this [moment on stage] isn't quite specific enough or sharp enough or multi-dimensional enough so we'd change the music for that reason. The same thing with the lights. The lights were sort of like certain kinds of artists might draw on charcoal then smudge some of the lines to get a tonal feeling and the contour and so forth. The lights, especially the lights in [audiences'] eyes were sort of like me smudging certain things in the play also. The rest of it was to increase the complexity, the density, because the density of experience is what I'm after. Most theater I used to go see just wasn't dense enough for me; they were almost like cartoons.

I remember seeing a play when I was quite young. I used to go to the theater all the time in high school and college and I remember going to a specific play where two guys are talking but seem to have no knowledge, feeling, or relationship to the set. They are doing the play *in front of* the set. There is no unity between all of that. I was always concerned with making it all one.

SHAUNA KELLY: My impression is that visitors to New York miss out on opportunities to see downtown theater. Is that because they are not looking hard enough?

RICHARD FOREMAN: I think that no, most people from out of town—why would they want to go see some strange things in some uncomfortable theater? I can't blame them. I think I sense they wouldn't like the work. If I was not in the theater I doubt that I would have done that; I would have seen if there was something interesting on Broadway. Now downtown there is a lot of commercial stuff downtown but I think you are talking about the plays that try to be more experimental and what have you. But no, it doesn't surprise me that people don't get to see that. And the people who come will have been taught about it in school, and there are a few people who are just interested in art. But what percentage of the American people are really interested in what we would call serious, advanced art? No not many.

SHAUNA KELLY: Is that for lack of exposure to it? Because people can't like what they haven't seen.

RICHARD FOREMAN: No because any interesting—especially in the twentieth century—important art is basically saying in one way or the other that the culture is wrong about everything. Now most people don't want to deal with that because if the culture is wrong about anything, well then I have to earn a living, I have to deal with a certain kind of . . . I don't want to be told that everything I believe in is wrong. That is just going to upset me and how am I going to replace that, you know. I don't blame them. Because I do think most things in our culture are wrong. I would do plays every year and I had a good relationship with the NEA where we got more funding than we were supposed to for the size of our theater. Every year I would announce before filling out the applications, "Oh, this year we are going to do a play about supreme beings"; and then we didn't do that play so I'd have to write a letter saying we didn't do *Supreme Beings*, we did *Lumberjack Messiah* and they would say "okay." Most of my plays are not very political but after *King Cowboy Rufus* (about George Bush and his ventures in war) we got a telephone call from the NEA (first time ever) and they talked to my manager Mimi. They said, "we see you didn't do the play you were supposed to do. We heard you did this political play called *King Cowboy Rufus*. How did that happen?" We said, "we changed it." Now we weren't punished but it was almost a veiled threat, like you better not go too far in that direction.

SHAUNA KELLY: Did any of your work ever have elements of persuasion or advocating for something?

RICHARD FOREMAN: I don't think I advocate. I didn't advocate anything in *King Cowboy Rufus*. I didn't openly say I didn't like George Bush—all symbolically really in terms of a myth. But yeah I have had, certainly for most of my life, a leftist political position and that would surface.

SHAUNA KELLY: What level of contentment in your life is due to your opportunity for self-expression and/or artistic expression as a theater director?

RICHARD FOREMAN: Oh well it's hard to answer because I was making theater from the time I was eleven years old. I've been thinking about it a lot these days since I'm getting old and very involved—I edit my films for like, well, this one for two years. I shoot very fast and then edit until I'm convinced gold has hit me. But if I weren't editing every day, I'd feel terrible. I've recently been reading this famous French guy, [André] Malraux, who started out being a novelist and then became a Minister with [former French President Charles] de Gaulle and he was responsible for cleaning out the buildings of Paris but he also wrote in the later parts of his life these books about art and he goes a long way in demonstrating, in saying that artists really are driven not by subjects but just by the need to create and I feel that very strongly. If I can't create every day I feel lost and unhappy. I really do. And that's what sustains me. Without that I think I would deteriorate very fast. And I think most real artists are the same way.

SHAUNA KELLY: If you hadn't processed the world through theater, how else might you have gone about it? Maybe your writing because that is such an integral part of your work?

RICHARD FOREMAN: Possibly. Possibly, or through film which is related in a way or through art. Painting, even though I don't think I was really that good as a painter. I couldn't have been a world class painter, which I would have wanted to have been. But I never looked back.

SHAUNA KELLY: How do you like to spend your time?

RICHARD FOREMAN: My time is spent mostly reading. I'm the kind of person that will get infatuated with a writer or a thinker and that infatuation might last two days, four months, and then it's always like I've had too much chocolate cake—I get sick of it so I pick somebody else. I was thinking the other day, I'm really like a ping pong ball, boom to the other side of the net, kaboom to the other side of the net, Norman Mahler, and I just get bounced back and forth by all these people who momentarily seduce me and yet I know that in the end, that is debilitating also; the only way my mechanism stays attuned and healthy is through creating. You know I've never gone to the gym and I'm suffering from it now I suppose but creating is my gym. If I just read, pretty soon I get flabby, mentally flabby.

SHAUNA KELLY: I think of original plays like Ryan Holsopple and Shannon Sindelar's *Metronoma* which was based on stories by HP Lovecraft. To what extent have you incorporated ideas from literature into your writing and plays?

RICHARD FOREMAN: Oh well it bleeds through but sometimes there are specific echoes yes. I mean a play like *Lava* was very directly influenced by my memory of [Jacques] Derrida, another French thinker. A lot of my work had incorporated my memory of things but became very distorted from different things that I've read but I've never said, "hmmm let me look up so and so and put them down." Certainly, many of them had allusions to different thinkers and writers.

SHAUNA KELLY: Is mindfulness and being present something you achieve in your life?

RICHARD FOREMAN: No. That's why I do the work; because I'm not satisfied. It doesn't happen in my life, but my work is a kind of spiritual discipline where that is more available to me.

SHAUNA KELLY: Our job as performers was to carry out simple and specific direction in an interesting way . . .

RICHARD FOREMAN: Did I tell you to do it in an interesting way?

SHAUNA KELLY: No.

RICHARD FOREMAN: If you have an actor and I say, "Go over and take the book from the bookcase" and you do it in a way I don't think is particularly interesting, I think, okay, what if we add a thud just as she is approaching the bookcase? Then we think, I don't know what she was going to do. That might make it more interesting. Or other things like that—the lights and what other people are doing. Maybe someone is pulling away from you. It's my job to make it more interesting, not really your job as a performer.

SHAUNA KELLY: Looking back over the years, what are some of the highlights for you—be it a particular production, rehearsal, audience? What stands out for you?

RICHARD FOREMAN: No. Nothing stands out. It is a continuous river. I stand back and watch it go by. There are no particular highlights. I guess a highlight was at the start of my career, I went to work in Paris but that was the peripheral glamor. In terms of the work itself, no. At the time of *The Cure* I remember saying to myself I think that is the best thing I've done so far but I was pretty young in those days. It would be sad to look back and say that was a highlight because my god, you're not at that highlight now. Then you'd be trying to recapture that highlight which is a mistake so you shouldn't have a highlight.

SHAUNA KELLY: Why are we not more creative in the theater world about how we advertise shows? It's just here is the general storyline or here is the actor or here is something.

RICHARD FOREMAN: They used to always ask you what's the play about. It used to be so frustrating being asked that question. And I didn't have the courage to say "go see the show and figure it out." [*Laughter*] You've got to say something. I've always thought, whatever publicity you do, it's always going to be vulgar so what the hell. Just embrace the vulgarity and give them what they want.

2017

SHAUNA KELLY: In our last interview you mentioned your belief that artists, including yourself, are driven by the need to create. You need to do it every day or else. I wonder if you could extrapolate on that.

RICHARD FOREMAN: I think I was reading Malraux at the time. I think that's who I was referencing. As time goes on, yes, I still have a need to create but I don't know if I think of it so much as creating. In other words, because I'm working in film and I shoot film very fast—I film in three or four days—then all the work is taking the material and editing it and reediting it and changing it and changing it and changing it. And I don't know if that's creating or not. I mean obviously it is on one level but on another level it's more like polishing and polishing and polishing to see what's really there.

SHAUNA KELLY: You get a base amount of footage to work with and don't reshoot?

RICHARD FOREMAN: Yes. I've always said it's like shooting a riot. You know, I get my footage like somebody who's shooting a riot, like a person who makes a documentary film and has to go home and edit that riot. You know I edit much more because I change all the parameters of the image. I mean, I change everything. Whether what I'm doing is good or bad, I'm doing something different from what other people are doing in this process. But I don't reshoot. I mean I don't reshoot because I don't have the people around. I don't have the equipment. I don't have all the setup. Whether I would . . . I would like to think I wouldn't. Because in a philosophical sense I think that the spiritual task is to take what you've gotten very quickly and then prove to yourself that great stuff is there. And I think it's always hidden away. Now in a sense that's very close to what I was doing when I started making theater. The first couple of years that I started making my own theater I would have all this stuff in my notebooks and I would say okay I'll go from here to here and I won't change what's written and I'll prove that I can direct, as crazy and as useless as this material seems. I'll prove that I can direct that block of material and make it into a successful work of art—you know, having faith that somehow it can emerge from that. And that's sort of akin to what I'm doing now in film.

SHAUNA KELLY: I remember in rehearsal sometimes you'd take out a very poignant moment or a touching moment or something the audience might feel rewarded by and relate to. You might take it out. Is that happening in film?

RICHARD FOREMAN: Yes, if something seems too easy or too cliched—I think audiences often like cliches but yes, I want it to be tough. I want it to be gritty. Will audiences like that or dislike that—I don't know. European films back in the 1960s and 1970s were relatively gritty and that's what I always liked. I have very little urge to get my films out in the world because I don't know who my films are for though I will have to eventually. I know they're for me and I think that's the healthiest way to proceed as an artist if you can. In the theater that's very difficult because there are all the practicalities of having enough money to put on shows. It's not really true in film now with digital media because it's so cheap to film. It really can be for you, in the way that a painter can paint for himself. And that's the history of painting—painters were starving because nobody liked their work and they were doing it for themselves. Very few people are using film in that way. There are still experimental filmmakers but they're generally making short, very abstract films.

SHAUNA KELLY: Are your films abstract?

RICHARD FOREMAN: I don't think my films are abstract because they have variations, recurring performers, and a thematic center.

SHAUNA KELLY: How long ago did you shoot?

RICHARD FOREMAN: The last time I shot was two and a half years ago. I'm reworking a whole block of material, some of which was used in some of the plays as background footage. Like the film I'm finishing now was shot in this loft two summers ago and I'm going to shoot again in October. There are some people, believe it or not, they're sending actors and some technicians from Slovenia to come and work with me because I was supposed to go to Slovenia two years ago and I couldn't go at the last minute. And Sophie [Haviland] went and I tried directing on Skype. It was pretty crazy. But they said, "Oh no. We really want to work with you. So we're going to organize it so we can send people to New York to work with you." So they seem to be coming.

SHAUNA KELLY: Would you talk about the commonalities and differences of how you use actors in the mediums of film and theater?

RICHARD FOREMAN: I use actors in film like I did in theater because I'm still very interested in having them do behavior like, "Okay, lie on the couch and have trouble getting up and then fall down." The vocabulary was the basic grammar of the moves that are available to human beings. And then those moves later on as society and human beings—as people maybe get more civilized, which is maybe a bad thing, the basic moves are then plugged into various aims that you want to achieve. "Okay, you want to get up from the couch so you can go over and turn on the TV." Well, I don't want to go that far. I want to just deal with you getting up from the couch and having problems. If you have an aim, it is not as interesting as the basic grammar of the moves that are available to you.

I'm using the actors in vaguely the same way. Of course, the use of the actors was very much controlled by the set on stage. In film their little limited environment keeps changing. The big difference is in the editing. When I rehearsed in the theater, I was editing to make it work and to make it seem like a cohesive whole of a certain kind. In film I'm not editing to make it work in the same way. I am still trying to make it seem like a realized work of art. When you're working in the theater, it's spinning around the center. In film, it's spinning off and discovers a new place far away. You don't think about where you're going; you discover where you're going. But this is all very amorphous. If you know what you're doing it seems less interesting to me—like painters of the twentieth century—like Picasso saying, "I don't search; I find," and he went out to find.

SHAUNA KELLY: Some people don't think to create because they probably feel they need to have a fully formulated, fully confident idea.

RICHARD FOREMAN: Oh, that's horrible. That's ridiculous. That's ridiculous. Now I understand why that generally pertains to the theater because one of the many corruptions in theater is—especially young people making theater—they have all these committees, these internships, these people looking and saying, "Well you know it was interesting but I think you could have focused more on this character and you could have made it this way" all this stuff, so it's clarified. It's ridiculous. It destroys the art of the theater. Now maybe that's what Sophocles did okay. But that was a different time, in a different environment, for different needs.

SHAUNA KELLY: What is your current film project like?

RICHARD FOREMAN: The film that I'm working on now is *I Slept Myself Awake*.[1] The last line, the guy says (they don't talk very much), "that woke me up." And that's what it is. It's about trying to be awake.

SHAUNA KELLY: Awake to anything in particular?

RICHARD FOREMAN: You don't have to be awake to anything in particular. You are awake to whatever is there. And it's very hard to know what's there because you're seeing through glasses of expectation that have been bred in you through all your conditioning and through all the media and by what everybody around you is saying.

I have been influenced a lot in the last two or three years by Guy Debord. He was a French guy who drank a lot, hung around, did nothing but wrote three or four very important books including one that a lot of people claim was sort of behind May '68 called *The Society of the Spectacle*. He turned out these books and made five films (which I think [Jean-Luc] Godard stole a lot from). I have been thinking a lot about him because he started a little group. It was ten people, at times fifteen people, called the Situationists and they had no use for art really—said art was dead. I think it's true. So the art of the future is situations—just creating situations. Was May '68 a situation? Yes. They didn't really create it but a lot of people in May '68 referenced him and his book *The Society of the Spectacle*.

I feel increasingly problematic about making art, about making films even, because I think the time has passed for art really but I'm not mobile enough to go out and make situations. I don't know. So I don't know what I'm doing.

SHAUNA KELLY: Most people are on their phones instead of sitting and talking to each other. How is the demand and the need for art any different now?

RICHARD FOREMAN: Someone like Debord predicted this sort of society with cell phones and so forth and he said that the media and all these things that you're buying are ways that separate people from each other. That's why he just liked sitting around with his dissolute friends in cafés drinking every day and talking.

SHAUNA KELLY: Are you writing much?

RICHARD FOREMAN: No.

SHAUNA KELLY: Do you miss the writing?

RICHARD FOREMAN: No. I mean I have to read a little bit occasionally for the film but I don't miss the writing at all. I have no idea what I would want to write and indeed I'm looking for text to use in the film all the time that are not my texts.

SHAUNA KELLY: You and I talked about your work as a spiritual discourse in a sense—you're a religious writer. Does that influence your filmmaking? Do you still explore that?

RICHARD FOREMAN: Much less than I used to just because things shift. Was my last film about getting ready for death? Does that make me religious or spiritual? I don't know. Waking up—I think that's spiritual—*I Slept Myself Awake*. I don't worry about defining that anymore because the minute you're defining it you're putting yourself in this box that is not particularly useful.

I was trained by my father, who was a lawyer, to have these big, logical arguments [but instead] I wanted to weaken those things in me because they interfered with pure instinct. I think that to be an artist, which was very important to me in those days, I have to proceed much more by instinct.

SHAUNA KELLY: How would you weaken those things?

RICHARD FOREMAN: Just by remembering that I should try and not let everything be controlled by logic.

2018

SHAUNA KELLY: What film are you working on? What is your editing process like?

RICHARD FOREMAN: We shot in this very spectacular location (a brownstone up in West Harlem, which was a gorgeous place) with actors from Slovenia and three actors from my entourage in New York. I can see the location is dominating the way I use the performers and what I'm trying to extract from the raw material. I just sit down every day and try. . . . See I'm at the stage now where I'm just correcting all the exposures and different things. But I am putting it together scene by scene so I'm not able to see it as a whole yet. People who make normal films know what they want their film to be about and they try to realize that and I don't. I have all this footage and then I try to go through it again and again and again to see what emerges. It takes a while to see what it's about.

SHAUNA KELLY: Would it ever be a fun experiment, just like someone directing your play, to have someone edit your footage just to see how they would use it?

RICHARD FOREMAN: Sure that would be okay. I wouldn't have any objection to somebody doing that if they wanted to. Some people did make films out of the footage I used in my plays when we filmed in other countries. I know one of the girls from Japan made a film that won some sort of prize. And I think in a couple of other countries there were one or two people who made things out of it. We always encouraged them—we told them that we'd be happy to have them do that.

SHAUNA KELLY: Previously, you said, to be an artist you have to proceed by pure instinct, not reasoned arguments like a lawyer would do. Would you expand on that?

RICHARD FOREMAN: Well since I don't have normal narratives, I don't know what it would mean to use logic. I guess back in the days when occasionally I would do a classical piece of theater—it's not really logic; it's kind of an intellectual justification for what is happening or what might happen. You have to be able to justify it emotionally but it's different from logic. Sometimes when you have a very recalcitrant actor who's a problem and wants an explanation of everything then you have to invent logic but I don't even then. I never use logic. But again, I'm not bad at logic because I come from a family of lawyers and we used to have a lot of arguments around the dinner table where I would try to use logic and I remember my father always saying, "No. What you're doing is you're using analogies. And that doesn't count. It has to be pure logic." As an artist you use analogies more than you use logic.

SHAUNA KELLY: It requires more creativity to draw a parallel than it does to construct a logical argument.

RICHARD FOREMAN: Yes. With art you are picking metaphors out of the air that are applicable to the situation you're trying to deal with. It's closer to poetry of course because poetry is built on metaphors and I've always said that my theater, certainly in its structure, was closer to the structure of poetry than the structure of narrative. Narrative that I've never been interested in, never, maybe makes more use of logic. Now if Jack has this kind of character structure would he do this? Is that logical? I would never refer to that. I would never go in that direction.

SHAUNA KELLY: The act of getting off the couch and struggling to do so but never actually getting to the point of turning on the TV (which is why you were getting off the couch) is more interesting to you—the smaller moments and detailed physicality instead of the uninterrupted, fluid action of getting off the couch to go to the TV.

RICHARD FOREMAN: And that is intensified now that I'm working in film because of course in film you're able to capture all these small twitches and so forth and zoom in on them as it were, in the way that you're not quite able to in the theater even though I had techniques in the theater that could do that.

SHAUNA KELLY: Is it a common mistake in narrative theater to not take the time to focus on the interesting moments that don't necessarily move the narrative?

RICHARD FOREMAN: Well that's what I've always rejected about the theater. If you talk about the influence of the [Actors] Studio and [Konstantin] Stanislavski, they're essentially asking the actors to find moments of truth within the narrative. I'm not particularly interested in that approach but there is some great narrative theater.

SHAUNA KELLY: Would you speak about the stylistic trait of repetition?

RICHARD FOREMAN: I've never been very much aware of the repetition. I'm not denying it. People see it—it must be there I guess. But I never think about repetition. That's an exaggeration. I'm sure I do occasionally because repetition is a rhythmic resource—somebody says, "I don't want to go to school. I don't want to go to school. I don't want to go to school." Okay, that's repetition. But it is used also as a rhythmic, musical thing.

Now why did I choose that phrase "I don't want to go to school"? Because that's how I always thought the audience would respond to my plays—like school. I'm putting them in school and so they're all thinking, "I don't want to go to school" because I am teaching them.

SHAUNA KELLY: Your work has been described as disorienting in a way that recalibrates the brain.

RICHARD FOREMAN: There's some work of art, and maybe it depends on what medium you're working in, that is recalibrating in terms of—here I'm making a big wad of clay and I'm throwing it at you. Wow. You get hit by something that is totally disorienting. I never thought of my work that way. I thought of the disorientation coming in the little steps—this step followed by this step. "Oh, how does that step follow that step?" So it was the calibration of minute things rather than a big whop.

SHAUNA KELLY: It gives us a chance instead of just knocking us down.

RICHARD FOREMAN: Some great art does knock you down. It wasn't what I was mostly interested in. I'm trying to think of the last thing that knocked me down. It's been years since I've seen anything. I see a lot of movies—some movies impress me a lot. Have you heard of the dancer Sarah Michelson? For years I'd been hearing about it—somebody said you've really got to go see this, and they dragged me. I saw her for the first time and it was a revelation. But anyway that was the last experience I had of seeing something that was challenging.

SHAUNA KELLY: What are you liking these days?

RICHARD FOREMAN: At the moment I like this French director Bruno Dumont. I think he's pretty good. Just two weeks ago I discovered the films of Kathryn Bigelow. I hadn't really known her films and I think she's a pretty good director. I have become totally enamored with this French writer who won the Nobel Prize years ago: Patrick Modiano. I read his books again and again and again like a child would say, "Oh daddy, read me that story about three bears again."

It's about Paris which I love. And it's like quicksilver. They're easy reads in a way—sort of faintly like detective stories. But everything slips through your fingers. You read it easy to get it and then you can't quite remember, "What was it?" So I go back and read it again. I wonder if he ever saw any of my plays. You know, I did like eight plays in Paris.

SHAUNA KELLY: Why don't we ask him?

RICHARD FOREMAN: I don't want to know. It's embarrassing. What am I going to do, write him a letter saying, "I like your books; did you ever see any of my plays?" If I ever met somebody who knew him, I would ask, do you know if he saw any of my plays? There was a writer I thought was great—Edmond Jabès who was an Egyptian Jew who spent most of his life writing in French in Paris. He's sort of a poet. And somebody told me maybe fifteen years ago that, "Oh yeah, he saw a lot of your plays," and I was floored.

SHAUNA KELLY: The MoMA right now has *The Long Run*, featuring artists with breadth over time: "Innovation in art is often characterized as a singular event; a bolt of lightning strikes once and forever changes what follows. But the long run provides an alternative view by chronicling the continued experimentation of artists long after their breakthrough moments. It suggests that invention results from sustained, critical thinking, persistent observation, and the countless hours in the studio." They go on to say that they're not featuring the artists' best known works but rather what emerged after such a full career. I was trying to think about what that would look like for you. I was imagining stage pictures from your plays and even still frames from your films on exhibition in a museum. Has that ever happened?

RICHARD FOREMAN: Oh, there's been a few little group shows of things but not quite the way you're talking about it now.

SHAUNA KELLY: Was there a point in your career where you were happy but kept experimenting?

RICHARD FOREMAN: Yeah. I did. I mean I never thought of it in terms of a point where I was happy. It was like a continual task. I've got to try to make something that does what I want art to do. And I know that I changed and evolved over the years. As I got older, the work got gentler in a way. It's not for me to say.

SHAUNA KELLY: You got to a point of satisfaction with a system, a practice.

RICHARD FOREMAN: Well obviously I did have a system, a practice, but I always thought you're starting from scratch each time. I mean the first day of rehearsal, for instance, I would always think, "Do I really know how to do this?"

SHAUNA KELLY: Having such a long career in the theater versus having only done it for five or ten years . . . what does that mean to you as an artist?

RICHARD FOREMAN: Nothing. Nothing. It's all gone. It's all gone. I'm convinced that everybody has forgotten about me. They've moved on to other things and that's okay. It's all gone.

SHAUNA KELLY: My project proves otherwise; it details your influence.

RICHARD FOREMAN: I'd like to think that but it is not present in my life here. I don't think, "Oh yeah, I have a lot of influence. Everything's great." No. I tend to think nobody thinks about me anymore.

SHAUNA KELLY: I would beg to differ.

RICHARD FOREMAN: Well people have told me that but I have no way to know. You know. I have no way to know.

SHAUNA KELLY: How would you want to know?

RICHARD FOREMAN: I don't know. I'd want to go online and see thousands of people writing things about it and saying, "Oh,

Richard thank you." [*Laughter*] I don't know. I don't think there is any way.

I mean for a person like me—the only thing one can look forward to is when books come out about you and your work. There are a couple more books coming out so that's good. That means maybe you'll have some presence. Maybe down the road somebody will pick up some of these books and say, "Hey this seems interesting. Maybe I should try doing some of his plays."

SHAUNA KELLY: What books are in the works besides mine?

RICHARD FOREMAN: There's a guy in England who just wrote a book which I think is the best book ever written about me. It's called *Richard Foreman: An American (Partly) in Paris.* It's a good book. I mean, basically it's very laudatory, but it's the only book that talks about the work being difficult and how it gives room to people who have really not liked the work. It's just about my work in Europe and he's writing another book for a series about contemporary directors. And then Stefan Brecht's book is supposed to come out. Those are two more books that I know about.

SHAUNA KELLY: I am so grateful you take the time to do this with me. You could easily just say, "No. I'm too busy" or "I don't feel like it."

RICHARD FOREMAN: I don't think that too many people say things like that. Their ego needs to be stroked as much as possible.

SHAUNA KELLY: Whether it's for the documentaries people have made about you, or D.J. [Mendel] bringing his class here, and whomever else—just thank you for continuing to make yourself available. You've influenced people so much and as I'm reaching out to people, they are happy to have this more focused reason to reflect and to think about you and their time working with you. They miss you. They loved hearing your voice on the audio recording. I'll keep you up to date about how it's all going.

RICHARD FOREMAN: Hopefully I'll be here still for a while.

2022

SHAUNA KELLY: You said on the phone that you're not editing film as of late? You're writing now?

RICHARD FOREMAN: Rewriting old things. Snatches of things I already had. They're texts. Essentially they're poems of a certain sort—not the sort anyone is used to. Letting language do the work on the page and in the head.

SHAUNA KELLY: What's your writing process like?

RICHARD FOREMAN: These days it's not very rigorous. The process of a lazy writer. Returning to old things that I have from notes and making those a little more pithy.

SHAUNA KELLY: Do you write in longhand?

RICHARD FOREMAN: Not anymore. I'm reediting text on the computer.

SHAUNA KELLY: Have you shared the writings with anyone?

RICHARD FOREMAN: Eventually I will. I look at them and they're pretty good. I transitioned from film because as I became more and more immobile, it was not sensible to think of shooting film that would require being physically active.

SHAUNA KELLY: What is going on with your health if you care to answer?

RICHARD FOREMAN: There is nothing spectacular to say. I can't walk. What can I say? I can't easily read books anymore. The contrast of the print and the page has become less. But I can read things online. I'm thinking about cataracts surgery but I don't know if that will help.

SHAUNA KELLY: Are you still watching films nightly?

RICHARD FOREMAN: Yes, but it's just habit. It's often the same films.

SHAUNA KELLY: I know David Herskovits was checking in with you regularly.

RICHARD FOREMAN: There's really only two people I'm in contact with regularly and that's David and Charles Bernstein.

SHAUNA KELLY: This project shows how vast your work was and the plethora of people who worked with you and valued the experience.

RICHARD FOREMAN: It's all in the dim dark past. I can hardly remember, but I think my work was good and brought out interesting things in different people.

SHAUNA KELLY: What keeps you in New York?

RICHARD FOREMAN: Inertia. I would go to Paris but Kate doesn't want to go because all her friends are dead. Though Paris today is not what Paris was when I was a younger man.

SHAUNA KELLY: I saw you did an interview entirely in French once (or many times) and I was impressed with your French.

RICHARD FOREMAN: Oh, I haven't spoken French in a long time.

SHAUNA KELLY: When I read your plays, I think the text is profoundly interesting.

RICHARD FOREMAN: I think the text is good. I assume one day people will pick up on that. I'm not shy about saying that.

SHAUNA KELLY: Do you still think about having attended Broadway shows as a kid?

RICHARD FOREMAN: I remember only one or two shows that had an impact on me. One was [Elia] Kazan's production of Tennessee

Williams's *Camino Real*. I was very shocked later when I read an interview with Kazan who said, "I failed that play because the text was so poetic and I did it so realistic." And I thought that was crazy because that's what made it great because in later years I saw certain productions that were sort of more symbolically oriented and they were awful. What made it great was the combination of the phantasmagorical text with Kazan's very nitty gritty, lower Manhattan sensibility.

When I was young, like in high school and college, I was impressed with Kazan's productions. Which I don't think I would like these days. You know, people thought Kazan was a great director and I guess I did too.

There was always [William] Faulkner's *Requiem for a Nun*, which I saw in what was probably not a great production—I don't know. It was by Tony Richardson and it was written for and starred Ruth Ford who grew up in the south and knew Faulkner. I always thought that was great. I just remember being so thrilled seeing theater lights go down. It takes place in a trial setting, "I judge so and so of the Yoknapatawpha County." Yoknapatawpha, oh wow! I was hearing the term Yoknapatawpha, which I never expected to hear on Broadway. The only place that had been successful was Paris where [Albert] Camus did a production of it. I have no idea what it was like.

SHAUNA KELLY: You have quite the titles for your plays.

RICHARD FOREMAN: Yeah they're good. They're good.

I was really unhappy about *Old-Fashioned Prostitutes (A True Romance)* because I thought it was my best play and for a year or two I had been talking to an actor [about being in my show] who would say, "You know Richard, I'm excited; it's going to be great." And then at the last minute he said, "You know Richard, I can't do your play," I said, "What? Come on, we're friends. Tell me what's the problem." "Well you know I work in a certain way and I need a kind of freedom and I see you control things a lot and I don't think I could work that way." I wasn't going to persuade him. I had always imagined him in the play. [For other reasons once we found a replacement] the rehearsal process was agonizing and I was not able to do a lot of what I would have done in terms of staging it and that was a great disappointment for me because I thought it was my best play.

SHAUNA KELLY: Why was it your best play?

RICHARD FOREMAN: It came from the heart. It was essentially a monologue. Not completely, but it was this main character that was me talking a lot. Was it my best title? I don't know.

SHAUNA KELLY: What are you reading?

RICHARD FOREMAN: I am flabbergasted by what I think is the best book I've ever read. *Death of Virgil* by Hermann Broch. I think that's an amazing book by a very great writer. There are some books that are pretty good but nothing compares to the *Death of Virgil*. It's a long sort of monologue meditating on death. The waves lapping on the shore. There is a section in the middle that is a dialogue where Caesar is trying to persuade Virgil not to abandon his *Aeneid* but to finish it. Because Virgil thinks—sure, I've had it. Caesar persuades him to finish. It's a great scene that I had thought if I found the right actors, could be done as a play someday. But that's just a third of the book. The rest of the book is just this ongoing meditative thing that goes on about what Virgil sees around him as he's approaching death. Broch wrote an easier to read book—*The Guiltless*.

SHAUNA KELLY: What's on the table [a large table in Foreman's loft completely covered with intricate models]?

RICHARD FOREMAN: That's when Kate was making trays a long time ago.

SHAUNA KELLY: There are a lot of great stories about actors coming to meet you in this loft.

RICHARD FOREMAN: Auditions are absurd. Really absurd.

SHAUNA KELLY: Your auditions were not typical. You use actors in such a different way. You believe in people's versatility. You'll hire Colleen Werthman to be your sound technician and then switch her to an assistant and then put her in the cast. Do you miss the ritual of the theater?

RICHARD FOREMAN: Not in the slightest. Performances I hated—having to depend on people coming to the theater. Rehearsal was just trying to get the piece to where I wanted it.

SHAUNA KELLY: You've had a massive impact on people.

RICHARD FOREMAN: Working with me didn't make anyone a star. While I hate normal theater and the whole system [that says the goal of an actor is to become a star], that's my automatic response. It's not that I think that much of movie stars.

SHAUNA KELLY: Better than being a star is they had a precedent for a certain level of—

RICHARD FOREMAN: Oh, there's many things better than being a star. But [you often hear], "Oh, you're in the theater. Are you a star?"

I'm neither bitter, disappointed, or surprised about who responds to my work.

It's exciting for me that you're doing something on me. I hope it gets out there.

SHAUNA KELLY: I will make sure that it does.

RICHARD FOREMAN: [*Laughter*] Okay.

Part II
Performing Richard Foreman

Working with the Ontological-Hysteric Theater

The OHT offered theater experiences distinct from those many of us have had. The theatrical or directing style, lifestyle, and social aspects of working on the shows, Foreman's fame, and the rehearsal vibe are especially memorable.

Foreman was involved in every aspect of the show. His attentiveness to every detail and his total commitment were things that made the OHT exceptional.

DENISE LUCCIONI: From the start, Richard designs every aspect of a production, and carries it through with a very hands-on approach. He's "on deck" the whole time.

JAMES URBANIAK: I suppose it has to do with how personal and hands-on Richard's approach is. I have a fond memory of walking into rehearsal one day and he was on stage painting the string that hung across the set.

JAN LESLIE HARDING: He did all the sound cues and the light cues to the show. He would just do them himself which was great. You come back from a break and the entire set would be striped with Gaff tape. Those were the kind of joys he had in store for us, to keep us going.

Foreman had a unique way of working in that he was solely in charge of, and privy to, the total artistic vision because most of it was in his head. He did not work from a polished script and previously determined list of props; rather, he continuously, instinctually, reworked his ideas for a play during rehearsal.

CHRISTINA CAMPANELLA: It had Richard Foreman at the helm—a seasoned theater-maker and intellectual titan. It cemented my understanding of the practice of making avant-garde art as something that requires the highest degree of patience and discipline. I had great respect for his commitment to the trail of his subconscious mind. It seemed very honest to me. I felt that he was just as honest about even his darkest proclivities as he was about his disinterest in explaining them to anyone. But even within that, the way he worked, things were always in conversation. There was never any question about who was in charge, but he worked out his ideas with us and through us. The process was very interactive, constantly trying things, throwing them out, trying other things.

JOHN COLLINS: The intensity around Richard's philosophical relationship to his work was unique. There was very much a sense that he always knew exactly what he wanted. It was a very singular kind of leadership which is quite different from what you will experience in other experimental theater settings. A lot of downtown New York City theater directors cultivate a kind of creative chaos around their development processes. I count myself among those! But with Richard there was always a kind of quiet intensity where everyone was in a kind of hyper-aware state awaiting what came forth from Richard. Not that he always took himself so seriously, but WE always took him very seriously and waited for his direction. Richard always seemed to have a very clear idea in his head about what he was after and a very particular language for articulating it.

DAMON KIELY: In some ways the OHT was a cult of personality—but in this case, one that was totally justified—he was and is a genius and his way of working meant that everything had to come from him. Also

Richard Foreman (date unknown). Photo by Paula Court.

I think it was the only place that truly embraced the weirdest, most experimental theater in town. It wore confusion as a badge of honor.

KEN NINTZEL: The Ontological was unique in that it was Richard's theater. It was his theater for him to create and present his work, and there was definitely a cult of personality there. Most of the people working/interning for Richard were Foreman super fans and there was a lot of idolatry involved. People wanted to be around him and the rehearsal process. I mean, he's Richard Foreman. And Richard loved this too. On breaks or at lunch, people would ask him all kinds of questions about his work. There were plenty of times he would reminisce about all sorts of people, places, and things.

Being a part of an Ontological show meant we had ample opportunity to enjoy the East Village or SoHo depending on where his shows were performing at the time. The lifestyle was especially charmed if we lived in the area.

ROBERT CUCUZZA: I lived a block from the theater and many of my friends at the Ontological lived within walking distance. It was surrounded by cheap bars and cafés and restaurants, where we'd gather before and after rehearsals and shows. It was community theater, in all of the best ways. Members of the community got together to make art, often for little or no money, just because we had an idea. It had a real "Hey kids, let's put on a show!" feeling, but with an absolute titan of the avant-garde, in his home. It was indescribably fantastic, especially between 1992 and 1998. It felt like Paris in the 1920s—just crackling with creativity and excess and intoxication and fun and competition and controlled chaos. I miss it terribly. Before the money started to pour into New York and rent got out of control, life was very geocentric.

DAVID COTE: Felt like a club, a home, a party place. The social and artistic were intertwined in a really fun way.

JAN LESLIE HARDING: It was like this loose group. Back in the days before the turn of the century, you'd socialize with your cast a lot, I found, especially in downtown theater in New York. You'd always go out for a drink after and you talked about the play and you'd have these pseudo intellectual, drunken conversations with cigarettes and all the good stuff. You were going through this shared experience. Of all the people I had a shared experience with, I think only Henry Stram had done something with Richard before. And David Patrick Kelly had done a few of them before. But otherwise we were all newbies.

As we got older, all these healthy people started acting so we no longer went out after every performance to get drinks. They were like "I have a spin class in the morning" or "I'm eating a salad" and I'm like "what?" It's true. This whole generation has their own identity. I mean I grew up in the eighties where we did every drug and had sex with everybody and we just talked a lot and dug down into deep questions. We were artists and we didn't even know that we were in some manner like a Bohemian or like a beatnik. We didn't have a name or label. We were just these downtown avant-garde theater artists. We were really young and we had a lot of energy. We crossed over into everybody's pieces like Cucaracha and Soho Rep and all those. We would eat, live, breathe, shit, fuck theater. Everything you saw, everything you heard just somehow got fed into your work. You were hearing about everybody else's experience and you all had a common love and you all had a common drive. Nothing was like anything anybody else was doing but [the work] was all new and it was all reaching. It was reaching to have a type of an expression that hadn't been put on stage before. I was especially lucky because of Richard Foreman using me multiple times and Mac Wellman using me dozens of times. I would just eat it up with a spoon. I came home one day and there were scripts all over my apartment and I thought, I have never been happier, riding my bike everywhere, footloose and fancy-free. There was constant, not only intellectual stimulation, but joy. The joy of seeing performances; joy of seeing performances with friends in them who you could tell were thrilled that they were up there. It was great. I just hope that there's some way that . . . I just miss it [while theaters are closed due to Covid-19 precautions] and I hope that it comes back with a vengeance. There's a lot of places that just died. I know there'll be a lot of things cropping up but I miss going to the theater. You know Richard is not going to do another play. You were either there or you weren't and I was lucky enough to be there.

Foreman's shows were devoid of any hype, superficiality, or prohibitively expensive ticket prices. The shows were astoundingly reasonable at $20–$25 a seat. Foreman always wanted to keep the price down so even students could afford the tickets.

MANUEL IGREJAS: There was a purity to it all. Keeping the focus tight and small made the Ontological experience different as a publicist. There was no idea of taking over the world, just to do this show brilliantly and get it the attention it deserved. I always enjoyed working with Richard's crackerjack production teams. We were happy to be in the service of The Maestro.

DENISE LUCCIONI: Working for Ontological-Hysteric in France, I was impressed by their competence, and non-emotional attitude toward the work.

SOPHIA SKILES: It has a sense of purity, poverty, and history to me. It held tight to a sense of experimentation but at the same time it was also one of the most affordable places to see theater. It really insisted on being accessible in that way, especially to young people.

FULYA PEKER: Expanding an experimental vision along with an underground stance for many years, without giving in to the commercialized theater scene, is really hard, and quite rare. Because once underground art gains some visibility, once it appears in *The New York Times* every season, once it has enough economical means, it inevitably rises above ground, it is forced to become a "brand," and its original version gets drastically distorted according to the rules of the common market. Because of that, there are many cultural philistines out there. I am not defending a romantic "suffering artist" view, but I truly respect OHT, for it was able to sustain its artistic integrity for almost fifty years, and with great dignity. Its works never looked over-polished or pretentious to me. It always continued to represent a historical and genuine example of that dusty, rusty, underground feeling. The only theater in New York where I truly experienced that was the OHT.

MARY EWALD: This is a quote in an article that ran in *The New York Times* after the death of Jonas Mekas, in addressing "The Budget Myth": "The low budget is not a purely commercial consideration. It goes with our ethical and aesthetic beliefs, directly connected with the things we want to say, and the way we want to say them."[1] [Our company] New City Theater has always worked in a poor theater vocabulary, both out of necessity and a commitment to using the imagination over using technology.

Over the course of his career, Foreman directed at a variety of venues but none as consistently as the St. Mark's Church or the Performing Garage in SoHo, New York.

DAVID HERSKOVITS: Moving into the St. Mark's church in 1992 was a significant transition in Richard's life. The last show I did for Richard was *The Mind King* and it was the first production he did at St. Mark's. It was a pretty straightforward deal—he had to rent it and he just continued to rent it. At the time, I didn't know that he was going to stay there for the next fifteen years or so until he retired. It felt like just one more place.

My introduction to working with Richard was not at the St. Mark's Church. We worked in larger theaters, even the shows at the La MaMa Annex, now what they call the Ellen Stewart Theater. It's a vast space; it's a great big ballroom of a space. We had good experiences there. One thing I was conscious of when we were in larger spaces was that he was always trying to bring the entire audience into the strange environment and feeling of it all. He would suspend strings way out into the audience of these bigger theaters to try and embrace the whole room.

When we moved into St. Mark's—it's not just that it's a small room—it's that the walls were very present. It's the box of the room that is really what you experience. The Shiva [Susan Stein

Shiva] (the smallest space at the Public Theater)—the set certainly connected to work we'd done in other places but it wasn't the same as the very compressed feeling at St. Mark's. Similarly, for many years, as early as *Angel Face* in 1968, Richard had this loft on Broadway that was an extremely long and narrow space. So the shows were these kinds of cascade of planes receding in space. So much of the staging was about the telescoping of this space with curtains and barriers and framing devices that would sort of recede into this tunnel-like loft that he had on Broadway. This was back in the day when being in SoHo meant something artistically. There were these crazy raw spaces down there.

And certainly the set Richard designed when we were in Houston for the opera was in a big outdoor, summer theater. It was like a bowl; it was an amphitheater that was quite large and a totally different feeling from St. Mark's. In terms of the evolution of his own work, the feeling of St. Mark's was really just the last phase in what had been really quite a long journey.

WILLEM DAFOE: What I really loved about New York when I first got there were the small spaces. The limited audience really kept corruption at a minimum. I just love the fact that Richard was always there and the fact that he made this beautiful little jewel of a theater, you know, a chamber theater. He really was sharing his work in a very clear way. There was no way you couldn't experience his work. Some work, particularly in bigger theater spaces, you don't experience it at all but at least you'd punched your cultural event ticket; you've knocked that off the list. You never had that with Richard. When you went to his plays you were all in because of the close physical proximity. You had no choice. Of course he performed in other, larger spaces but that classic St. Mark's and the Wooster Street stuff before—there was no escaping it. It was always a great event.

PAULA GORDON: Every theater and company has its own personalities and quirks. As far as the physical space of the theater upstairs at St. Mark's, my memory is that the space was small, dark, and soft, especially in comparison with the Performing Garage, which was open, grey, shiny, and full of hard surfaces of wood and metal.

T. RYDER SMITH: The space at St. Mark's was narrow, with a consequent steep rise to the seats, as opposed to the more standard gradual slope of most theaters, and the chairs were close together, which given the fact that the audience was always fully illuminated—the houselights remain on through all of Richard's shows—gave the impression of a literal wall of bodies. The back row was 10 feet above the actors' heads and the front row at the level of their waist, so the wall seemed very close, uncomfortably so. There was a feeling for actors and audience of being trapped, almost trussed, somehow. And the space quickly became hot under the lights, which never dimmed.

RICHARD FOREMAN: *I didn't like St. Mark's because of the pillar. I always had to figure out how to deal with it. The last two plays I did at the Public, I was working in a space I didn't like too much but I tried to deal with that in creative ways.*

My ideal theater is just a small theater like St Mark's because I like everyone to see what I see when I direct it. If you're working in a big theater some of the audience in the back sees a totally different play and no director goes and sits in the back in the balcony. If you're sitting in one of those seats, you're not seeing the play. So my theater would be a small theater. Everybody in front. I remember that's what I used to want.

THERESA BUCHHEISTER: [St. Mark's Church] felt like a home. Maybe because of the hours spent there. Maybe because of the intimacy I experienced with every piece of that space—lofts, dressing room, office, front graveyard, back graveyard, all of the various stairs and doors, the bathrooms, the box office, the risers (above and below), the paint room, the booth . . . all of it. I could draw you the most detailed picture. It holds ghosts and memories that I hope to never lose. I got kicked out of the back graveyard in November 2019 by the very young person running Poetry Project . . . I just wanted to stand back there again after not doing so for five years.

There were many particularities, even climate control.

CHARLOTTA MOHLIN: The temperature was kept extremely low so it was quite uncomfortable at times. But that was part of keeping the performance electric.

DAMON KIELY: Oh well, he always wanted things a certain way. The theater was always hot and the office was always cold. If you ever turned the heat on in the theater he got mad. So I remember feeling like Bob Cratchitt in the back room trying to keep warm next to a space heater as I tried to balance my receipt. Then there'd be the crazy yell—"DAMON"—and I'd scurry out and he'd say, "Uh, I think we need (and he'd trace the air with his fingers a bunch) about fifteen garlands of flowers in red and yellow to hang from the ceiling there, there, and there." "Okay when do you need them?" "Well immediately of course." "Okay Richard!" Then back to my cold office with an intern—to send them out with some cash to go to Canal Street on a crazy errand.

SOPHIA SKILES: [I recall] the feeling of the changing temperature of the fans to almost freezing before the show "to wake up the audience" and the desperate heat of the accumulated lighting instruments by the end curtain.

SHAUNA KELLY: He said he kept the theater cool for rehearsals so no one would fall asleep.

Theater artists could put their many talents to work at the OHT.

BRENDAN REGIMBAL: The working aspect is something that I love about it. I've always cherished that the OHT interns didn't sit in the office and just type up spreadsheets. They were expected to paint, learn to cut wood, drill, help track the blocking, etc. It was almost an apprenticeship. And it's something that I think certainly has fallen out of favor [elsewhere], which is a bit of a shame. [Typically] it's a specific type of apprenticeship where, for instance, you're going to learn to be a carpenter. You're going to summer stock and you're a carpenter intern, whereas at the Ontological everyone does everything. Everybody learns to climb a ladder and focus a light or plug in a light or paint something. Obviously, some people are better at some things than others but there was parity in that you were there to learn and everybody was going to do something to help make this thing that is so complicated. I mean, I had never done any of those things before I came to New York so it was extremely valuable to me. It was just an experience—like sitting at the foot of the master and watching him for four or five months.

THERESA BUCHHEISTER: [When I learned I was going to perform in the show instead of intern] I asked if I could still help build the sets and props, which was baffling to everyone but me, I guess. But I am so glad I did! I met all the interns and technical staff and grew quite close to most of them before we even started rehearsing.

Foreman had his own theater to use for extended rehearsal and performance periods. It allowed director, cast, and crew to experiment with costume, props, lights, sound, space, and set from day one.

KEN NINTZEL: I like to think of the theater as being the most multidisciplinary of the arts. As a place where visuals, sound, music, movement, and dialogue come together to create an entirely new world. *Gesamtkunstwerk.*

I always appreciated the fact that Richard created his productions in the theater space where they were performed and not in a sparse rehearsal room with a taped floor and prop stand-ins. It is quite a luxury to basically be building a piece involving the set, décor, lighting, costume, sound, actors, etc. simultaneously. It was like a giant moving three-dimensional painting that each day Richard would come to the theater and work on a little bit more. It was his living canvas—the place where the work was created and rehearsed, tried new things, restaged scenes, rewrote dialogue, reblocked. . . . Obviously, this is a totally impractical and expensive proposition but also completely brilliant and perfectly natural. I think I was spoiled in many ways by being around Richard and his creative process.

MIKE TAYLOR: What got to me in a big way was having the chance to work on something for a long time, with the tech and design developing alongside the show. The Woosters [the Wooster Group] and the Ridiculous [Theatrical Co.] worked that way too. It makes it possible to do so much more to get there. But that is a luxury for most, including me, since having a performance space with all the tech for the full, very long process of building a show is not a standard option. But it is a great way to work. And I think it's the only way Richard likes to work and the only way he can make the theater that he wants to make.

TRAVIS JUST: The luxury of several months of six-days a week of rehearsal with a fully formed technical situation is something that I doubt I will ever experience in my own work.

JULIANA FRANCIS KELLY: Twelve weeks of rehearsal . . . not "development," full on rehearsal . . . with constantly changing tech. Yikes. Rehearsals were bananas: six-days a week for twelve weeks and enough changes to generate at least twenty plays. They also blasted away one's confidence—RF had a knack for destroying all attempts to feel comfortable inside a play. But that's a great thing. Why make experimental art for $180 a week if it isn't going to force one to grow?

———

RICHARD FOREMAN: *Even though I had a long time, in the back of my head I was always still thinking "I've got to be ready in 14 weeks." Everything in the society in which we live is a commercial product; that's part of the corruption in my opinion; that's part of the evilness of this society. But to not have to get things ready in four weeks means that you don't have to make a lot of the spiritual sacrifices that you have to make when you're going to do it in four weeks. When doing* *it in four weeks, you're looking quickly at what will work. And when you have fourteen weeks you can spend a lot of time on—"It might be interesting to try this. What do you know, it works, even though I thought it was crazy." A lot of the time I used to sit there, week after week seeing all kinds of things and saying, "Oh stupid. Stupid." You don't have that luxury when you're working for four weeks.*

THERESA BUCHHEISTER: We rehearsed forty hours a week for months and then got to do the show five times a week for months. That is not normal! But it is very special. The thing is, Richard used that time and all of those resources with a deep brilliance honed over time and a complete brutality to his own words and ideas.

CHRISTINA CAMPANELLA: The OHT at St. Mark's Church became our home for those six months. It was a full-time job. [It required] research and study to try to understand what came before you and be aware of what your peers were doing. It takes commitment to forge ahead when there really is no clear path.

BRENDAN REGIMBAL: Its length. Its duration. You're all together so long and you all work so many hours so it creates a family, to include the army of interns that I was originally a part of and that I eventually managed.

It's a beautiful thing that he created in those weeks of rehearsal. It probably ruins you from making any sort of semblance of traditional theater because Foreman's work is so long, drawn out, and iterative. And it gives you a sense of a creative freedom and of creative work that is rare in a process that doesn't have that time allotment. It lets ideas, emotions, feelings, and even just constructions take the time they need to develop. I think it's much closer to what a sculptor in their studio can feel than what most theater people get to experience.

Foreman's prestigious work was in demand. We felt like we had clout working with him during his illustrious career.

JAN LESLIE HARDING: When you worked with him you felt like a rockstar. You really felt like there was something more going on than just theater—there was thought. It wasn't just entertainment. It was a thesis on humanity and existence. It was great.

He was pretty high profile. Every single performance at the St. Mark's was sold out because it was such a small house.

JOHN OGLEVEE: It was the first time I'd toured with a known quantity and it was quite nice to be respected simply by being associated with the piece.

FULYA PEKER: The OHT had a loyal audience base as well as devoted patrons. There were some people fervently following Foreman's shows, showing up every season, along with newcomers. With the giant black and white posters appearing around town, people would know that it was the time of the year to witness yet another Richard Foreman "theater machine." From January till May, every night, except Monday, we were performing the shows, and the house was almost always packed. That is not very common with New York experimental theater. Attracting a large audience has always been an issue for many underground venues; so to be able to reach that many people was a privilege.

The people Foreman assembled to work on his shows shared his intellectual curiosity and artistic gravity.

FRANK BOUDREAUX: Everyone involved was very smart. That may sound like a stupid statement. Most artistic teams I have ever encountered feature artists of varying types of brilliance. But in the Ontological, there was just an extra degree of plain-old intellectual sharpness, and that environment was led, naturally, by Richard and his concerns.

The breaks were full of discussion, including, usually, directly with Richard. Everyone involved—actors, the interns (all artists themselves), the designers/design-support, and Richard himself— were intellectuals.

I was particularly bold among our cast, crew, and interns in asking the maestro direct questions, and Richard never failed to engage. It was a heady experience to have that kind of direct access to his thinking and his process.

ROBERT CUCUZZA: I never have and never will work with anyone as intelligent—he could reference anything at any time, from [Michel] Foucault and [Alejandro] Jodorowsky to Mookie Wilson and Howard Stern's *Butt Bongo Fiesta*, and somehow make it all seem accessible and relatable.

Foreman produced high art in a professional and focused setting. He set the bar high for making theater.

STEPHANIE SILVER: The Ontological was very artful. Something about being in an old church maybe, like a 1970s performance art cliche. All we were missing was some nudity.

COLLEEN WETHMANN: There was a sort of optimistic devotion and quietude that I've rarely experienced anywhere else in my life.

KARL FRANKLIN ALLEN: There was a history there but nothing was precious. It was an amazing space to get to learn, be creative, and experiment—all qualities that are sorely missed downtown. It's passing, and now the passing of PS 122 has left a great gouge in the East Village and the performing arts.

JOHN MATTURRI: The atmosphere was much more professional than in most productions I've been involved in. The times were set and things were done much more efficiently.

CHRISTINA CAMPANELLA: We all worked very hard, but no one was over-tasked, meaning there were separate people employed to do all the different jobs (a luxury in downtown theater). Everyone was extremely competent and fully committed to working at a very high level. It was an incredible thing to experience that level of professionalism and experimentation at the same time.

It was on both those fronts that it differed so much from other places I'd worked: it was a more creative environment than what I'd experienced in mainstream commercial theater, and a more respectful, mature, responsible one than I'd experienced in downtown experimental theater.

During rehearsal every cast and crew member were needed almost constantly so everyone shared a sense of responsibility and reward.

BRENDAN REGIMBAL: I think there was a lot of ownership for the people that made the show and that includes actors. There was sacrifice on all sides. Which I know you can find in many theaters but it was certainly very true of that tiny room in a church in which everybody was giving up quite a bit to be there.

CHARLOTTA MOHLIN: You needed to be on stage at all time since we were all part of the picture being painted.

SUSAN LATHAM: You were encouraged—implicitly—to be creative. I don't know if this was true for the performers and crew, but it was true for me.

ETHAN GOULD: I remember a conversation in rehearsal with Foreman involving the angle that French bread should be inserted into a giant human heart framed by an invisible box on wheels and thinking, this is terrifically validating to be having this conversation about putting fake French bread at the right angle into a human heart.

It felt very natural—like, of course I would be spending the day looking for oval frames or constructing geometric shapes out of foam core and gaffer's tape. That's just what a person is supposed to be doing. It's a sort of, "This activity is perfectly natural and right." It was my first experience feeling that and it's been a compass in work settings since then.

Watching Foreman's Theater

DAVID PATRICK KELLY: It was a wonderful, yearly cultural event to be in the audience for Richard's plays.

JAMES URBANIAK: [Being an audience member was an] absolute delight. I think in the first Foreman play I ever saw (*What Did He See?*), one of the characters used the word "enchantment." It was apt.

DAVID COTE: Since I knew Foreman was a big deal and making mind-blowing work, I had to see it firsthand. *Samuel's Major Problems* was my first one. It was like someone was making theater from inside my brain. I was instantly addicted and went nearly every year to see what Richard was cooking up.

SHAUNA KELLY: Foreman's plays were one of the things that made life in New York something to celebrate, indulge in, and be rewarded by. It was an experience in the city that invites you, dares you to go see the next chapter of his artistic pursuits.

DAMON KIELY: [My experiences as an audience member at Foreman's shows were] always the same—engaged in the music and spectacle and philosophy—eventually overloading at some point and typically falling asleep at the one hour mark when my brain couldn't take any more—and then waking up for the exciting conclusion. It's the theater where my mouth gapes open in the best possible way—my brain is engaged in "What is happening?," but not just, "Oh what the hell is this?"—it wants to know and keeps leaning in.

T. RYDER SMITH: I worked up the courage to get tickets to finally see one of Richard's shows. I invited a friend, with whom I was just starting to become romantically involved, to see it with me. We were going to meet at the theater, St. Mark's church. I had done a show there the year prior, when it was still a rental space, just before Richard took it over as the new home of the Ontological-Hysteric Theater, so I knew the entrance was tricky to find. I had given my friend directions and arrived early, to wait in the lobby for them, not knowing that Richard basically manned the theater door for his shows. So as I walked up the last stairs to the second-floor box office there he was, this artist I had read so much and thought so much about, who was acquiring something of a legendary status in the arts world, and certainly in my mind, standing there in shapeless grey clothes. Photographs always made him look glowering or disdainful, and didn't capture what I saw was his actual, unique, energy: shyness, boredom, fury, contempt, curiosity, disappointment, torment, and a mystical kind of gentleness and humility, *simultaneously*. And his voice was remarkable, which I heard for the first time as he greeted a few people entering, deep, thick tones. So I was pretty much petrified, standing there, as if I was auditioning for him somehow, auditioning *as a human being*. But in reality he paid little attention to me as I stood looking out the window of the lobby, hoping to see my friend arrive. The clock moved closer to curtain. This was in the days before cellphones, when you actually had to experience life without instantaneous updates, and wonder where people were. I went out on the street to look for my friend but worried that I might miss them somehow, or lose the tickets entirely, and so went back upstairs.

It was then just a few minutes before the start of the show and I was the only person still in the lobby. Richard came to the door once more and glanced at me with what I worried was a bit of sneer. Here

I was at the fabled Ontological at last, and instead of swanning in and taking my seat with effortless downtown cool, was awkwardly pacing the floor, staring out the window with my forehead in a knot. The box office started to pack up, and the manager told me gently that there was no late seating, once Richard shut the door I wouldn't be able to get in. I said I understood and sighed. The door drifted half-closed. Two minutes to curtain. Richard suddenly emerged, scowling at me as he crossed the lobby to what I realized were the dressing rooms. He was calling the actors to the stage and they all had to pass by me, with bothered glances, as Richard escorted them through the doors into the theater. I felt bad for them to have been "seen" by an audience member offstage, their makeup garish in the fluorescent light, and embarrassed, as if I had somehow blundered backstage in the middle of the show.

I looked out the window at the empty street and, appropriately, the graveyard next to St. Mark's. I wondered what would happen to my budding romance if they showed up and the door was shut, with me having chosen to see the show without them. Perhaps they would innocently try to enter anyway, or knock to be let in. How mortifying that would be! At that very moment, the door flung open and Richard stood there looking at me. Richard Foreman himself. "You have to *choose*," he said slowly. I opened my mouth and squeaked out some random syllable, gesturing to the dark lobby window and street beyond, and Richard, without taking his eyes off me, slowly stepped backwards into the darkness and shut the door with a loud click. I stood in the sudden silence feeling horrible, exposed, discarded. And of course at that moment the downstairs door clanged open and footsteps rushed up the stairs and there was my friend, breathless and happy and utterly charming. I could hear music and actor's voices inside the theater and explained that we were too late for the show. My friend looked distraught and apologized profusely and asked if I was terribly disappointed, was it something I'd really wanted to see? I said um . . . no, it was fine, we could see it another time, but inside myself felt like I had been flung from the temple, refused participation in some unrepeatable mystic rite. I didn't go back to try to see the show later. (And the romance fizzled out a few months after, too.)

I was starting to get more work as an actor, then, often out of town, and missed the next couple of Foreman shows, but when his subsequent play opened I bought just one ticket, and arrived early, rushing past Richard inside the door hoping that he didn't somehow remember me as that fool pacing in the lobby years ago and missing the show. I took a seat in the upper rows so I could see the entire wide space and was completely surprised at the work, at how much denser and starker it was than I had imagined it would be, and also how funny. I thought certain things were hilarious but no one else was laughing. I don't have a loud laugh but still felt odd being the only one to find certain things hilarious. The acting style was abstracted, spare, and the actors seemed severe, removed, as if they disdained the whole idea of "performing." I wasn't sure what to think of them. And then there would be moments of intricately choreographed movement, or bursts of frenzied gestures. It was unlike anything I'd seen, and I had no idea how one would "act" any of that. It all seemed like codes, obscure translations, transmitted messages about something happening elsewhere.

PATRICIA YBARRA: I loved them. They made me laugh harder than almost anything else I see. But, also sometimes, there are moments that make me cry. This was more true of moments I had seen multiple times during a rehearsal. There was a moment in *Maria del Bosco* [which opened in January 2002, just months after the 9/11 attacks] when a plane goes into a window. It was so quick, I am not sure everyone got it, but I still think about it all the time. He did not back down from that, which I thought was brave.

COLLEEN WERTHMANN: I was haunted by them, tickled, intrigued. I liked the chaos of a whispery quiet interlude followed by a cacophonous insanity parade or gross dance. And after I'd seen ten or fifteen, they didn't affect me as deeply as those first ones had, though I enjoyed them all. It made me sad to realize I was becoming sophisticated as a theater person.

FRANK BOUDREAUX: I'm a big fan of what his work did to my head. I would not say that Richard's aesthetic is mine at all—the clutter, the shabbiness, the leftover imagery from the failed nineteenth and early twentieth-century Western myths. However, I was in awe of his "reverberation machines" when he hit it right (*Lumberjack Messiah*, for example). Some of his work was less successful for me, but I would see anything that Richard made, ever. It would always be instructive, searching, and rigorous. In short, I am on board with his artistic *project*.

TRAVIS JUST: I loved his shows. As a composer and musician, I came to them quite late via my wife (writer/director Kara Feely). I found them exciting and utterly unique, shot through with an energy that I have never been able to replace with other theatrical experiences.

ETHAN GOULD: The first time I saw Richard Foreman's work was *King Cowboy Rufus Rules the Universe*, and then I watched reels of his work at Lincoln Center Library. It was pretty galvanizing. I wasn't a stranger to experimental work at that point but didn't know much about how it fit into the contemporary world. The intimacy of the performance and space was something that made the material feel haunting in a way.

JAY SMITH: The first Foreman play I saw was *My Head Was a Sledgehammer* in February of 1994. I was on the waiting list and got in at the last minute, sitting on the stairs. I went back every year thereafter, more than once. The thing that I came to understand about Foreman's world was that nothing in it was gratuitous. Everything was totally heartfelt. If there was violence against, say, a stuffed animal on stage and it elicited chuckles from the audience, I knew that he meant that action as a true expression of real violence. On another director's stage there would have been verisimilitude and lots of stage blood to achieve that effect for viewers. Foreman didn't resort to that kind of stagecraft, but I always felt that the intent was the same. It upset me when that stuffed animal was punched because it was a statement about how badly people behave in real life.

SOPHIA SKILES: I love them. They baffle and surprise me and also make perfect sense.

MARY EWALD: I found them fascinating, and always loved the sense of humor behind them. I also appreciated what sometimes seemed like a menacing sexuality that you can't quite identify. I also loved the poetic quality of his texts. Who else could come up with the name Ontological-Hysteric Theater? It's got to be the greatest name for a theater of all time. I'm not drawn to naturalism, partly because I can see that in movies. I want theater to take me somewhere else that only live bodies in space can take me.

SUSAN LATHAM: The audience member is a performer—we often watch ourselves reflected back from the stage in a piece of plexiglass.

STEPHANIE SILVER: The very last show of his I saw was *Old-Fashioned Prostitutes* at the Public Theater and it was a somewhat awful experience for me. The space was too big and I was sitting too far back. The confrontation was lost in the sea of audience. And I missed the intimacy and seeing the details of the stage. It was, however, cool to see the set on a bigger scale and it did remind me of watching *Penguin Touquet* in the NYPL [New York Public Library] and how oddly exhilarating that was.

JOHN OGLEVEE: I've always found as a Foreman audience member, I tended to get frustrated when I heard someone "laughing knowingly." On the one hand, everyone should be free to react as they so please, but there was as certain amount of "Oh, I got that reference" that I found to be disingenuous. It was a place to be seen and it was certainly a "scene" as well. The irony, I believe, is that as opposed to the "cool kids" over on Wooster Street, Richard cared very little about the cool factor. The "scene" was less high-end cocktails and coke and more PBR and weed.

CHARLOTTA MOHLIN: I had never seen anything like it. It was ninety minutes of constant impressions! Both visual and auditory. I left not knowing what to think but loving every second of it.

CHRISTINA CAMPANELLA: Richard never wants the audience to be lulled into a dream like they are peering through the darkness at delicate fiction unfolding behind the fourth wall . . . no. He wants you to stay awake and be aware that you are experiencing something, even if you don't know what it is. Especially then. Hence the Dada-esque theatrics (flashes of light popping in your eyes, strange props appearing and disappearing, loud, disjointed sounds crashing in, etc.). I liked this.

KEVIN HURLEY: Glee . . . humor . . . amazement. [The shows gave me the sense that] something was going on that I was unfamiliar with.

T. RYDER SMITH: I regularly saw Richard's plays and was particularly impressed by *Paradise Hotel*, and Tony Torn's performance in it. I actually waited in the lobby afterwards to introduce myself to him and tell him how remarkable I thought he was. He was very gracious; a bit amused at my enthusiasm, maybe, but kind and sweet. He was wearing a cowboy hat, I remember. That performance remains a touchstone for me, and I think Tony is one of the great actors alive today, truly exceptional.

DAVID COTE: Mesmerized, amused, baffled, bored, thrilled. Certain lines lodge themselves in your memory and you repeat them to yourselves or savor them with fellow Ontological veterans like your favorite lines from movies. One of mine is D.J. Mendel stomping around at the end of *Permanent Brain Damage* while the basso profundo voiceover keeps repeating, "No magic. That's the magic. No magic. That's the magic."

DAVID HERSKOVITS: I saw *Symphony of Rats* at the Performing Garage on Wooster Street. It starred Ron Vawter who has now passed away and who I was very lucky to have seen in it. He was an amazing actor. I watched it and introduced myself to Richard. I loved that show. It was very challenging and exciting in a good way and I remember thinking about being inside the brain of the show—the sort of weird, idiosyncratic sensibility of it. I remember being fascinated by that.

The people who saw Kate Manheim in *Rhoda in Potatoland* talk like it was a massive cultural event for the ages in New York theater.

CHARLES BERNSTEIN: *Rhoda in Potatoland* was my first Foreman show; I went to every Foreman work in New York after that and loved them all—though missed the sublime Kate Manheim after she stopped performing. While Foreman's work is "difficult," in the sense of its aversion of conformity and nonlinear structure, its jolts are ravishing. It's not disorienting but *reorienting*, opening to new possibilities of experience.

MANUEL IGREJAS: I saw all the shows several times and each time I found something new in them. And I could never predict what would happen next. It was being scooped up in a benevolent cyclone and dropped some place . . . more interesting.

SUSAN LATHAM: I always loved Richard's shows. They were intellectually stimulating and made me feel alive. I would often go to a show multiple times, to see what I missed the first time around, to see how the show changed as the actors grew into their roles over the course of a run, to re-watch a favorite scene or rehearse a favorite piece of dialogue.

DENISE LUCCIONI: I feel I was able to follow his work, like you follow the life story of a close cousin, and see it develop and change. His work has grown familiar, just as you revisit an attic in your home or in your memory and you are confronted with your past, your dreams, your life. . . . Whenever I had a chance, I would go see his new work, in New York often, but also in Rotterdam, or Lille, or . . .

If I try to imagine myself sitting and watching a performance, I guess it feels like getting a taste of what I already know, what I've come to see, or taste, and taking delight in it (like my favorite Dutch salted licorice!); I know it, I recognize it, YET I am surprised again and again, by the pace, the layers of language (ah the sound and the rhythm!!!), by how far he allows his imagination to push, the richness of every inch of set, the sequence of myriad cut-outs embodied by the actors, like faux robots developing into utmost expressions of life and aliveness and realness, I guess, stemming out of deliberate artificiality.

ROBERT CUCUZZA: Going to see his shows was like Old Home Week. It was the most fucked-up family reunion—like taking a spaceship to an entire alien galaxy that you once inhabited. You saw old friends up there on stage, as well as new additions to the family. You saw old props that had been recycled. Sometimes patches of dialogue or sequences that had been cut from shows you were in. There was a "coat scene" that he tried to work into several shows I was in. I think it finally ended up in one.

One of the most remarkable things about seeing his shows after being in them was how impossibly similar they were in structure and timing. Traditional movies and plays have a clear act structure, which if you understand, you can see as plain as day in everything you watch. You can see the shifts between Acts 1 and 2 and Acts 2 and 3. Richard's shows had no traditional story structure; in fact much of his discipline was hammering against that. What I started to see, though, was that he had developed, no doubt unintentionally, his own narrative structure. Each show was about the same length—seventy to eighty minutes. They would have these flare-ups of action and sound that happened at about the same point in each show, followed by a darkening and slowdown. At around the sixty-minute mark there were a series of false endings where more shit than ever would be happening on the stage and a *deus ex machina*—some new character, action, element, sound that came in, not to wrap up but to kick the whole thing into some new plane. Structurally, it served the same placeholder as the "11:00 number" in musical theater, where the main character crystallizes themselves onstage, alone. Then, after another slowdown, the whole thing would ramp up into ecstatic chaos—with ear-splitting sound, the entire cast on stage often yelling or chanting, crazy repetitive choreography, and the lights would fade as the fevered action continued into the darkness.

And I remember walking out of the theater each time having been moved in ways that I didn't expect and having no idea how he did it. It was like he was able to get into the marrow of the theatrical experience. Nothing you saw made any logical "sense," but it made *a* sense within itself. People who saw me in his shows would sometimes ask if we were just making it up as we went along. I would just laugh. It was as meticulously structured as the most crowd-pleasing, irrefutably-entertaining Broadway musical. The narrative structure that he found carried an emotional impact—somehow. I'm sure that he couldn't even tell you what he did or how he did it. It just always ended up there. It was also apparent in the way that he executed comedy in shows. In rehearsal, he'd create these hilarious, impeccably timed moments of physical comedy (which he'd often jump up on stage to demonstrate, and perform brilliantly). They'd get a huge laugh from everyone in the room, every time. Then, over time, he'd bash the shit out of them, leaving the structure and timing, but messing with the content. Then in performance these unlikely illogical moments that made no seeming sense whatsoever would get scattered laughs from the audience (sometimes and sometimes not). People were responding to the structure of the comedy—setup, beat, punchline—but with the actual jokes replaced with something else.

He really was as much of an unabashed theatrical showman as David Merrick or Flo Zeigfeld. I think he wanted the same effect as them—this theatrical euphoria that sends the audience out of the theater having had a transportive experience. It used to be that the sign of a successful musical was if the audience left the theater whistling the tunes from the show. With Richard, I think he wanted to leave the audience with their heads buzzing like a hornet's nest. At least that was my experience. I'll never forget the full-on theatrical assault at the end of *My Head was a Sledgehammer*: Thomas Jay Ryan, center stage wearing a feathered headdress and standing on *cothornos*—foot-tall wooden platform shoes—swinging a long staff and screaming "ONE MORE TIME!!" until his voice was hoarse, all while an insane pounding loop of music got louder and louder, the lights blazing right into your eyes. It was as hard to watch as it was to look away, and I think that's exactly what Richard wanted. He always rejected when people referred to him as a "master." But he was a master at using the tools of theater to elicit a reaction from the audience—positive, negative, or otherwise. He shook you the fuck up. I'd walk out of the theater sometimes just reeling—mentally, physically, emotionally, psychologically. And other times I didn't.

———

RICHARD FOREMAN: *Normally you [the spectator] expect the move goes from A to B and I've always been interested in going from A to minus B or B off to the side. I've never been interested in going from A to Z. It is just sliding off to the side. It's like a slippery surface rather than absurdist theater which goes from A to X or from A to number seven. I think you've got to keep the next step close enough to something logical so it's close enough to something anticipated, so that it's distance from that is what is shocking. It's being slightly off the mark. Always slightly off the mark.*

You know all my life even from very near the beginning I had ambivalent feelings about the theater. I didn't like having people there responding. The whole idea of the theater appealing to a group of people, and they have a group response—aw! I found that always very problematic, very disgusting. So I wanted to make something dense like a sparkling crystal for myself. And then I just said, "Anybody else have any use for this?" I never thought that you could have the aim of achieving something or being able to make something and put it into the audience's head. No. This thing I made is over here, if you want, see if you can make use of it.

I used to go to the theater as a teenager. I'd go to see all the Broadway plays with my friend and I'd walk out of the theater saying, "John, if that's what they like, I can't do that. It's terrible; it's hopeless. I can't do that because it's so repulsive to me." So I thought, you know maybe it was impossible. And the thing that gave me the courage to do it was meeting Jonas Mekas and the people around him and seeing the early underground cinema where all these people were taking their little home movie cameras and making films that

I just thought were breathtaking. And I thought, could I do that in the theater?

JULIANA FRANCIS KELLY: I absolutely hated the first Richard Foreman play I ever saw. I felt completely shut out from it, and I had always believed that even if an audience member isn't schooled in all the philosophies in a show—that there is a way in for everyone. . . . I was FURIOUS about this play. I hated seeing myself reflected in the plexiglass. I hated the other audience members, who seemed to me like a bunch of pretentious jerks pretending to understand what was going on.

I complained about this show to Reza Abdoh, and he listened to me for a while, and then said, "Well, Foreman creates a world that is complete." That stopped my rant. What did Reza mean? What is a "complete" play? I started trying to think about the play through that idea, and I felt less angry . . . enough to go see the next play Richard Foreman did, *Benita Canova*.

Again, I felt excluded by the philosophies . . . but there was a moment in the play, in which Benita was violated somehow by an actor in a gorilla costume, and then she had to get up and continue as if that hadn't happened. I didn't understand that moment, but suddenly tears started rolling down my face . . . not for her violation, but for the fact that she had to continue. And from then on—I felt a kind of reverence for Richard Foreman's work, because I think it is a rare and important aspect of theater to allow an idea or a SOMETHING—some MYSTERY—to flower in a heart or mind for which that mysterious idea is completely foreign.

KARL FRANKLIN ALLEN: Initially I was confused and annoyed. Over the years seeing the annual shows became a great ritual, one that I miss, and the understanding of the larger visual vocabulary he worked with was a great lesson in dedication and style.

JOHN OGLEVEE: I was mostly baffled by the early work of his that I saw in my twenties in the early 1990s but I could tell he wasn't trying "to be cool" or trying to be deep. I was struck by what I saw as an intimate display of the inner workings of the mind. Richard's work resonated with me on some kind of subconscious level.

JOHN MATTURRI: My first exposure to Foreman was the rather light entertainment of *Dr. Selavey's Magic Theater* and aside from *Paint(t)*, I did not really experience his work as an audience member until I stopped performing in the plays. But in general I enjoyed them, and enjoyed being confounded by both the complexity of the plays and their spectacle and continued attending the plays yearly until Foreman stopped giving them. But in a sense, I feel, night after night for months on end as a performer, and year after year as an audience member, I may have become something of an ideal audience member as the characteristic rhythms and textures of buzzers, lights, music, etc. became as comfortable as an easy chair, which is somewhat ironic for a theater that trades off a degree of audience discomfort.

WILLEM DAFOE: When I see his shows I'm like a perfect audience for him. When I watch his shows, not only do I get the pleasure of seeing funny things, seeing colorful things, seeing beautiful design, and hearing interesting fragments of thought—sometimes being titillated by nudity or sexual innuendo—all these things are in his shows often and I feel he taps into what I loved about the theater—that it's not at all like life. It's an invention and it's an inquiry. When I'm sitting in his theater I never tried to make connections. I never tried to understand anything and that's a real liberation. Anytime you can stop thinking but be totally engaged is a beautiful place to be and I appreciate it so much. So all of his darkness and all of his intellectual questioning and his kind of restlessness is all worth it both as an audience member and when we're working on a piece [as a performer]. It pays off in the respect that I like this place where I am when I'm watching his plays. I miss seeing his shows.

KEN NINTZEL: I had only seen one of Richard's shows, *My Head was a Sledgehammer*, before I went to work for him. I don't remember any of it except for the classic Foremanesque things like lights shining in your eyes and loud and abrupt sounds. I wasn't a Richard Foreman super fan like most of the people who worked for him. After seeing the show I was temporarily overwhelmed and intrigued by the bizarre nature of Richard's work but it didn't necessarily make me want to see another.

As a stage manager watching the shows night after night I did begin to create a narrative that linked all the actions and dialogue that occurred into some kind of convoluted story. But having stage managed the rehearsals my head was already chock full of what had gone on to get to this point. *Underpainting* is a concept that Richard had often spoken about in relation to his work—that all the activity and dialogue that had come before, and was subsequently cut, is still all there under the surface. Whether you see it or not, it still creates a resonance, which was another concept Richard also referred to—a vibration. After my stage management years I did go see Richard's plays. I think my favorites were when he began to incorporate video into them. To me it really brought out the ritualistic aspects of his work.

BRENDAN REGIMBAL: Once you've created [a Foreman show] you can't go back to unseeing what goes into the making of it. You appreciate it on a different level when you don't know what it is; it's very destabilizing. Once you've worked with Foreman you know some of the dark secrets. You appreciate it for different things because you can see the depths. But it's hard to go back to that feeling of being lost at sea which is something I think he's trying to achieve.

JAN LESLIE HARDING: I'd never seen a piece by Richard before I worked with him. By the time I saw his stuff I think the fact that I had experienced working with him and gotten to know him, I was probably enjoying the piece triple because it would be reminiscent of previous work. He has a certain style. I saw him do a piece at the Public that he directed but didn't write, but his stamp was still on it so you just love it.

JOHN COLLINS: I find his shows exhilarating. I also think they are cut through with a wicked sense of humor and absurdity; two traits that will tend to make me love a show. When I first saw his work in *Eddie Goes to Poetry City*, I was a bit perplexed but I still found something utterly revelatory and joyful about it. That was the only show of his I saw before working on one, so after that I had a kind of insider perspective and had a better sense of what to expect.

DAVID HERSKOVITS: After I'd worked on many shows with Richard, I realized my connection to the shows as an audience member had become very personal and my reaction was not typical. I loved watching things being reworked from other shows that were coming back or being developed or it was a departure from earlier work in an interesting way.

FULYA PEKER: As an audience member, I remember getting bored by my own mind trying to figure things out. The constant failure of reasoning, that non-victorious comprehension, helped me let go. I became childlike. . . . Then the whole show began pouring over me. It was not answering my questions; rather, it was questioning my answers. It was allowing the stream of consciousness to function on its own. It was as if I was witnessing someone else's dream while simultaneously observing myself doing that. Foreman patches together theatrical elements in such ways that his shows alter the audience's sense of the real, the symbolic, and the imaginary. He is expert at *metis*. I remember him saying something like, without caring about the audience's response, he makes things for himself, but *for himself as an audience*. Considering the eternal arguments about artist-audience dynamics in "director's theater," it is a rather clarifying point of view; and a strong clue about his creative process. Foreman is very good at "watching himself watching something," and he compels his audience to do the same. Later on, I used this clue as a performer and interpreted it as "performing myself performing something." The following line from *Deep Trance Behavior [in Potatoland]* summarizes my initial confrontation with his mind: "I hear you knockin' but you can't get in!" I always found getting in that mind, in that realm as a performer, more stirring than knockin' on its doors as an audience member in his shows.

SHAUNA KELLY: When I begin reading a book, or watching a movie or play, I look for the heartbeat so I can attempt to live in those worlds. With Foreman's plays, there was no such acclimation. Being in the audience was like witnessing a secret ritual—worried you'll be found out as an intruder but happy to stay and risk it.

The characters were uncategorizable but that was intriguing, not straining. The physical agility of the actors performing with their whole bodies and hyper-detailed movements was fascinating! And sometimes acting with their whole bodies revealed—the superb Tony Torn stomping steadily around the stage fully nude with the accompaniment of deafening crescendo and lights ablaze at the end of *Paradise Hotel*!

THERESA BUCHHEISTER: I liked letting them wash over me. I liked feeling free to laugh. I would jot down phrases on my program because I did not want to lose them to space and time. I would bring friends and tell them that we could talk about it after, so they should try to be present and not try to get it while it was happening. I loved watching the actors' eyes and hands.

PAULA GORDON: Attending a Foreman show was work! Total sensory engagement. But I was often conflicted between wanting to connect the dots intellectually and wanting to soak it all in as a visceral experience without thinking at all. Often my face would hurt afterwards from smiling (or mouth agape) for eighty minutes straight.

JAN LESLIE HARDING: Every single person in the audience is taking a subjective ride, which everyone does anyway, but he's not spoon-feeding them laugh lines. He's not spoon-feeding them feel good/ feel bad like other types of theater.

BRENDAN REGIMBAL: I loved it. It was everything I wanted—to not know where to grab hold. I didn't know where to come at it especially coming to it after having read so much of it and putting it into boxes academically and then being confronted with how loud, how fast, how bright, how disorienting it was—everything

I'd written about. But to write about joy or euphoria and then to actually experience it are two different things. "Oh this is what it's supposed to feel like. This is what's disorienting." It's like sitting there and being like, "This is all happening too fast and I'll never capture it" and then releasing—being like, "Don't. Don't chase it. Just let it wash over you."

RICHARD FOREMAN: *A couple of people said about my plays, "You know I liked your plays but when they're over I find them hard to remember." They thought that that was a criticism but I didn't. I thought, well, they're hard to remember because they're opening a new door that you haven't gone through yet.*

RYAN HOLSOPPLE: In Richard's manifesto in the collection of plays *Unbalancing Acts*, he describes his shows as a toy, like a top or a dreidel. When you hold the dreidel in your hand, you can see different images on each side—like a butterfly or a boy fishing, but when you spin the dreidel, it becomes a blur.

I was swept away [seeing Richard's work for the first time]. *Permanent Brain Damage* was all voiceover, in Richard's own ominous growl. There was a love of life and a dread of living in each sentence that was uttered. At the same time there was phantasmagorical choreography billowing around the stage. I was in my early twenties at the time so the angst and chaos I witnessed really spoke to me. This was also one of Richard's last shows to have a *full* plexi-glass barrier between the audience and the stage and I was sitting in the front row, this allowed me to see the reactions of the people seated behind me, reflected in the glass. I remember thinking at the time that this was like looking at a Francis Bacon painting behind glass, melting in front of my eyes, I loved it.

WILLEM DAFOE: To see his theater is to know what is possible in the theater. He really taps into what I love about theater so it's a theater that I enjoy. While a lot of theater is very dead, I found his theater always very alive. People sometimes admired his work very much but they were always a little snooty about how from piece to piece—they were quite similar—because he uses the same language; it's very coded and very familiar and he recycles gesture and certain elements in the scenography. Similar complaints have been made toward Bob Wilson, someone I've also worked with.

DAVID HERSKOVITS: Working on and seeing the shows over the years, I could see the work change a lot. I was frustrated because the reviews about those shows over the years were very admiring, very positive but basically always talked about the plays like they were all the same. They would say, "Oh yes he's doing that thing he always does." And I always thought that was crazy; I felt like the work was changing so much: the rhythms of it, the way the language was used, the way video imagery came into it in very particular ways and stayed in, the subjects, and the content of the plays themselves. In that sense, I always think Richard is a playwright. By the way, he's a completely conventionally trained playwright. At Yale School of drama, he was writing plays like Boulevard comedies that he thought might be done on Broadway. The dramaturgy of those plays is quite conventional.

In Richard's work, the structure of it and the way that all of that is refracted, as it were, prismatically, is very challenging but essentially there is a shape and an arc to them. There is even a thematic content that is quite present in the text but the reviewers would never really get that. I can see that this is a play about memory and that play is more about politics. *Symphony of Rats* was really a response to the Ronald Reagan era. Ron Vawter played a crazy president who was tormented. Even though it was also very personal to Richard's psyche in other ways, I just saw the work as changing so much [over the years]. There were some I really loved and there were others that didn't grab me as strongly but I always responded emotionally to them because of my relationship to the work and to him. I think a lot of the work is very poignant and emotionally naked. People think the work is being very intellectual but that's not my experience of it at all, really.

———

SHAUNA KELLY: *Some commentary on your work calls you innovative even though they say you're doing the same thing year after year.*

RICHARD FOREMAN: *That's the great misunderstanding. Except at the very beginning I never claimed to be innovative. That's not what's interesting. What's interesting is every artist has very limited material that he works upon and it's a matter of down through the years if you can work on it deeper, if you can find new angles to it. But the attempt to be innovative is silly. I'm only interested in getting to some kind of truth. And in my case getting some kind of truth meant a kind of electricity, a kind of density, just capturing a certain vibration. I'm well aware that there were people who used to say, "Foreman is okay but he's always doing the same thing." That's ludicrous. Take painters—I mean was Francis Bacon always doing the same thing? No. He had a style and his style was recognizable. Because he had such a strong style, if you didn't know much about him, you'd say, "Well yeah, he's making the faces like that." But that's not the point. I mean that's just a reflection of the stupidity of people who don't understand what making art is about.*

SHAUNA KELLY: *You said every artist has limited material?*

RICHARD FOREMAN: *They return to certain themes, to certain clusters. I mean it depends on what you know about a poet or a novelist or playwright or a painter or whatever it is. I mean the work is recognizable because it's always built around a certain stylistic cluster that occurs again and again in their work. I mean Merce Cunningham—if you saw Merce Cunningham Dance and then you saw a lot of other dance and then ten years later you saw another Merce Cunningham Dance—If you didn't know much about dance you would tend to say, "Oh yeah, well I've seen that. Yeah. He's doing the same thing."*

SHAUNA KELLY: *Why does your work feel familiar? Or exotic?*

RICHARD FOREMAN: *It's familiar because I think I'm working in the area of: "What is the neural network inside human beings? What happens when the brain is stroked in a certain way?" So it should be familiar. Exotic? I've always been interested in exotic art essentially.*

You know the only thing I ever wanted people to say was, "Wow, that's the greatest, most profound thing I've ever seen in my life." [Laughter] That's all I care about.

———

Foreman's Character

COLLEEN WERTHMANN: I was always a bit shocked whenever I saw him eating strawberry-banana Light & Lively yogurts. He had a lot of those. It seemed like such an out-of-character, regular-person-ish thing for him to eat.

DAVID HERSKOVITS: Richard was so straightforward. There was no affect. There was no performance. There was nothing he was putting me through personally.

Many years after I stopped working with him, I lived in the East Village (when people could live in the East Village). I had a rent-stabilized apartment, which would be insane now. I mean, that was like the early 1990s. I would just call Richard up and ask if I could come by rehearsal. I'd say I'm free today and I'd come and sit in the back of the theater and watch it just because I liked it. I liked just checking in and saying hello. And by the same token, I'd have people calling me saying, "Can I talk to Richard? How can I reach him?" And I'd give them the phone number because it was in the phone book (there used to be this thing called the phone book). People were terribly scared and worried about that. But I appreciated that. I think Richard is amazingly available to help people.

JAMES URBANIAK: I quite liked him personally. Before I met him I used to go to all his shows and you would see him there, sitting in the audience with a deadpan expression, seemingly glowering behind his mustache, an intimidating figure. But once I got to know him it was clear he was just another goofy theater dork like all of us. He was funny and energetic. He was a bit of a showman as well; sometimes he'd jump on stage and strike a pose or gesture for us to emulate in our own style. Despite his avant-garde trappings, he sometimes put me in mind of an old-time Broadway impresario like George Abbott.

SHAUNA KELLY: Foreman was an exemplary leader—personable and professional. He was captivating and entertaining—he'd jump to the stage to choreograph a dance for an actor. His unassuming demeanor didn't reflect the charisma and command he exhibited in rehearsal. He was a likable, sometimes mysterious, brilliant person to work with. He was a gentleman and an enigma. When interviewing him in his loft, he was candid and easy to laugh with. He was courteous, present, and genuinely happy to know I was interested in digging deeper about him and his work.

JAN LESLIE HARDING: People totally revere him. He's pretty special. He's non-wavering.

People's perception of Richard is so much more simplified than anything you experience when you spend three months everyday with him.

KEN NINTZEL: I remember going to Richard as I was establishing my own personal directing style and asking him when—and what—prompted him to start doing things his own way. I remember him saying that he was dissatisfied with the theater he was seeing and wanted to create the kind of theater he would want to see. This had a profound effect on me as I was developing my own style and approach to theater. It gave me the permission to make the type of theater I wanted to see. I think this was just before I created my piece called *Opera Queen* for the Seven Minute Series. It was my first personal work in my own idiosyncratic style. Richard was kind enough to record a voiceover which was used at the end of *Opera Queen* to great effect.

From left to right: Amy Perry, Ben Prager, and Mary Ewald in *Eddie Goes to Poetry City, Part 1* at the New City Theater, Seattle, 1990. Photo by John Kazanjian.

Richard didn't—and doesn't, as far as I know—like going to the theater. It was always the running joke that Richard only likes one kind of theater—Richard's. So if he wanted to come to one of your shows or a series at the Ontological that you were a part of, it was a big deal. An even bigger deal for me, at least, was a phone message on the answering machine Richard left for me after seeing *Opera Queen*. He told me how amazing he thought it was, although he didn't use the word "amazing." I don't believe he had called and left messages for other productions I had done. I will always remember, all in all, Richard was very supportive of my work.

MARY EWALD: Richard was kind enough to write a letter of support for the New City Theater, stating that he appreciated how the collaboration allowed him to explore his "most adventurous impulses." The "sympathetic and talented artists" there helped bring his work to a greater depth. During his time with the New City Theater, he was able to discover "a new tonality that allows my art to expand in ways rewarding and unexpected. Even to myself."

COLLEEN WERTHMANN: I'm embarrassed to recount this, but a little while after I got "cast" in Richard's play, I told Richard that I wanted to be an actor, and I asked him, since *The Mind King* was being produced on an Equity contract, if he would sponsor me for my Equity card. He said yes, sure. I found out later, to my embarrassment, that it must have cost the production some money, but he never said a single word about that to me. His willingness to help me start my acting career was a significant, and touching, kindness on his part that I've never forgotten. I'll always be grateful to him for that.

DAVID HERSKOVITS: Richard was always so supportive. I landed in New York and was working for the guy. I didn't direct for like a year because it is so hard to figure out who you are and what you are doing but finally I did. The Yale Drama Department hired outside directors to direct student shows for a couple productions a year. I was hired to direct Frank Wedekind's *Spring Awakening*. I told

Richard about it but it was in New Haven, Connecticut, so I didn't expect the guy to come there, but he came. He was making a trip to Boston. I think he was still working at the ART [Harvard's American Repertory Theater] or something. He had some gig there and on his way back he stopped in New Haven to see the show. And the next morning I saw him in the bookstore. I had just wandered in because I like browsing in bookstores. And the show was performing so I was still there and I had free time and Richard was there browsing. So he had stopped in New Haven to see the play and he had stayed in a hotel overnight. He didn't tell me this. I had no idea he stayed overnight in a goddamn hotel, and the next morning he was hanging out in New Haven and he was on his way home. And that was the first thing of mine he ever saw and he liked it a lot and was very supportive of it. I think probably because of that he started to take me seriously in a different way as a young artist. He was just incredibly supportive; he really was.

JAN LESLIE HARDING: When we were in Montreal [for the Montreal Theater Festival], Richard and I had a huge existential, intellectual argument about filming the performance. I wouldn't sign the release to do this video section of it. After we'd been fighting about it for a week he came to the hotel breakfast and he brought a letter of apology and asked me would I do it as a favor for a friend and I said, "Oh yes. Why didn't you say that a long time ago?" They wanted to film and at that time I was so mad at the Lincoln Center for wanting to film everything but not wanting to give a copy to the actors. It's like, "You can't have a copy of your work." I mean, what are we going to do, sell it? Theater, it's ephemeral. The thing is, he knew what I was arguing because he believes the same thing about live theater. I thought it was really sweet that he wrote me an apology and then at the end he said, "Would you just do this for a friend?" Then I said, "Absolutely." That trumps the purity of the art form. Our friendship is more important. But I think of that and he said, "I can't argue with you because you're right."

I loved to irritate him with the small talk. I would just be so mundane just to fuck with him because I knew he hated it. And sometimes after I'd mention the third or fourth thing he'd talk about [*impersonating his grumbling*], the cauliflower he had in the refrigerator, and I was like, he's telling me the mundane stuff even when he's got a persona to uphold (not that he actually ever cared about that), but I felt privileged. Afterwards, when we weren't working together, I would be like, "Richard can we meet for lunch? Can we get dinner?" Like Henry Stram and I would go out to dinner with him but that all faded off when his health was so bad. He was like, "I'm in bed at six" and I'd say, "Okay then let's get dinner at four."

During rehearsals for Kathy Acker's *The Birth of a Poet* we were way out in Brooklyn and everyone would go out to lunch on break and I would sit in the rehearsal hall eating my lunch because I was a poor person. So Richard and I would sit on the bleachers and I would bombard him with small talk, which he hated. Like, "What did you have for lunch today?" and he would answer me and indulge me. It became a thing with us. I would be like "it's a nice day we're having" and he would look at me, "yes" or "no."

I loved the conversations with him on the breaks. I would always just sit in the seat and talk with him. You got so much more [insights about the play]. That's why I liked doing new [original] plays too—just talking to him about it.

We [myself and Richard included] went out for Valentine's Day once with Willem Dafoe who worked with the Wooster Group. [*Excitedly*] "Oooooo what are we going to talk about with Richard and Willem Dafoe?" Richard did say when people who make theater get together, they talk about funding; they talk about grants. They don't talk about, "Oh my great philosophical ideas!" I thought, yes there is a whole group of people out together on Valentine's Day but Willem Dafoe is the only one I'm going to talk to. But it was funny: [*Impersonating Richard's voice*] "We don't talk about the substance of our plays, we talk about funding," which is something they always had to think about. If they were the artistic director of their theater, they needed to talk to other artistic directors of theaters about who to get and what to get. [In contrast] I mean the actors go out after the shows and get drunk and talk about the moon and the sky, which is kind of great.

SOPHIA SKILES: I remember hearing how much he loathed being asked, "How are you?" So I always remembered to greet him with, "Nice to see you," which was true. I think he enjoyed a strong sense of privacy. To me, he cultivated a very strict sense of self and at times, seemed very shy.

JOHN OGLEVEE: His self-deprecating manner was mostly amusing and his disdain for small talk was both intimidating and refreshing.

DAVID HERSKOVITS: I remember really loving that he would always mean what he said. I was very comfortable with it and I think that's one reason we got along very well right from the beginning. The culture of the institution I was in at the time was not that way. People didn't know what was being intended (I'm making a general comment about that particular theater); there was paranoia and weird feelings because it was unclear what people meant, but with Richard I felt, "This is great; He actually means everything he says."

I'll never forget showing up at the airport in Houston for the opera [*Where's Dick*, Houston Grand Opera, Texas]. Richard had arrived a day or two before me. Usually in the first phase of rehearsal of an opera, everyone will just sit and sing. They will sing through the score at the piano. Because I was going to be working on the staging I came a little later but Richard went a little early. I landed at the airport and I was met by the production manager of the opera, and she walked up to me and grabbed my hand like I was a life raft. She said, "We are so glad you're here." She was in a panic about Richard. His affect had sort of freaked them out just because he hadn't done all the little social things that people do. I swear to you, we would be in rehearsal and Richard would say, "Well, ah, I don't know. For tomorrow, let's make this chair green." After the meeting everyone would run up to me and say, "What did Richard mean? What is Richard saying?" And I would say, "Well, I think we should make the chair green. Can we make the chair green for tomorrow?" I mean it was just ridiculous. It's really pretty straightforward here. It's just the way he is; he seems very forbidding or something like that. But the truth is, once you get him talking, he loves talking! He loves to tell stories if you scratch him a little bit. He's actually quite social and quite sociable and he will open up and tell you all kinds of things. He's not a closed person at all. But he'll come in and sit down and say nothing and that makes people think, "Oh my god. Something's wrong." Because he doesn't come in and say, "Hey. How are you doing today? Great! What did you do over the weekend?" None of that. And I just never cared about that. I was like fine. Fabulous. No problem. He just doesn't make small talk. He's not interested in sitting around in all of the social interactions people have where we kind of stoke each other or reassure each other that "oh we're nice." He just didn't do that. There wasn't a lot of chitchat. It's not that he meant anything by it.

———

RICHARD FOREMAN: *I was adopted. I didn't know until I was thirty-two. I remember the first nurse, who wouldn't let my mother near me for the first couple months until they fired her, and I'm sure I was not breast fed. I wonder if that distancing made me be a more aloof person. But you know, it doesn't bother me. In life you play with the cards you were given. You play with that hand. You don't say, "Oh, I wish I was dealt a king of spades." No. What can you do with the hand you were dealt?*

———

MANNY IGREJAS: Working with Richard was clean, honorable, and gentlemanly—rare qualities in entertainment. Richard was remarkably funny during the rehearsal process. Richard never smiled in photos and when we did production shots, I liked to see him smile between shots.

T. RYDER SMITH: Richard would sometimes joke that he had a twin brother and on occasion would announce in the morning that Richard couldn't be here today, he was Richard's brother Dick, and he was going to direct for a bit. At which point, we would work on more antic material, songs, sequences of slapstick. Richard would say that it was his wife, Kate Manheim, who had made his work interesting and funny. "But Richard," he reported her as saying, "it has to be *theater*, too."

DENISE LUCCIONI: Richard is an amazing human being. His work is his life, but he would never be insulting or even tough on somebody. Demanding, yes, but that's the game.

SUSAN LATHAM: I watched him in action—especially with funders, he was incredibly charming and disarming, self-deprecating and confident at the same time. I learned from his example and have tried to incorporate elements of that into my own dealings with funders.

PAULA GORDON: I did appreciate that he was not above a corny joke or a pratfall, and it was always a point of pride to be able to make him smile or laugh during rehearsal, especially during that first Wooster Group production.

DAVID COTE: He is a big fan of lack of affect, which he often adopts in his personal speaking style. Of course, Richard can also be very warm, goofy, sweet, and vulnerable. But he can also sound austere, withholding, and emotionally cold.

T. RYDER SMITH: Richard was gruff and sometimes awkward socially. He didn't do "emotion." Someone asked him which country he most enjoyed touring his shows to. "Austria," he said. "Because they are so unfriendly."

DENISE LUCCIONI: *Café Amérique* [Cafe America] premiered in the fall of 1981, and played for four weeks in Gennevilliers, France, before touring to Strasbourg, Lyon, Torino, Nice, and Amsterdam. I have many memorable stories of this tour, hilarious ones, mostly. I believe almost everything that could go wrong, did. And I discovered a fatalistic Richard, always ready for disaster, and pretty damned serene about it, or resigned in a way.

JOHN OGLEVEE: Richard expressed his great love of creating the work, but then not so much enjoyment in being witness to his own subconscious night after night. Certainly, the rehearsal process was in many ways more interesting than the performing.

DAVID PATRICK KELLY: Like Hitchcock doing cameos in his films Richard always had his voice and, sometimes, image in the plays. Kind of "Richardus ex Machina."

JAMES URBANIAK: He once mentioned that when he was younger people said he looked like the movie character actor Henry Jones. I always remembered that for some reason.

JAN LESLIE HARDING: He wouldn't let anyone [audience members] in after eight. Doors close and he has educated his audience, "We are not starting at ten past" like every other theater in the world. You're there before eight or you don't see the show. There was a big thing one day when someone was banging on the door and he got up on the stage and said, "Should we let them in or should we not let them in." He loved those little controversial things. He loved the little controversies among cast members. He preyed on them. One time an actor fell asleep on stage [during rehearsal] and Richard loved it of course.

DAMON KIELY: Every year toward the end of the rehearsal process or on the second day of tech if we were abroad on tour, he would inevitably have huge doubts and threaten to cancel the show. He was never kidding and he wasn't being dramatic. He was just totally unsatisfied, afraid, vulnerable, and not ready to open. That's because the work was personal. I always admired that panic at the end and his ability to push through and find the solution that only he could figure out.

JAN LESLIE HARDING: One thing he always did three-quarters of the way through the production, he would throw his arms up and say he was going to cancel it. This happened every time I worked with him. He gets to a certain point where he'd hit a wall and get sick of everything he was seeing. But he'd come back and change it. Everybody was terrified until they'd seen it once before. When it happened the third and fourth time I said, "Okay we're going to get past it." You always get to the point you have to bust through the wall and transcend it.

We were out of town somewhere and I was sitting next to Richard while the other actors were doing a part of the piece and he just kept talking [to himself], "Missed opportunity. Missed opportunity. All I see up there is missed opportunity," and I was just like "holy crap!" It was really interesting to sit with him. We were out of town so he didn't have the light and sound board to be behind—no control panel. Just to sit back there with him while he had this running commentary about everything that was happening on stage—I just felt really privileged to have those kinds of moments with him.

COLLEEN WERTHMANN: [In rehearsal] I remember him frequently saying things like, "This is awful. This is horrible. This is all terrible. We're going to have to cancel the show," and his constantly being miserable and dissatisfied.

————

RICHARD FOREMAN: *I'm editing the film I shot in West Harlem [in 2017] with the cast and crew from Slovenia and I will be editing it for a while. It generally takes me a year, two years to edit. This seems to be going relatively quickly but that's suspicious so I suspect after I'm done I'll look at it and think, "Oh my god this is terrible." Who knows?*

————

ROBERT CUCUZZA: The runs of the show from start to finish in rehearsal were some of the greatest shows I've ever been a part of as an actor or audience member. Hilarious, moving, beautifully lit and composed, comically—and emotionally timed—like Broadway musical-level of delivery and execution of theater. Then, all four times—and as far as I know—every single time, the same thing would happen. We'd come back from break and with a somber tone he'd say, "I'm terribly sorry, everyone, but this is not at all what I had in mind. I've made some terrible mistakes here—it's not your fault; it's mine—and I just don't know how we can fix it. Unfortunately, we need to cancel the show. We'll have to send a press release to *The New York Times*. And I'll pay you all for the remaining rehearsal weeks but I just can't put this in front of an audience. I'm sorry."

We'd all sit there in stunned silence, not sure what to do next. The show was cancelled. Should we leave? Should we protest? Then, out of the unbearable silence, Richard would kind of mumble: "Well, maybe there are a few things we could change." Then he'd kind of look at the lights or the set or something. Then, he'd send us all home and tell us to return the next day.

The next day, we'd walk in and he had done something dramatic. Like, maybe he collapsed the depth of the set in half. Or added tons of impeding shit all over the stage. Or threw out the play. Or took down all of the theater lights and replaced them with fluorescents. Then we'd start at the beginning of this beautiful, incredible, crowd-pleasing show that we had created together and he would spend the next six weeks bashing the living shit out of every single moment so that no two audience members could experience the same thing the same way. That crowd-pleasing show was in there— just buried inside of a battered and beaten and disjointed shell. I believe that those layers are what defined his aesthetic. A lot of it was based upon the amount of time he gave himself to rehearse— six hours a day, six days a week, for three months. He gave himself the opportunity to create an entire show, let his shit indicator blare like a fire alarm, and then throw everything out and start over. He even said one day, "If anyone took as much time as I do, they could create work like this." That's true and not true. But it's more true than not true.

During *Panic! (How to be Happy)*, the stage manager, Evan Cabnet, called his bluff. Evan had been through this at least once before and did not suffer Richard's foolishness gladly. After the full run-through finished and Richard wrapped up his "we need to cancel the show" speech, Evan started to pack up his gigantic SM [stage manager] book, thanked everybody for their work, and got up to leave. Richard burst out: "Whoa, whoa, whoa! What are you doing, Evan?" "You said the show was cancelled, so I'm going home." "Well, I mean, there are probably a few things that we could do." "No, you said it was cancelled." And Evan was truly pissed. It was so manipulative and infantile to pull this same stunt every time and terrorize everybody involved. With *Panic!*, we got right back to work, starting from the beginning. It was one of my favorite moments from my time there.

DAVID HERSKOVITS: There was always a point a couple weeks into rehearsal that he would have staged the whole play. He would look at it and say, "Well that's terrible. We have to change everything." And he would. And that's the kind of thing the actors would take very hard. He really didn't mean *you* are terrible; he just meant his own work. But he wasn't smooth at making them feel good about it; some of them would be just in agony because you've been working for a couple weeks and then it's all just thrown out.

Richard, I know he knows this story because he tells this story, there was one time where he scrapped the entire show and he just told everyone, "Do whatever you want to do and we'll see what happens. David, just take a note about everything they do." I was frantically trying to track the random stuff they [the performers] did, and only partially successful [in tracking it], I'm sure. But then we went back and basically based on what they had invented, and the notes I had taken, we worked through everything using that as a new basis. He had completely worked the play and it all got washed away and he just let people do whatever they wanted. He just didn't know what to do so he honestly said, "I just don't know what to do. Why don't I just try letting them follow their impulse and see what comes of that." I remember there was another month or more of rehearsals when we were still reworking everything so it's not like he didn't manipulate everything [eventually] but that was a crucial phase of what we were doing.

ROBERT CUCUZZA: Shit Indicator—One day he said something about that he wasn't talented, he just had what [Ernest] Hemingway called a good "shit indicator." He could look at something he made and recognize it as shit. He was merciless in this way because it didn't just apply to what he was creating, it would also apply to what we were doing and who we were as people. It felt like he could see your core being, he could x-ray through the layers of shit that surrounded you in a rehearsal room—years of being told that you were good or talented or funny or "an actor." I desperately wanted to please him—heck, all of us did. But he seemed to think that I had this unquenchable desire to be liked and he hated that part of me and would punish me in rehearsal for it. And I hated him right back for it. (Because he was right.)

SOPHIA SKILES: His bullshit detector is so resolute, at least to me.

THERESA BUCHHEISTER: He was capable (it seemed) of seeing and hearing everything at all times—the sound loops, voice overs, text spoken by actors, props, set, costumes, reflections in the plexi[glass]. It all mattered and it could all be cut.

MIKE TAYLOR: Richard notices everyone in the room and also notices what they seem to be able to do.

FULYA PEKER: Foreman was always in the house during the shows, sitting in his renowned seat. I remember him even stepping on stage during one of the shows to fix an entangled rope. It was intense to always be watched by him, sensing his constantly editing gaze. Actually, that was something that I reconsidered while working on his film project, as I was being watched by him through the camera, as a condensed image. On stage it was somewhat possible to follow his built-in zooms and framings, the moments he was adjusting the focus, as well as his entire editing process. But in film, because he was not watching us directly, but via a screen; and because he would edit all the collected material later, he wasn't spending too much time on details; he was capturing certain moving images and we were moving on.

FRANK BOUDREAUX: Two moments of direct testimony stand out from my time as a performer in *Maria del Bosco* that I think represent Foreman's artistic morals:

During a post-show talkback, I heard Richard draw a revealing comparison between his experience watching a [Jean-Luc] Godard film and a more conventional piece of cinema. Leaving films by Godard, Richard said, he usually felt a disgruntled sense that the film was "pretentious," sometimes "obvious" and/or obscure. In contrast, Richard readily admitted that he succumbed to the manipulations of conventional cinema—often leaving a film "deeply moved," crying or laughing at the intended times, etc. Yet, emerging from the "emotionally moving" world of a conventional film, he would be struck dead in his tracks with the thought, as he put it, "After Godard, it's irrelevant!" Richard left it implied in the talkback, but the point being, of course, that Richard's intentions were like Godard's. Sure, audiences might have more emotional experiences at other theatrical productions perhaps, but once exposed to Richard's work, the magic of those experiences would be unmasked as . . . well, manipulated. Less-than-authentic, exploitative. Irrelevant. This was revealing about Richard's intentions, and it stuck with me as a supremely high standard for any artist to aspire to.

In 2001, I remember Prada, the fashion brand, pioneering a kind of . . . how to put this? . . . nihilistic advertising style. This was back when glossy magazine ads were still the main delivery system for fashion announcements, and Prada's full-page ads were nearly without product content—perhaps a toe of a shoe or the button of a collar would poke into an otherwise moody (non-)scene of, say, a wall or a corner of a wall? One day during lunch where several of us, including Richard, were eating in the Ontological, I proposed that this was how far late-capitalism had come: I regarded the campaign as a self-aware, sly critique of the very consumer culture it was designed to promote. Essentially, I was arguing that there was a respectable artistic intention involved in the ads' creation even as they were strictly a commercial production. (Kind of, a proto-[Takashi] Murakami move, but even bolder given it was on the actual side of commerce, not art.) I didn't notice it at the time of the discussion, but Richard must have been agitated by this argument. I left the discussion to use the bathroom and just as I started pissing, Richard pulled up at the urinal next to mine, himself immediately beginning to pee while, simultaneously, asking in a fervent, concerned tone (as if there had been no break in the conversation whatsoever), "Yes, but is that a legitimate artistic goal? Can advertising for brands designed to create class-division possibly ever be considered a moral practice or valid artistic intent?" Right there at the urinal, so urgent was his need to address what he considered my uncritical argument! At the time, still peeing, I babbled some qualifiers as best I could, kind of, immediately sensing his point in the rhetoricals. To some extent, this was a generational divide: My generation grew up in the ironic world of Warhol's creation, whereas Richard was a stalwart of 1960s art and activism—his generation's attempt, to transcend the necessarily corrupt world of commerce. Nevertheless, I ultimately always want to side with Richard. I respect some of the sophistication and engagement with our moment that contemporary art stars like Damien Hirst and Jeff Koons exemplify (and Murakami). But ultimately it can't help but be shallow; like Prada's campaign, it's *designed* to be shallow. Richard never gave up on depth. Yes, his work (repeatedly) diagnoses our culture as shallow. But in that diagnosis, he always reaches for depth. He always acknowledged the dubious motivations of his own artistic practice—self-glorification, egoism, assertion of cultural privilege, and hierarchy. However (as is evident in his urgent need to address my youthfully misguided elevation of an advertising campaign in a bathroom!), Richard's work was always striving to do more than sell itself, do more than reinforce what the audience walked in believing. Perhaps this sounds incongruously precious, but I think my moment with Richard supports my idea that he wanted his art to change the audience *for the better*. He always believed it valuable to challenge received wisdom, reveal corruption, ever with the goal of awakening consciousness ("Wake up! Wake up!"), if not achieve, then *point at* enlightenment . . . even as he believed that it was our human lot for that enlightenment to be ever elusive.

KEN NINTZEL: Especially when he was in the moment, he hated the fact that there were equity rules, that people needed to take breaks.

KARL FRANKLIN ALLEN: We were rehearsing the year that Obama was elected. Richard didn't seem to think it was a big a deal but after much debate he finally agreed to pause rehearsal so we could watch the inauguration and sat with us to watch it.

T. RYDER SMITH: Sometimes in rehearsal Richard would just start talking about life. A moment we were working on would prompt him to tell a story, or a joke, which would lead to another story, or a reminiscence, or a confession, or an explanation of a philosopher's system, or a show he had once seen, or food he had once eaten, or a story about his wife, or the plot of a film he liked, and on and on. Everyone would begin listening by standing or sitting where they were, expecting to momentarily return to the performed moment, but as it became obvious that Richard was riding waves of thought, people would sit, settle, gather around him. He would talk for as long as forty-five minutes sometimes, saying remarkably hilarious or provocative or profound or bizarre things, and he was spellbinding. I tried to remember some of the stories to write later but they were inimitable. I would sometimes try to surreptitiously scribble some down, like dictation, my pencil moving over the page in my lap without me looking down at it. I can decipher some of these notes, often written on top of stage directions or text, but others are lost. Eventually, he would say, "Well, I guess we should get back to work," and we would reluctantly stand and return to the stage. But we wanted him to keep talking.

Those spontaneous talks were moving, too, because it was clear that for Richard, who had no children, and was something of a recluse, this was his family. His children and grandchildren, briefly, were listening to him speak.

His face was more often than not glum, the corners of his mouth turned down and eyes deeply sad, but when he told an anecdote or spoke at length, he smiled and laughed throughout, and his eyes brightened and face became jolly. He has a lovely smile.

But things could be difficult, as well. Richard was viciously critical of his own work, which was part of the live-composition process, and he often made a point of saying that the problems with the show were his fault, not the performers'. Yet sometimes he would say cruel things to the actors or staff, or would lose his temper, in a sudden, surprising, paroxysmal way, at someone who had missed a cue, or written down a note wrong, or failed to perform a requested task. He could single people out—as he did me, at least once—for long scoldings, as the room stood still around the shamed individual, silent but for Richard's cold, precise voice—a miserable experience—or could shout an insult or infuriated command in his deep tone which echoed off the walls. (He did this to me once *in performance*.) And on some occasions his jokes or passing comments were malicious, uttered without hesitation and perhaps without better forethought. A veteran actor of his told me that I was lucky to be working with Richard "after he started the brain drugs," and Richard himself on a few occasions after some production mistake would refer in passing to a regimen he was on, and chuckle darkly what he might have done or said "before" at such a moment. One former actor of his said that he still, years later, couldn't pass by St. Mark's without shuddering. And on a daily basis, personally, Richard was rarely a "warm" personality, having little patience or sympathy for anyone's private troubles, losses, concerns, romances, money worries, etc. None of that had anything to do with the work, and so, in his view, had no place in the room; he had no capacity for or interest in engaging with it. Privately, he was respectful of such things; mildly disdainful, perhaps, but respectful. In his public "performance" of himself in rehearsal, though, he was always bleakly, sardonically, misanthropic. It made for some painful moments.

"I am not in the theater because I love people," he once said.

JAN LESLIE HARDING: He demanded a certain rigor to getting it right and showing up. Like he had us all get a flu shot. He couldn't lose one piece of the puzzle. He couldn't lose one of the chorus or you wouldn't be able to rehearse. Everybody was so integral to what everybody else was doing and god forbid . . . so we all had to sign a waiver, we were not going to quit in the middle of show, that we were going to get the flu shot, and that we were going to show up (I think it was four days a week) and everybody was there every day except for when I remember Thomas Jay Ryan's father died and Richard was like, "Oh my god, what's going to happen to my play?," and I was like, oh my god, you just got demystified in front of me, man. I was like "Richard!" I became a "mom" because it was all guys and me and this was *Sledgehammer,* and I said, "He'll be gone for three days and he'll come back. Richard, it's his Dad." He became so human at that moment. I was like, "Shit, Richard!" And we were fine. We missed a day of rehearsal and he came back and Tom was ready. And you felt like, oh, Richard is growing *with* us here. There are places for all of us to go.

People think of him as a very heady artist but he had very practical problems that he would dwell on. When Tom's father died he was like, "What's happening to my play?," and I was like, "Richard, if there's any time you're supposed to be philosophical and existential it's when someone's father died. Don't think of the minute; think of the big picture." He immediately went to this petty little place and I was like, "Richard, not now." To a certain extent you have all these different types of relationships—you'd be the student and then you'd be the sister and then you'd be the mother and the wife and the student again. My relationship with Richard was just whatever was needed at the moment. I would go with whatever he put out there (when I wasn't being mundane with him).

But I adored him from the minute I met him. Absolutely loved how he irritated people [in the audience] and didn't compromise.

Finding Foreman

Those of us who worked with Richard Foreman had varied career paths before joining one of his shows. Working with him for nine months needed to be a firm commitment because every person was indispensable in a Foreman show.

T. RYDER SMITH: One day in 1976 there was a theater review in the *Village Voice* newspaper with a photo of an actress named Kate Manheim leaning backwards at an odd angle and the review described something entirely new to me, and utterly bizarre: an event, or ritual, or initiation, it seemed, more than a play, written and directed by a guy named Richard Foreman. I was fascinated as I read and thought about it, but also unnerved, even a bit frightened by the whole thing.

I'd just graduated high school and had vague, or better to say diffident, plans to be an actor, "someday." I was in lower New York State, about 25 miles from the city and I would have missed the last bus home if I were to have seen this odd *Potatoland*. It was a kind of relief since my psyche told me to be careful about this "Richard Foreman" fellow and his strange *Rhoda* events. I read other reviews of Richard's work in the next few years with a mix of awe and dread and some feeling of fatefulness. I looked for articles about him in magazines, and read interviews, and his essays, and his plays, which were striking but still opaque to me.

A few years later I moved to New York City to seriously pursue, with great misgivings and with little sense of any sort of aesthetic clarity, an acting career, and started to hear more personal things about this Richard Foreman person, stories which made him seem like a combination of a mad emperor and a mystic who spoke in tongues.

Later in my career I was only really happy as a performer doing "weird stuff downtown," even when few people saw it. Some of the actors I worked on those projects with were veterans of the Ontological. I started to hear stories about what it was like to work for and to audition for Richard, and they made him sound simultaneously like a tyrant and a holy pilgrim, and sometimes like a vaudeville comic, too, and also a nineteenth-century actor–manager.

A few months after seeing *Paradise Hotel* I received, suddenly, a message from Richard. Richard's stentorian voice said "This is Richard Foreman. If you'd like to audition for a role in the tour of my play, call me back." It was as if Zeus had called me. Here it was twenty years since I'd seen that odd photo of Kate Manheim and read that review, twenty years of varied and challenging work as an actor, and twenty years of personal explorations and setbacks and discoveries and crises, and an attempt to craft an artistic sensibility and a politics, and those doors, which had symbolically closed, seemed to be cracked open a bit. I felt ready. I felt *called*.

And so I looked at the script pages that were sent to me, and they were for a role in the European tour of *Paradise Hotel*, replacing an actor from the New York City run. I found out later that Tony Torn had mentioned me as an actor Richard might want to meet.

JAY SMITH: As I recall, this is what happened: Richard wrote *Paradise Hotel* with the idea of casting five actors from the late Reza Adboh's Dar A Luz company. I had worked in L.A. with one of these actors, who told me months before rehearsal started that another Dar A Luz actor was going to withdraw from the project. I called him and asked him if I could audition to replace the departing actor.

Unfortunately, I was booked to fly to California and would not be able to audition immediately, so the role went to Gary Wilmes. A couple of weeks later, the Dar A Luz actor with whom I had worked told me that he had decided to drop out as well, and that he would recommend me to be his replacement. I called Richard and said, "I understand you've lost another actor." He said, "I don't know what you're talking about. What do you know?" I muttered something about getting bad information and quickly got off the phone. The actor had opted to quit not by telephone, but by sending a letter of resignation and Richard had not yet received it. A few days later I got a phone call from Richard; the letter had been received and I was invited to come and audition. He later told me that he cast me because (1) Kate Manheim told him to cast the giant guy, and (2) he called Anne Bogart (from my resume—I had worked with her while in grad school at Columbia) to find out if I was crazy and she said no.

FULYA PEKER: After graduating from the Theater Program at H.U. Ankara State Conservatory in Turkey, I went to New York in 2003 to pursue an MA at Brooklyn College focusing on ancient and avant-garde theater. I started exploring experimental theater in New York City, and after discovering Richard Foreman, I began following his shows. I remember sitting right behind him during a performance of *King Cowboy Rufus Rules the Universe* in 2004. In front of his seat there were tiny volume control buttons that he was playing around with. It was a powerful experience to witness some of the avant-garde elements in practice that I had previously only read about.

DAVID HERSKOVITS: I was a student fellow at the Institute for Advanced Theater Training at Harvard at the American Repertory Theater (ART) in 1987–8. Richard led a workshop production with the students of one of his own texts—a play called *City of Amateurs* (which has never been done aside from that production). And then he directed a production of a new opera by Philip Glass that was based on Edgar Allan Poe's story "The Fall of the House of Usher" and I assisted.

ROBERT CUCUZZA: They had a few books by and about Richard in the "experimental theater" section at Carnegie Mellon. I found his ideas to be impenetrable and the pictures of his shows to be off-putting and I veered more toward Robert Wilson. Then I traveled through Europe for a year, saw theater from all over the world and had my mind completely shattered apart by all different superstar theater-makers. [After reading] *Breaking the Rules*, about the Wooster Group, I walked to the Performing Garage, the home of the Wooster Group, rang the bell and asked if they needed any help. I started interning for them and running their box office . . . and hearing more about Foreman and that he was doing shows at St. Mark's Church in-the-Bowery.

I saw Foreman's newly published book, *Unbalancing Acts* in the Strand Bookstore in 1992. I brought it home and read the fantastic opening interview between him and Ken Jordan. He described his idiosyncratic process and theater in such a way that it felt like he was unlocking *my* way of thinking about process and theater. I had to work with him.

DENISE LUCCIONI: In 1980 I was working with Bénédicte Pesle at Artservice International in Paris. Among Bénédicte's numerous claims to fame was introducing Merce Cunningham to European audiences starting in the 1960s and Robert Wilson, Philip Glass, Yvonne Rainer, Trisha Brown, Meredith Monk . . . from the 1970s onward. Having first seen Richard's work in the late 1960s, Bénédicte was responsible for Richard's first two invitations to Paris in 1973. That was *Une Semaine sous l'influence de. . . ou Thérapie Classique* [A Week under the Influence of . . . or Classical Therapy], then in 1976, *Le Livre des Splendeurs* [The Book of Splendors]. At that time (late 1970s), Richard wanted to move to Paris, because he was explicitly infatuated with the French "intelligentsia," and what he imagined of cultural life in the country. In 1980, Bénédicte worked out a different scheme for him: she helped him create a French nonprofit, named OH (for Ontologique-Hystérique), so that he might apply for French funding. She convinced Michel Guy to produce three works over three years in a theater run by Brechtian director Bernard Sobel, in Gennevilliers, in the immediate outskirts of Paris. Each new work would premiere with Festival d'Automne, and possibly tour in Europe.

I had never seen Richard's work. I had absolutely NO IDEA what it was like. Before Richard came to Paris, Bénédicte asked me to translate articles and reviews about his work from English to French, and to compose a presentation that would help her find sponsors (other venues in Europe) and start raising interest with the press. I very much enjoyed what I was translating, and writing. Then Bénédicte asked me whether I wanted to work with Richard on his production *Café Amérique*. I would have two jobs, officially: "assistante de production," [assistant to the producer] and "assistante du metteur en scène" [assistant to the director]. I gladly accepted.

———

RICHARD FOREMAN: *When I first went to work in France, I thought that I wanted to be in France to draw from the energy of that society and that culture. It's changed a lot but at that time, I did think that I was in a fantasy.*

———

DAVID PATRICK KELLY: In the 1970s, when I arrived in New York City, there were many companies I admired . . . The Open Theater, Circle Rep, Living Theatre, Performance Group, La MaMa (Wilford Leach and Andrei Serban), Ridiculous Theatrical Co. (Charles Ludlam), Mabou Mines (Lee Breuer), . . . and Ontological-Hysteric Theater. I had seen Richard's early essays and sought his theater out when I came to New York. Before I worked with Richard I would regularly attend his shows in the 1970s like *Rhoda in Potatoland* with Kate Manheim and *Hotel For Criminals*.

I worked as a dishwasher at The Mercer Arts Center where Richard's *Dr. Selavy's Magic Theater* had its successful first run (1972–1973). I auditioned for [Foreman's direction of Bertolt Brecht's] *Threepenny Opera* and did not get it. The next year I was hired by Richard's musical collaborator Stanley Silverman for his musical with Arthur Miller that we did at the Kennedy Center. For that audition I sang a song by the great Bert Williams called "I May

Be Crazy But I Ain't No Fool." Six years later when I auditioned for the *Dr. Selavy* re-do (1984 show), Stanley remembered that and I think it contributed to my first gig with Richard.

MANUEL IGREJAS: Because of my work with Blue Man Group, a lot of downtown artists approached me. I had heard of Richard Foreman but never saw his work. In preparation for the meeting I read *Unbalancing Acts*. I was excited by it and his approach to theater. I saw *The Universe* and loved it.

JAN LESLIE HARDING: Resa Bramen had been the assistant director of my first show in New York at Ensemble Studios theater. Richard was directing a Kathy Acker play *The Birth of a Poet* at BAM and Resa brought me in originally to be in the chorus. Richard auditioned me when he lost his lead actress and I became the lead, which was fantastic. So that's how I met him—working with him at BAM.

I'd never seen any Richard Foreman shows before I worked with him so I had no preconceived notions of what we were doing. I was just doing what he said purely and not thinking that I have to affect some kind of Foremanesque thing. I had a loose way of working with Richard.

CHRISTINA CAMPANELLA: Joanna Adler recommended me. Jo and I had worked together in *Boys in the Basement* at Mabou Mines/Suite and HERE Arts Center as well as in a production of *Pericles* where she played the title role and I played her wife. I'd also worked with David [Greenspan] before on a piece he wrote and directed called *Start from Scratch*—a play with chamber music at the Greenwich House.

SHAUNA KELLY: When I met actor, director, and writer D.J. Mendel in 1998 he had been, and continued to be a lead actor in Foreman's plays: *The Universe, Permanent Brain Damage,* and *Panic! (How to Be Happy!)*; and directed Foreman's film *Planet Earth: Dreams*. Mendel cast me in Tennessee Williams's *Small Craft Warnings* which he directed with certain Foremanesque elements. He introduced me to the work of Claude Wampler, Cynthia Hopkins, Elevator Repair Service, Wooster Group, and Foreman (I saw his show *Paradise Hotel* in 2001). Mendel graciously contacted Foreman about my interest in performing in one of his shows, and Foreman brought me in for an audition.

COLLEEN WERTHMANN: I was a huge fan of Foreman's work having seen *What Did He See?*, *Lava*, and *Eddie Goes to Poetry City*. When I was an undergrad drama major at NYU, for my last semester I decided to pursue an internship.

RYAN HOLSOPPLE: I came across Richard Foreman's trademark black and white advertising, tri-fold flyer for *Permanent Brain Damage* on St. Mark's. I was familiar with the name and had read his play, *Pandering to the Masses: A Misrepresentation*, in a collection of plays that I had found at Mercer Street Books called, *Theater of Images*.

PAULA GORDON: My first show with Richard was *Miss Universal Happiness* in 1985, when I was a staff technician for the Wooster Group at The Performing Garage and they brought him in for a coproduction. Richard wrote the play and directed the company, and Wooster Group design and technical staff and regular freelancers did the design and tech.

WILLEM DAFOE: I was aware of Richard very early when I was still in Milwaukee, Wisconsin, working at a theater called Theater X. I remember we had a small press bookstore in the lobby of our theater to include many volumes of the Tulane Drama Review and I think that's where I read about Richard first. I hadn't seen his pieces until I came to New York but I certainly sought him out very quickly. And when I came to New York in 1977 and started working with the Wooster Group they were all great fans of Richard's, particularly Liz LeCompte, the director. She started taking me to the shows at his Ontological-Hysterical Theater. Also, her sister Ellen performed with Richard as well as Peyton Smith, who both worked with the Wooster Group, so I had those kinds of connections and I got to know Richard. I got to know

Kate Valk (left) and Willem Dafoe (center); against wall (left to right): Jeff Webster, Peyton Smith, Nancy Reilly, Anna Köhler, Elizabeth LeCompte, and Ron Vawter in *Miss Universal Happiness*, 1985. Photo by Paula Court.

his work and I remember he always was a little jealous of Liz having a fixed company of performers, at least that's what he would say. And he talked about collaborating with the Wooster Group's performers. So we did that in 1985 on a piece called *Miss Universal Happiness*. That is how I came to work with him. The Wooster Group also performed/collaborated with him on *Symphony of Rats* in 1987[1] but I didn't perform in that because I was away shooting a movie.

JULIANA FRANCIS KELLY: Richard had seen one of Reza Abdoh's last plays (*Tight Right White*). I was asked to join the cast of *Paradise Hotel,* along with several other members of theater director Reza's Dar A Luz company, shortly after Reza's untimely death.

CHARLOTTA MOHLIN: I was a teenager working in a café close to the Ontological theater. One day Richard came in, stood in the door with his hair standing up, and asked me: "Are you an actress or do you want to act?" I said yes.

JAMES URBANIAK: My own mentor, the director Karin Coonrod, with whom I'd co-founded the theater company Arden Party in the late 1980s, took me to my first ever Richard Foreman show in 1988, *What Did He See?* at the Public Theater, a mind-blowing experience. I recall watching that show in dazed rapture while thinking, "I could be in one of these."

In 1994 Foreman saw me in a play at the Ontological-Hysteric called *Parlour Problems,* written and directed by Robert Cucuzza who was one of the many young directors Foreman had mentored at the theater. Sometime later, Foreman asked me to audition for his next show. I'd seen every Foreman play since 1988.

DAVID COTE: Through Eric [Dyer, a classmate at Bard College] I got my first glimmer of Foreman's work. He carried around a copy of Reverberation Machines and his senior project to get a Theater BA bore a very strong Foreman influence. Eventually, Eric and his friends would form Radiohole, one of the most original and

Willem Dafoe (top) and Kate Valk (bottom) in *Miss Universal Happiness*, 1985. Photo by Paula Court.

exciting performance collectives in what I call the "third wave" of New York City avant-garde theater. My biggest regret is not seeing Reza Abdoh's work in person. In 2000 I joined *Time Out New York* as a theater critic and made sure to write about Radiohole, ERS [Elevator Repair Service], NTUSA [National Theater of the United States of America], all these companies whose work I admired so much.

MARY EWALD: John Kazanjian is the producing artistic director of the New City Theater in Seattle (John and I are married, and I was a co-founder of the theater). He was familiar with Foreman's work from living in New York City and attending work dating all the way back to 1973 and seeing *Vertical Mobility* in Richard's loft. I lived in New York City after college in the 1980s and saw whatever Foreman was doing.

John commissioned leading experimental writer/directors to come work with us. He produced Richard Foreman's world premiere of *Eddie Goes to Poetry City* with a $50,000 grant from the Ford Foundation's National Alternative Arts Organization Commission Program.

STEPHANIE SILVER: I found Richard through Shauna [Kelly]! She invited me to see her in *King Cowboy Rufus*. She was a most excellent chicken; I didn't even recognize her. I was so relieved when I walked into a church for the play instead of a normal theater and even more relieved when I didn't see a living room set. I remember Juliana Francis appearing like an apparition from a sad, terrifying dream singing "Wake Up" in the most piercingly beautiful voice.

JOHN COLLINS: David Herskovits taught me at Yale when he was Richard's assistant and stage manager and he had invited his Yale class to see Richard's production *Eddie Goes to Poetry City* at La MaMa ETC [Experimental Theater Club]. When I was working for David that fall as a sound designer on *Titus Andronicus* at Target Margin Theater [TMT], he introduced me to Richard who was looking for a sound operator for his next show. I gladly took the job.

FRANK BOUDREAUX: Evan Cabnet, now artistic director at Second Stage Theater [formerly artistic director at LCT3 at Lincoln Center, New York] was stage managing Richard's show, *Now That Communism Is Dead My Life Feels Empty* in 2001, in his first year out of NYU's Tisch School of the Arts. Richard, was looking for "dwarfs,"—the name, for the initiated, of those performers who are basically chorus members in his shows, billed as "Stage Crew," for his next production. Being a dwarf meant following Richard's minutely specific and always evolving directions for manipulating his shabby-surreal props and scenery for the main performers, and involved minimal speaking lines (to not run afoul of Actors Equity rules). Evan knew myself and another NYU peer and colleague of mine, Thom Sibbit, to be hard-working and capable so he recruited us for the upcoming production. The insane hours, months-long rehearsal schedule, and absolutely insufficient wage did nothing to deter us: we agreed immediately!

The show became *Maria del Bosco* (we began rehearsals just days after the 9/11 attacks hit the World Trade Towers). True to his description, the leads were played by Juliana Francis Kelly (Obie winner for the role later that year), (the incomparable) Okwui Okpokwasili, and Funda Duyal. The dwarfs were a chorus of five young guys—myself, Ryan Holsopple (of 31 Down, Radiohole, etc.), Zachary Oberzan (Nature Theater of Oklahoma, Rambo Solo creator, etc.), Youssef Kerkour (international man of mystery), and Thom Sibbitt (who later founded the experimental performance company, aetherplough, in Omaha, NE).

PATRICIA YBARRA: When I was finishing my doctorate in Theater History/Theory, I was an intern for the Ontological-Hysteric Theater for *The Universe*. I was making a decision about whether to stay in mainstream academia, or to go into arts administration/ curation. I applied for and became the administrator of the Ontological Theater. Ultimately, I chose a career in academia, but I learned a ton by working with Richard.

From left to right: Juliana Francis Kelly, Okwui Okpokwasili, and Frank Boudreaux in *Maria del Bosco*, 2002. Tina Barney, Cotton Candy (photo originally in color), 2002. © Tina Barney. Courtesy of the artist and Kasmin, New York.

DAMON KIELY: I saw *My Head Was a Sledgehammer* as part of a class through Columbia University where I was getting my MFA in Directing. I was blown away. I felt like my mouth was agape for an hour. We needed to do an internship and so I joined him the next year as an intern.

THERESA BUCHHEISTER: I read *Lava* by Foreman and was very intrigued. In college I met Patricia Ybarra, a brilliant teacher and director to whom I connected pretty massively. In 2004, we came to New York at the same time and saw *King Cowboy Rufus Rules the Universe* on opening night. I was HOOKED.

BRENDAN REGIMBAL: When I was a junior in college I read Foreman's plays and decided that I was going to write my thesis about him. I spent the next year of college reading every play he wrote and everything anybody had written about him, writing about him, and watching videos of him. Then I saw his show live.

Casting and Hiring

DAVID COTE: In late 1995 or early 1996, I auditioned for Foreman at the Public. It was the world premiere of Suzan-Lori Parks's *Venus*. I didn't get it, but when I was on tour with Assurbanipal Babilla's company, bringing a show called *Suddenly Something Recklessly Gay or Cirque de Ca-Ca* to Portland and Seattle, I got a message that someone dropped out of the production and would I be interested? I was devastated! My big break, and I missed it!

Eventually, I got a call out of the blue from Sophie [Haviland] about a new show at the end of 1996, *Pearls for Pigs*. It was going to open in Hartford and tour around the world. I don't even think I had to audition. Rehearsing in January, and the job would be off and on for the whole of 1997. I quit my job at the Soros Foundation, since this was the first "professional" acting job I ever had.

COLLEEN WERTHMANN: I walked down to SoHo, and met Foreman at his home, a huge loft on Wooster Street with periwinkle blue walls, a tiny model of a set on a huge table, and (to my mind) more overflowing bookshelves than The Strand [Bookshop]. It was the first artist's home I ever went to, and I was pretty nervous, and also super excited to meet someone who was so mysterious and legendary to me. We sat for maybe fifteen or twenty minutes. I told him that I had no sound experience, but was a fast learner. He said, "Well, you seem like you have a sensible sense about you," and that was that. A week or so later, Foreman decided to hire someone with more sound experience to be his sound op[erator] and asked if I would be one of the show's production assistants. I said sure, of course, because I wanted to witness the process no matter what.

About three weeks or a month into rehearsals, Foreman was blocking a scene during which Henry Stram and David Patrick Kelly pulled a female CPR dummy out of a suitcase, and Foreman decided it unfortunately looked like their characters had murdered a woman, and he needed to counteract the image with an actual woman onstage. He said, "Ah . . . Colleen . . . you're going to be in the play."

DAVID PATRICK KELLY: In the early 1980s I auditioned for Richard's re-do of his hit 1970s musical *Dr. Selavy's Magic Theater*. I sang a Schubert song, "Who is Sylvia?" which was based on Shakespeare. That was my last audition. All subsequent work was by request only.

JOHN OGLEVEE: Richard had me walk onstage as if it were covered in glass, walk close to the edge of the stage, realize that my stench repulsed the audience, and then there was an explosion and I was to exit the stage. My training at NYU was from the Strasberg Institute as well as European clowning. After graduating I'd been doing lots of psycho-physical training from SITI style viewpoints, to Min Tanaka style butoh, and a little bit of Noh mixed into the highly stylized work we'd been doing with GAle GAtes. I don't exactly recall what I did in the audition, but I do recall that following my two- or three-minute audition, Richard said to someone offstage, "Yes, he can do this, he'll be fine."

JAN LESLIE HARDING: Richard asked me to come in for *My Head Was a Sledgehammer*. He invited me to his apartment and I read a snippet from his play. I mean what can you do? You just read it. There's no character you put on. Luckily, I got that.

CHARLOTTA MOHLIN: I had an audition in his loft where I was asked to say some random lines. Later I auditioned in the theater and

Richard told me, "A train has just come down from the sky and hit you in the head, as you say the line, 'I want to go to Istanbul.'" I got the part.

KARL FRANKLIN ALLEN: I spent about an hour at his place taking direction and talking. I remember distinctly at the end he said to me, "Well, I think you can do it. Do you want to do it?" I was so excited!

CHRISTINA CAMPANELLA: When I auditioned and he gave me the part, he walked me to the door, said he'd send me the script, etc., then added: "Oh—and there will be no improvising."

JAMES URBANIAK: He called me at home [asking me to audition] and I was so stunned that at first I thought it was a friend playing a joke on me. The audition was at his bookshelf-lined apartment. I read some scenes and he gave me some simple physical direction. I had a sense of his style [from having seen at least six of his shows]. I had the feeling it went well. Later, he called me on the phone saying he had really liked what I'd done but that the actor David Patrick Kelly (with whom he had worked several times) was available and he was going with him based on their history, etc. It was a disappointing phone call but for some reason, as soon as I hung up, I thought, "Well, David Patrick Kelly will get a movie and then Foreman will call me again." Which is exactly what happened. A few weeks later, Richard called me again to tell me that Kelly had gotten a lucrative film and had dropped out of the play for which rehearsals hadn't started yet. He asked me back to his apartment for a callback and when it was over he said, "Well, I think you could do this part."

ROBERT CUCUZZA: He'd cast the show with a collection of personalities who were able to perform with a certain amount of intensity. That was really the main criteria. It had nothing to do if you could act, could move, could speak well, or embody "the character." He seemed to want an almost menacing amount of inherent focus, and then he'd work with whatever else you brought.

T. RYDER SMITH: One actor told me that he had auditioned for Richard in his apartment, standing under a skylight in his kitchen, and that he'd read the audition lines in a standard, earnest way and that Richard had said, "Try it again. But this time . . . say it as if a friend of yours is standing on a ledge about to fling themselves down to the street and in order to save his life you need to speak in code, a code the police and fireman trying to rescue him must not be allowed to understand." And I thought: what a brilliant bit of direction. And the actor said that he did the lines that way, speaking "normally" but with an elaborate set of secret stresses and emphases, and that when he finished Richard just looked down at the table and grunted.

And then another actor told me that he'd had to audition for Richard *in his kitchen*, under a *skylight*, and that he hadn't known how to interpret the part and so read it flatly and Richard said, "Try it again. But this time . . . do it as if there is a voodoo doll sewn up inside your chest and the pins are connected by invisible threads to the person you're talking to and you want to somehow find the words that will make them pull the pins out of you. But you can't let them know that." And I thought: what a bit of brilliant direction. The actor said they tried it that way and Richard just looked down at the table and grunted.

There were three of us waiting to read [for a role in the European tour of *Paradise Hotel*, replacing an actor from the New York run] and we lingered in the hall outside Richard's apartment, a loft in a converted factory space downtown, next to a rattling ancient elevator in a hallway with dark waxy floorboards which creaked at every step. The door opened with a long creak and Richard stood there. He spoke my name loudly, as if in quotes, and with a question mark at the end, like he was asking me if I really wanted that to be my name in life. I followed him down a hall which was lined with shelves, a pantry of sorts. There was a can of peas. I thought: Richard Foreman eats peas!

And then found myself standing in Richard's kitchen, in front of his refrigerator. This is *the kitchen*, I thought to myself, and there is *the skylight*! Richard took a seat behind a long table, with his assistant at the other end. I could have said any number of things at that moment, talking about how much I'd enjoyed watching his work, or reading his essays, or about his collaborators, or what an inspiration he'd been to me or how I shared his interest in certain artists and thinkers, but instead I handed him my resume and mumbled, "I know some of the actors you've worked with."

Pause.

Richard takes the resume as if it's a piece of wet paper I brought in from the street, holding it with just two fingers and setting it down far from him without looking at it. He asks me brusquely if I had seen the play. Yes, I say. Have I memorized the sides? Yes. Okay, Richard says, gesturing for me to begin. I read the lines in my best "Foreman" style, barely moving. Richard pauses and then says, "Try it again, but this time . . .," and I think: here it comes, here comes the brilliant bit of direction. "Try it again," he says, "but this time do it as if . . . you're scared." I stand there. Was that it? "As if I'm scared?," I ask. Richard nods. And so, for inexplicable reasons, I squat down behind a kitchen chair and read the lines with just my eyes appearing over the chair's back. I finish and stand up. Richard looks at the table and grunts.

I was resisting accepting that I had given a truly bad audition, and more than that, that I just wasn't right for the work, that I didn't possess the depth of soul or richness of character or wit or even the simple intelligence to ever do a Richard Foreman play. I did accept it when I saw one of the actors from the audition a few days later, at a commercial call, of all things, for some new car or shampoo, and asked if he had heard anything back from Richard. He laughed and said that the other actor [the first to read] had gotten the part [on the spot]. I nodded and waited to go in and read for the shampoo commercial, feeling bitterly that I was exactly where I belonged.

A few years pass, and I am in rehearsal, happily, with a "weird, downtown" play opposite an actor who had worked frequently with Richard. They say casually that he will be auditioning actors for the next play and that they think he'd really like me; would I mind if they mentioned me to him? A week or so later I get a email from Richard—the world had gone from answering machines to emails— asking if I'd like to audition for his new play. He doesn't send any material to prepare. I arrive early at his building and sit on a bench in a nearby park, waiting, telling myself to not try to make anything happen, just be there. Richard is waiting for me in the doorway, and greets me simply, almost happily. Richard ushers me beyond the kitchen to a couch in a small cubby of bookshelves and eases himself into a well-worn chair. "Tell me a little about yourself," he says, and I realize he doesn't remember me. Which is good, because I feel a different person from the one who entered that apartment years before. And so we talk, and talk, about art and philosophy and theater, about film and mysticism and religion. I can see beyond him long rows of tall bookshelves and that his entire loft space is set up like a library, a maze. We talk of collecting books, of certain writers, of online searches for obscure volumes, and whether or not one should ever make notes in the margins of a book. We talk for over an hour, and then Richard says, would you like to read? He hands me some pages of text and says to not look at the page too much, look at him, paraphrase the text if I have to. I somehow instantly memorize half the lines. The play is about a cowboy, it seems, and some sort of advisor and a woman, and it all plays with the tropes of the Hollywood western, gambling, shootouts, damsels, whiskey. Richard has me read the role of the advisor with various accents, various attitudes, and he reads the other parts, playfully, remarkably, hilariously, swaggering and speaking with a loose jaw as the cowboy, swatting at the six-guns on his hips, fluttering his eyelashes as an acerbic, seductive saloon hostess. We try a few more variations, and I am not deciding anything, I'm just living in the momentary moods and tones, and I'm not acting, I'm just playing, seriously playing. Eventually Richard stops and looks steadily at me. "That's very good . . ." he says quietly. We sit and talk a bit more and in an instant Richard's tone changes to fear suddenly and he announces, "I know what you're doing! You're trying to make me *like* you so I will cast you in the part!" I laugh and sort of shrug, thinking, well, yeah. Richard stands and says it was nice to meet me, and walks me quickly to the door, saying in a rush that he hasn't made any decisions about the role yet, he may cast an actress in it, he thinks maybe a South Asian actress should play it, maybe two actresses, so its all up in the air, and goodbye! In the doorway I say to him well, however it works out

From left to right: Juliana Francis Kelly, Jay Smith, and T. Ryder Smith in *King Cowboy Rufus Rules the Universe*, 2004. Photo by Paula Court.

is okay with me since it has been wonderful to meet and talk with him and that I think he is one of the great artists of world theater. Richard makes a sound like coughing and growling and flaps his hand dismissively at me and the door loudly shuts me out into the hall. I don't feel awful riding the coffin-like elevator down because I genuinely believe what I said, that no matter what happens, this morning was an extraordinary event in my life, the culmination of a thirty-year dream, to meet and talk and *act with* Richard Foreman, the creator of *Rhoda in Potatoland* and everything since, and to have him pause for a moment and *acknowledge* whatever it was that I had learned about acting and about being a person through all my bumbling mistakes and failures. I walk quickly through the lobby and don't care whether I am cast or not. The next day, Richard calls to offer me the role.

Roles

JAMES URBANIAK: I was in the cast of *The Universe* with Tony Torn and Mary McBride (plus a silent chorus of six "servant" figures, also known as "dwarfs" in Foreman parlance). I played a classic Foreman protagonist who was tormented/seduced by a man and a woman. Our characters had our own first names. Foreman, of course, does not write traditional plays. He achieves classic dramatic effects of tension and release but the meaning is veiled, cryptic, elusive. The characters, events, and setting exist in a wholly theatrical world outside the parameters of the naturalistic or recognizable. I say this because to describe "who my character was" is to engage in subjective interpretation. But since I was playing the part, I had to make those subjective interpretations. Essentially, Tony's character played taunting games that made my character question his own identity and decisions while Mary's character and I were engaged in a push/pull, love/hate relationship with romantic/sexual overtones. So my subjective interpretation was that I was a man at a psychosexual crossroads. But take that with a grain of salt. For the audience, our characters' behavior would have had its own meaning.

FULYA PEKER: I was an intern for *Wake up Mr. Sleepy! Your Unconscious Mind Is Dead!*, and I was a performer in both *Deep Trance Behavior* *in Potatoland* and *Astronome: A Night at the Opera*. Most recently, I took part in the film Foreman was shooting with the Bridge Project. I was the "black haired woman" in *Deep Trance Behavior* and "woman with the white blouse" in *Astronome*. Those were the names we put on the playbill, just to make clear to the audience who was who, since there were no "characters" in the traditional sense in either of the shows. Instead of assigning roles, I think, Foreman preferred to work on the textures he initially saw in each performer, to incite patterns or colors that he wanted to add to the fabric of his shows. What each performer represented was defined during the rehearsals with various transformative acting and design directions. The only initial clue I had about my part during *Deep Trance Behavior* was the costume note, a "femme fatale." There are two major female types that recur in his shows: a dark and a light lady, a "femme fatal" and a "coquette." According to some audience members, I was the menacing, elegant, dark lady who retained a secret in *Deep Trance Behavior* and a crazy magician or beastly alchemist who hid the truth in *Astronome*. . . . But who knows what I truly represented. It remained an unspoken secret. That very secrecy somehow helped me capture and sustain an uncanny attitude on his stage.

ROBERT CUCUZZA: *My Head Was a Sledgehammer* was the first show where he employed a team of non-speaking actors to assist on stage—"dwarfs." (I think Colleen Werthmann paved the way for this with her small role in *The Mind King*). When Richard approached me about being in it, he said he wanted some "non-speaking actors to move stuff around the stage and point at things with sticks" (or something like that). He went through a couple of names for us—"illuminati" (he was always ahead of the game) and "functionaries" (he was also not only unimaginative at times but almost "anti-imaginative"). Then one day he put us in pointy hats and started calling us "dwarfs." That's what stuck for this show and for many many years to come, even without pointy hats. To anyone outside, this was a miserable and thankless job. We had to be at every six-hour rehearsal, six days a week, for three months and I think we were paid about $100 a week. Me? I loved every minute of it and sucked up those rehearsals like a sponge.

My first "real" role was the Bell Boy Hat in *Permanent Brain Damage*. I was so excited to be cast . . . and then found out that this, too, would be a non-speaking role. Richard was at a transitional point, as was much of New York theater in the mid-1990s. I think I remembered that he had tired of working with "actors" and wanted to work more with bodies than on performances . . . which was frustrating. D.J. Mendel was undoubtedly the main character and we all revolved around him. We were on stage the whole time and had some featured moments but mostly the whole rehearsal process was a slog and the run was downright awful. I've never been so bored in a theater as I was performing in that show—and that includes as an audience member at shows where I fell asleep.

In *Panic! (How to be Happy!)* I was Umberto. This guy was a demented, falsetto-voiced "Renaissance fob in a pink doublet."[1]

As a playwright, director, and producer in New York, I spent six years as an artist-in-residence at Richard's Ontological-Hysteric Theater where I mounted many original plays and co-founded the Obie Award-winning Blueprint Series.

SOPHIA SKILES: As four women in *Now That Communism Is Dead, My Life Feels Empty*, we were costumed identically: loose white pants rolled at the knee, black knee pads, brassieres, wig caps, heavy dark red and black eye makeup, fanny packs, and animal tails—and significantly, face masks and heavy rouge on and around our belly buttons. I remember hearing that image described as open wounds, which felt like a displaced orifice for our hidden mouths. It was hard to get past the idea of being part of a harem, with our mouths covered. We toured to Amsterdam and Vienna.

JAY SMITH: In *Paradise Hotel*, I played Ken Puss Puss, a sort of simple-minded, simpering wimp with a cartoonish Spanish accent. I played Fred in *Now That Communism Is Dead My Life Feels Empty*, who had long hair like Fabio (which was attached to the brim of a little leather cap I wore) and spoke like a snide surfer. As Rufus in *King Cowboy Rufus Rules the Universe*, I was a prissy

English fop pretending to be an American cowboy. In *The Gods Are Pounding My Head (AKA Lumberjack Messiah)*, I played Dutch, a bearded lumberjack who was so withdrawn as to be practically non-functioning.

STEPHANIE SILVER: From 2004 to 2007 I usually played some kind of mischievous insider; a mysterious and ghostlike provocateur. My movements were like a creature that appears and disappears into the walls, very softly yet direct. I knew the number of steps between one place to the next and my eyes were almost always fixated on something or someone.

SHAUNA KELLY: I was "the woman in a white dress" in *King Cowboy Rufus Rules the Universe*. I wore a lacy, white, elegant, floor-length dress, and gold nose and lip jewelry. In one scene I played a chicken rolled out in a cart on wheels wearing a yellow feather headband, beak, and tutu over the white dress. I dismounted and walked around stage cocking my head at the lights and sound effects. My chicken was extremely lifelike with pecking and twitching. Perhaps it was the most naturalistic performance in a Foreman show? I'm not sure but at least it was a memorable enough part of the aesthetic that my chicken made it into the *New Yorker* cartoon for the show!

JULIANA FRANCIS KELLY: I played Julia Jacobson in *Paradise Hotel* (toured Europe), and the Beautiful Woman in *Bad Boy Nietzsche* (toured Europe and Japan). I played Suzie in *King Cowboy Rufus Rules the Universe*, a worker in the cigarette factory, and I got to wear a beautiful creamy crepe dress that had been worn by Richard's best interpreter, the great Kate Manheim.

Suzie felt different to me than the other three characters I played for Richard, because she was the only one who had a job. I can't remember much beyond that, because *Rufus* was the most explicitly political Foreman play I ever did. *King Cowboy Rufus* (embodied by the wonderful Jay Smith) was a kind of fractured funhouse version of George W. Bush. It was really exhilarating to feel Richard turn his gaze on the issues of the day. That and getting to wear Kate's dress are what sticks with me the most from *Cowboy*.

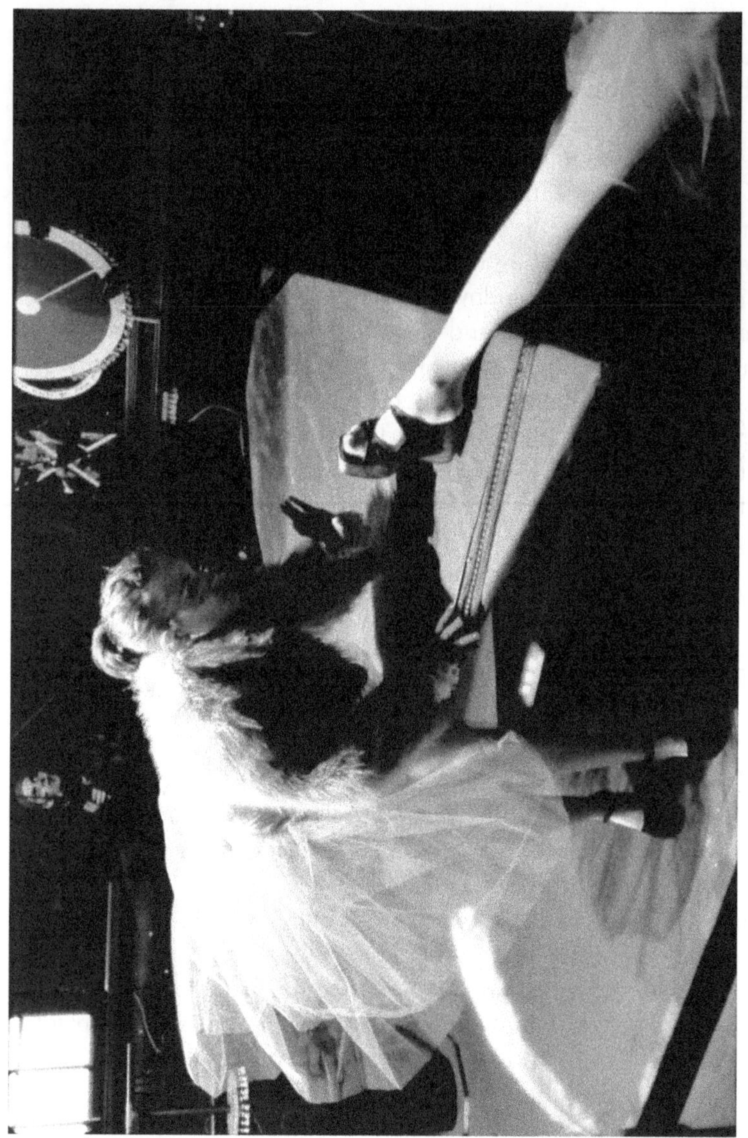

From left to right: Frank Boudreaux and Juliana Francis Kelly in *Maria del Bosco*, 2002. Photo by Paula Court.

I played the title role in *Maria del Bosco* (toured Singapore). Maria was my absolute favorite, because the play starred three women, Funda Duval, Okwui Okpokwasili, and me. We began rehearsals exactly one week after 9/11. Everyone was in shock. The bomb site continued to burn, then smolder for weeks. Trains kept stopping and actors would be delayed. Signs of the missing were posted everywhere, along with poetry.

One moment meant everything to me in *Maria*. . . . As Maria, Foreman directed me to place a baby doll into the pilot seat of an airplane that was about 4–5 feet long, and carry the plane overhead toward a large, paned window stage right. I placed the nose of the plane against the window, and—for me at least—that juxtaposition transformed the window into one of the twin towers. I held the plane there for a moment—then moved the plane away, and someone took it offstage and I don't believe it ever came back . . . It sounds mawkish to write it out—but I swear it wasn't, perhaps because it was so muted, and none of us reacted to it emotionally. The plane with the baby was there and then it wasn't, the window remained intact. I felt that moment secretly signaled the desire to reverse the calamity we were living with.

WILLEM DAFOE: In *Miss Universal Happiness* I played the role of the local psychotic. Later, I performed the title role in *Idiot Savant* at the Public Theater.

JOHN MATTURRI: In *Vertical Mobility* and *Pandering to the Masses* I was simply a member of the onstage crew, moving props and set elements around, posing in tableaus, and engaging in sundry actions. In *Rhoda in Potatoland* I was called Admirer in the script and at one point walked up to Foreman, who was sitting at the tape recorder in front to the side of the audience, asked him if he was the famous Richard Foreman, and for a moment exchanged places with him and briefly worked the recorder. In the same play, I also appeared in a giant potato costume.

KARL FRANKLIN ALLEN: In *Astronome* I had a bloodied butcher's apron, knee high leather boots, riding pants, and a sort of Egyptian hat

From left to right: Charlotta Mohlin, Jay Smith, and T. Ryder Smith in *The Gods Are Pounding My Head* (AKA Lumberjack Messiah), 2005. Photo by Paula Court.

with a snake on it. At various points in rehearsals I also had a little beard drawn on my face, a monocle, and a bald cap that was not glued down but those all got cut during the rehearsal process.

JOHN OGLEVEE: In *Pearls for Pigs* we were a motley crew of dung-hat donning, black-lace stockinged, white gloved, bespectacled, fake-buttocked, G-string wearing, stage attendants with our own highly subversive modes of being. In hindsight, I would liken us to the Koken from Noh or the Kuroko in Kabuki.

THERESA BUCHHEISTER: In *The Gods Are Pounding My Head* I wore blue shiny bloomers, a wrestling belt/brace, a black turtleneck with a medal velcroed on the front, fingerless leather gloves, a bowler hat with the rim cut off and white and black stripes along the bottom and a golden jeweled cross on top, John Lennon glasses, dangly earrings, a stippled beard, tights, and black dance shoes. I looked great. I still sorta dress like that. I would go all over the east village in costume. The deli guys knew my look and order—toasted wheat bagel with just tomatoes.

CHRISTINA CAMPANELLA: I played "Cristina, Her Chief Rival" in *Benita Canova (Gnostic Eroticism)*. The piece was very dark and I was sort of the comic relief: a big, loopy Valley-Girl who was the clumsily sadistic boss of the other girls but also sort of a big dummy. It was extremely fun (except when it wasn't, of course—as is the whole world of RF, I'd say).

The character mostly came from this weird voice we came up with. A valley-girl accent was the jumping off point (Richard's idea), which we then bent into something a little more surreal. I am also a singer, and Richard definitely had me work my full vocal range with lots of extended melodic inflections. I'd never worked with lavaliers before, nor experienced the intimacy of close mic-ing, and it totally changed my life. The ability to be super detailed with every aspect of my voice while not having to project any volume completely radicalized my way of performing. It was like allowing the audience to listen in on my thoughts.

FRANK BOUDREAUX: My "role" in *Maria del Bosco* was as one of the five supporting "Stage Crew" who worked as a kind of lascivious chorus, eyeing and enticing the lead women with consumer-era distractions and diversions against their struggle to transcend their limitations—both human/social and self-imposed. We five were the transporters of Richard's complex web of loaded and obscure symbology.

CHARLOTTA MOHLIN: I was the female lead in *The Gods Are Pounding My Head*. My character, Maud, was a sprite-like girl experiencing everything and every line for the first time. Very lithe and bouncing from one end of the stage to the other.

DENISE LUCCIONI: While working for Artservice International, I met Richard in 1980 when he came to Paris to cast his play *Café Amérique*. He seemed intense and shy, or enigmatic, and spontaneous. Kate was there too, impeccably bilingual, and I felt she was checking how I managed.

I assisted Richard in hiring a crew of builders for the sets he envisioned; a team of dressmakers to make the costumes he had designed; and I translated meetings, press appointments, texts, etc. . . . A couple of weeks before rehearsal started, Richard suddenly asked, "Who's going to translate rehearsals?" I said, "Well, I'm going to be there all the time, I can." Richard asked, "Who's going to write the book?," I said, "What book?" He said, "Well, you know, the book. . . . Who comes in where and when and how, what music is playing, how the sets are being moved, and the props, the lights . . . the book!" I said, "Well, if I'm going to be there all the time, and translating, I might as well write the book." Innocent little me had sealed her own fate.

Thanks to Richard I had a grant from the French ministry of culture in the fall of 1982 to work with him in New York. He was staging a Botho Strauss play for the Public Theater, *Three Acts of Recognition*. The fun thing was I was the European woman, AND I'd seen the production of that play by Claude Régy, a few years earlier. So I appeared very knowledgeable, and the actors would ask me details about the play often, and I felt allowed to answer spontaneously because of Richard's open-mindedness. I remember the day I thought of asking a Georgian cab driver how he pronounced the name of Pirosmani (Pirosmanachvili is the real name). Lo and behold, that very morning, an actor who had the name in his script came up to me and asked me how he should pronounce the painter's name. Perfect timing. I still hear the music of the word.

Looking back, this was a blissful and exhilarating time for me, I worked my ass off, pardon my French, and I could see every tiny result of what I was helping to be born.

SUSAN LATHAM: Working with him as a college intern in 1983 turned into a full-time job from 1984 to 1985 during which I assisted with publicity and fundraising. I began working as his publicist and fundraiser again from about 1990 to 1997, during the years that he was in residence on St. Mark's, and then transitioned to a board member (Board Secretary) for Ontological-Hysteric Theater—I'm still officially on the Board.

I wrote his grant proposals for the NEA and NYSCA [New York State Council on the Arts] about a year before each production and although the titles and names of characters changed, I remember the descriptions stayed pretty close to what he gave me.

MANUEL IGREJAS: I worked with Richard as the publicist from 1996 to 2009 when he stopped presenting his work at the Ontological. Richard would send me a wild description of what the show was about and I would trim and add a few details to create the first press release. After seeing some rehearsals I would add more information but always wanted to keep it in Richard's distinctive voice.

DAMON KIELY: I worked for many years with Richard under many jobs. I was the producer of the space and his shows for a few years—I ran the space for the six months he wasn't in—doing the 7 Minute Series, the Blueprint Series, renting space to Target Margin and Richard Maxwell and Collapsable Giraffe, and also doing my own shows. I also went on tour with Richard with *Paradise Hotel* to Paris, Copenhagen, and Vienna as his company manager. I was the assistant master electrician for *Permanent Brain Damage* in London.

SOPHIA SKILES: Uncharacteristically, Foreman committed to a project during the run of *Bad Boy Nietzsche* that would take him away from physically running the sound design live from his "penguin" chair in the audience. In preparation for his absence, I ran the sound and he trained me using various foam core objects to signify when the sound was too loud/soft or the changes too abrupt/slow. As one can imagine, he was exacting and quick to correct. But when the show showed signs of surviving without him, he was very appreciative. It was extremely challenging to fine tune my sensibility to his, but ultimately deeply satisfying and exquisite to run the show well.

———

SHAUNA KELLY: *Your being at the controls in the audience during performances was something special about your plays as if the audience got to watch you shape and control the show in front of their eyes. Could you talk about that element and the feedback you've gotten about it over the years?*

RICHARD FOREMAN: *In the beginning the sound was much simpler so I would control everything. By the time we got to* Cowboy Rufus *there were people controlling the sound, rolling the tapes, and so forth, and I was only controlling the volume.*

The only feedback I ever got was when I was in Paris and the tape continuously said, "Comprende vous," and at one point the guy in a tweed jacket sitting right next to me turned to me and said, "No! Ze no compra!" That's the only response I can ever remember. Of course there was the famous occasion in an earlier play, I sat in the front with a big sword dangling right over my head.

SHAUNA KELLY: *Why the sword?*

RICHARD FOREMAN: *To indicate that I was doing this thing. That I could fail at any moment. The sword could fall and pierce my skull at any moment metaphorically.*

MIKE TAYLOR: As technical director I'd come in and out of rehearsals. I'd watch to find out what needed to happen, maybe do something while they were on break, or be there to meet with Richard, or occasionally run the light board if necessary. I did most of the work after rehearsal when the stage was empty. It was super fun for me because I got to enjoy the process but I didn't have to be there for the grind.

DAVID HERSKOVITS: From 1988 to 1992 I worked on everything that Richard did in New York and some of the things he did outside of New York depending on the money basically. I would always be listed as assistant director but I would do some of the job of a stage manager in terms of tracking whatever happened in rehearsal (the blocking), working with the actors on learning stuff, calling cues, starting the show, and finishing the show.

Rehearsal

T. RYDER SMITH: [Walking into rehearsal you saw] the space was brightly and evenly lit, and a set of sorts had been built and decorated on the stage. Some music or sound was playing as you entered—often just long, wavering tones—and the tall, narrow theater's carpeted risers were empty of chairs except for two in the back where the stage manager and a sound technician sat, and a well-worn chair in what would be the second row, where Richard sat. That chair had a half-desktop on one arm, like the flip-up desks used in classrooms, and an old console held together with black duct tape which allowed Richard to adjust the sound and light levels. Richard was sitting in his chair almost all the time, and always dressed in similar clothes: gray, loose, sometimes with a scarf around his throat, completely nondescript. He was there when we all arrived, and stayed each day after we all left. It was rare to see him not in the chair.

You entered and found a place on the empty risers to put your things, and you waited.

In addition to the main actors, there was a company of what Richard listed officially as "stagehands" but who were the ensemble performers. They were often young, and not necessarily strictly actors—playwrights, directors, grad students from various arts programs.

Also in the room were the set designer and the props designer—who had the relentless and vitally important job of building or supplying everything Richard wanted to test out, often having to come up with them on just a few hours' notice, only to see them discarded after a single use. (The upper corner of the risers became the "props graveyard" and an archeological record of the process of rehearsal: on the top of the pile were the most recent discards and as you dug down you arrived at the first days of the work. Heads on pikes, weird flags, baby dolls with crowns, bloody buckets, stuffed birds, giant maps. . . . And some props actually survived into performance).

Lastly, in the room was a group of "observers," sometimes called "interns," who came from all over the world and from numerous disciplines and careers. Some were given small tasks, note-taking, or dramaturgical assistance, but most were just there, to be part of the work by witnessing it, and receiving it, and sometimes by offering a comment on it, or just reactions to it, laughing at or being moved by or engaged by a bit of stage business, an episode of choreographed movement, a new version of a scene, a sudden pause in the action, a sound cue. They helped make the room a dynamically creative space, and we thought of them—as Richard did, too, I think—as full collaborators, even if they didn't say a word.

And so the room felt full, with twenty or so people in a space that seated only 100 in performance, and the work began and ended promptly each day, 10:00 a.m. to 4:00 p.m., with brief actor breaks and a short lunch break, six days a week.

There were no windows in the theater and very little space backstage, and a narrow office only Richard and the stage manager ever went into, so everyone was in the room all day, in the house or on the stage, all of us sealed off from whatever was happening outside, "in the world." This was just prior to cellphones and news traveled more slowly, so you felt isolated working on the show. It was often a surprise on breaks merely to see what the weather was doing that day. The plays began rehearsing in the fall and opened just after the new year, running until April, so one experienced three seasons of the year only in a marginal way. You lived "at" the theater and "in" the work.

The workday proceeded like this: You were expected to arrive on time, if not early, and be ready to begin at 10:00 a.m. precisely. Richard rarely greeted you when you arrived, and whatever socializing there was among the cast and crew was always friendly but subdued. The actors and ensemble put on whatever costume pieces they were working with, and assembled on the stage.

DAVID HERSKOVITS: I would show up at the workshop [at the Institute for Advanced Theater Training at Harvard's American Repertory Theater] thirty minutes or an hour early, just to get there and be ready. Richard showed up early too and we would sometimes sit comfortably in silence. I would review my notes. I would make some coffee. Sometimes we would talk but often we would not. For a lot of people that would just freak them out but I didn't need any chit chat and neither did he. We were there to work and that was great.

When you start rehearsal there's no talk; there's no read-through. He just starts staging the play. "You come over here, touch your head and fall down. Okay let's do it again. Right. This time don't fall down. Touch your head and turn in a circle. Let's look at that. Okay." You go on like that until you've staged the whole thing.

ROBERT CUCUZZA: On the first day of rehearsal, you'd walk into the Ontological and the basic set would already be assembled on the stage, and there were rough stand-in props and basic costume pieces. He'd gather everybody together and then say something like, "Well, I don't really know what I'm doing so let's just start." Then he'd go to his chair in the house, next to his little jury-rigged sound board, the actors would go on stage, he'd put on a [sound] loop, and then he'd just start staging the show. We'd work like this until we got to the end of the show, usually for about six weeks, if I remember correctly.

It took a lot of structure and discipline to stage that chaos. Rehearsals started at 10:00 a.m. on the money. He'd be in his chair in the house a few minutes before, checking his watch. As soon as 10:00 a.m. hit, he'd say, "Okay, let's start," and he'd begin directing. Breaks were run the same. The stage managers were told by him to interrupt him to call break, which they did. We ended on time. Despite his upper-class upbringing and sophisticated aesthetics, he was very working class in ways that made him approachable. He was never not working. He was the first to arrive and the last to leave, putting strings and gaffe tape all over the set, turning it bit by bit into this baroque external manifestation of his mind.

JOHN MATTURRI: Arriving at the first rehearsal there would be the bare bones of a set and a script with lines assigned to characters and a few other notations but not much else. During the first period of rehearsals, Foreman would go slowly through the script page by page, setting up blocking, actions, and so on. This staging would change night by night as Foreman would slowly layer in visuals, actions, lighting, and sounds, gradually building up the final play. What struck and attracted me during this process was its ad hoc development: rather than impose a preset conceptual scheme on the script he would seemingly improvise the addition of these elements, constantly refining, adjusting, changing.

MANNY IGREJAS: I think I was at every first rehearsal. It was a way to meet the cast and get a feel for the show. I always made a note of when the first string made its appearance across the stage. Then the dolls, crumpled paper, artwork, and exotic props started to populate the stage. Richard knew where he wanted to go and it was exciting to watch him work his way there. He always had first rate performers and it was a pleasure to watch them dive into his work. I always looked forward to entering Richard's world.

FULYA PEKER: I had always been stimulated by his rehearsal process as much as, if not more than, performing in his shows. The first day of rehearsals felt rather like tech rehearsals. Because, unlike in conventional theater, on the very first day, the initial set, the lights, the sound loops, the costumes, the props were all present to be gradually deconstructed by the director. The performers would enter Foreman's playground and he would begin transforming things. There were moments when he would suddenly approach the stage with scissors and cut your costume, or you would return from a lunch break only to find giant letters on the walls that were previously covered with precise geometric shapes; or you would come the next day to find some "red pubic hair, which looked like a pizza pie," attached to your costume, or a "pink bra tied to the edge of the giant pendulum."

WILLEM DAFOE: The thing I remember most—the thing that is so unique about Richard is he writes a text without any character designation so basically first thing he's assigning text to different people or he's trying to make music out of what he has in the room with the people. Much of the beginning is just designating who says what because that's not clear immediately.

KEN NINTZEL: Not only were Richard scripts written by him but essentially they were bits and pieces that he had previously written and assembled. So there were always line changes and script changes with the new pages being brought in and sandwiched in between other sections.

———

RICHARD FOREMAN: *There are so many poets who say that a line just comes to them and then they build a poem out of that line. And it's not that they're saying, "Oh, I want to write a poem about my mother." Good poets don't do that. One day a line comes and they take hold— "That line is sticking in my mind. I've got to make a structure around it." Because the truth is any subject is as good as any other subject; if you go deeply into them, you end up always in the same place—the world, the way the world functions, and the truth of the world.*

———

CHARLOTTA MOHLIN: The script changed several times per rehearsal. As did the décor and our costumes. You never had a chance to be completely comfortable with your lines which made for a very electric performance. It was my first time acting and I took it for granted that this was how you rehearsed a play. It is unlike anything I have experienced since.

ROBERT CUCUZZA: Here's his process, as succinctly as I can put it. This pertains to the shows I worked with him on between 1992 and 2003. At home, he'd nap, read a bit, watch some TV, often soap operas, and jot down standalone lines or sequences of dialogue. As he was approaching the start of rehearsals for a new show in the fall, he'd gather lines that seemed to go together in some way into a "script," often without any characters assigned to them. So, it was just a string of lines. He'd also make a model of the set—a messy and unsophisticated 3-D representation of the field that he had in his head, made of jagged foam core and gloopy hot glue.

RICHARD FOREMAN: *. . . the texts are slightly . . . abstract is not the right word. I don't know what word to use but lines come in from left field, right field, all over the place, and the lines need something [the set] to bounce off of, to reverberate with so you have a sense there are many possible associations with each line.*

T. RYDER SMITH: You could have scripts in hand if absolutely needed, but one also learned to quickly memorize any changes since Richard needed to see the scenes played out fully. He would put a simple shape on a scene, and then repeatedly refine it, rewriting or reassigning dialogue, precisely choreographing movement to music and sound cues until every moment was simultaneously simple and intricately complex, connected to larger, more amorphous, patterns. It became clear early in the process that rehearsals were about Richard searching for something that was either immediately "a performance"—a moment or exchange fully lived in without obvious "acting"—or was the gestation of something which would be able to appear and maintain itself as "artless" or almost "random" in the actual performances. Richard used the stage and actors as a living sketchpad, drawing, erasing, crossing out, slashing, or just intricately shading, adding detail; he would step back, lean close, and then put it away, coming back to it with fresh eyes later, pleased with some of it, appalled at other parts, until things, as he said once, "made emotional sense." "My plays aren't intellectual," he insisted. "They're emotional."

JAN LESLIE HARDING: You have to learn the script before day one. You have to be off-book. Once you're on stage, if you're one of the main three characters you're on stage a lot. You're not running off and staying off for another scene or anything. Everyone's on stage a good amount of the time but when I would get off stage, I would look at my notes preparing for the next minute. Eventually it all comes together. It's not like we're rehearsing whatever scene tomorrow so think about it the day before. You go in and open yourself up—BOOM you're on stage and you start taking notes or doing things. And Richard's saying, "Oh yeah. Do that," or "No, no, no, no. Don't do that." That's another thing I really loved about him. He was really blunt. It was clean and clear and he would change his mind a lot so you never got attached to anything, like the monologue he's going to cut.

He would go through a big chunk of stuff and he would give notes and tell you to change the first five minutes of it, but not do it again with the changes. He'd move on without rehearsing to get it in your body so it was an exercise of all your acting potential when you finally did it again.

The interns would all be asleep on the risers. I think initially there was an intern that was assigned to the main characters and the dwarfs. He would have an intern for each actor, like seven or eight people, who would write down the blocking and changes for everyone every day. So someone could say, "What am I doing now?" and there would be someone on book immediately. It was really smart. But yeah, they would still fall asleep.

Things were modified constantly, which was great because it really felt like you were in a living, breathing thing that you had to be 100 percent present for because you might do something fabulous and Richard would keep it. You'd be like, "Oh I tripped on this thing and I didn't do it on purpose but he used it. It's my trip!"

In rehearsal for *I've Got the Shakes* he had me in these high-heeled, patent leather, thigh-high boots. One day I walked in in this 1940s little linen Chinese dress. It had ripped on the bottom so I had shortened it and he said, "Oh that's much more perverse.

Wear that." I was supposed to be in a red, vinyl, bustier corset thing but then when he saw me in this little Chinese dress he thought that's much more perverse to have this little girl dress on with these boots. That kind of thing he would change.

He was still constantly taking things in until after the big blow out when he was going to cancel the show, which happened every time. Oh, he would make the final chunk cut and get it down to time; it was always an hour fifteen at the most.

The first time I worked with Richard was the BAM piece and the script was set because he wasn't changing Kathy Acker's text. So I got his directing technique in that piece. When you start rehearsal for the plays he wrote, you have to be memorized on day one, which is fantastic in a way. I mean his scripts would be like three inches thick because they were all double-spaced and he would use a very big font so you get this thing that's three inches and you say, "Oh shit I have to memorize this." But there's a lot of space on those pages but it's daunting at first. But everybody does it and you don't question it because it's just the way he works. He's got a reason. It might be just a very practical reason for him.

There's these short back-and-forth lines, this repetition, little variations to the same line, so you come in perfect [perfectly memorized] with that and then it's really interesting to see what stays and what goes. He made little changes but I didn't feel like he cut a lot at all. He just tried things in different ways. He has the set completed from day one too.

JAY SMITH: I was surprised that there was no table work. We were immediately outfitted with body mics and thrown onto a built set with no scripts in our hands. You had to have excellent memorization skills just to keep up. It was like being a glob of paint on an artist's canvas. Dialogue was rewritten, added or cut on the spot and we had to write the changes into our scripts during the rehearsal breaks and memorize them overnight. I remember feeling like enough material for six plays had been rehearsed before the final script was settled on. The length of the rehearsal process starts to play tricks with your mind. Seasons change, holidays pass, and you're still showing up there six days a week for six and a half hours a day. I had never experienced anything like that.

JAMES URBANIAK: Rehearsing with Foreman was exhilarating. The actors were required to have their lines memorized on the first day of rehearsal, which is unique and unusual. (We were all cast a few weeks before rehearsals started so we had time to learn the lines.) Because rehearsal is so precisely physical, Richard didn't want scripts getting in the way, even from day one. We needed our hands free. The first week of rehearsal was basically Foreman blocking us. "Cross there, spin around, say the line." He said we didn't really have to think about it that much. We blocked the whole play. Then the second week, we'd run what we'd blocked and I remember Richard saying to one of us, "Now why are you doing that?" And one's initial response was to say, "Because you told me to . . . ?" But then one realized that Foreman was trying to make sense out of his instinctive blocking of the first week. And thus began the collaboration between director and actors to find the logic in the abstract.

The second week was about trying and discarding. Because the blocking was so abstract and seemingly "random," when we finished rehearsing a scene Foreman would have us get our scripts and write down our movements. At the end of a sequence, Foreman would say, "Okay. Write." We'd grab our scripts and notate. Early in rehearsals I sometimes had trouble remembering all this detailed blocking and I remember Richard asking if I was going to be able to handle it. (In a gentle way, he was never brusque or rude.)

Richard starts experimenting with the soundscape from the beginning. Musical loops and (famously) recordings of his own voice uttering mysterious phrases in his appealing lower register. One vocal loop that he used in rehearsal but got cut before we opened was him repeating "Break something." In our last week of rehearsal he added a new vocal loop for the end of the play, a recording of his voice saying "Empty space calling. Empty space calling James." I found this rather moving, to be honest. Richard's voice beckoning me from the beyond.

T. RYDER SMITH: [In contrast to working with Foreman] the standard method in commercial and even some experimental theater was to begin with a social event, a light brunch-like meeting of all the artists involved, listen to speeches by and watch presentations from the director and playwright and the designers, who had already decided on the costumes and set and lights and sound, and then to read the script aloud while sitting around a table and spend the next few days discussing and analyzing it, after which one began to tentatively stage and rework scenes, eventually running them all together, moving into the theater, adding and incorporating the design elements, performing a few previews for small audiences, and then opening the play. In many cases, all that happened over a period of only three or four weeks, and almost everywhere the unspoken rule was that the general atmosphere of the process was to be kept friendly and playful and positive. Which meant that it was sometimes easy to not take anything "seriously," even when the subject matter of the play was serious. Things were kept at a distance so as to not disrupt or delay the tightly-scheduled process of production: there wasn't *time* for that, one was sometimes told, but more than that, there wasn't imaginative space for it; nothing was allowed to be truly dangerous or unsettling, or unsettling beyond the level of titillation which sold tickets, and so there was no chance and no opportunity to—no grammar with which one *could*—question the work, the text, the design, or more importantly the entire enterprise of making theater. There was no time or space to dispute the foundational concepts of either the art or the culture it was a part and product of; you were locked into a conceptual apparatus of making "theater," and any existential questions about what theater *was*, or what acting was, or "what we were all *doing*" had no place in the process or the work. You were expected to have figured out any personal concerns long before. To disturb the established process of rehearsing or performing theater, even if you were striving simply to understand the work at hand, or suggest ways it might be done differently, was considered disruptive, and by doing so one was branded "a difficult actor." And yet it seemed to me that such supposed disruptions and questions were the entire point.

With Richard, one knew at the start that rehearsals were going to last three months, and that the work was going to be rigorous. You were to arrive "off-book"—with the text fully memorized—and be ready to rehearse on your feet from the first day. There would be costumes and lights and sound and a set, but everything was subject to change. Endlessly. And the run of the show was set to be four months, no matter what the critics said, and even if no one came, and the show would close on a fixed date even if there were audiences still clamoring to see it. Which meant that we weren't there to please anyone but Richard. And ourselves. And no one was there to make money—the job didn't pay much—and certainly no one was going to become famous doing the show; working at the Ontological wasn't considered a good "career move." And so we were all there, by whatever paths, because we wanted to be, or, really, for various reasons, because we needed to be. And also maybe to find out if we should be. And all that was the unspoken connection between everyone in the room: it was all an inquiry through the project into the project itself, an embodied, ongoing critique and exploration of "theater," of "acting," of "text," and "design," and "performance." We were all "difficult" and were in a place, finally, where we *could* be. And you felt that the moment you walked into the room.

JAY SMITH: I was and still am wildly impressed with the environment he was able to set up in order to make his work. He could practically see a version of the whole event fully realized from day one. Sure, the décor on the walls might change, and full costume and makeup only came toward the end, but I have never seen a director work with so many technical elements in place from the start. It seemed so luxurious to me. Add to that the interns who—functioning like a band of shoemaker's elves—would execute set and prop changes overnight, and you've got a kind of theater-making factory. In that sense, it was kind of magical.

KEN NINTZEL: Although structured like a typical rehearsal, the days were basically Richard working things out on stage in a way that was really a reflection of his own mind. There was little rhyme or reason as to the choices he made except to him and unless you were a super fan or a scholar of his work, it could become a tedious experience. There was also a particular kind of reverence for Richard among the interns and those who worked for him which often resulted in a competition of who could impress him. I often thought of Richard as the cold father figure and everyone around him, myself included, were the children constantly seeking validation.

Rehearsals were often terribly dull [for interns]—sitting and observing Richard's idiosyncratic, mysterious, and impenetrable process. When there were notes to take or props to make or errands to run, it was far more interesting because you were engaged. Otherwise, it was a lot sitting and watching. As a stage manager, rehearsals were the complete opposite of boring because you were so caught up in keeping track of all that was going on. As a stage manager I always equated Richard's rehearsal process to controlled chaos.

DAVID COTE: Oh, there was boredom in rehearsal, or envy that the other actors got lines but we, the Large Male Dwarfs, were stagehands in goofy costumes with deadpan expressions. But we still had to maintain intensity and focus.

FRANK BOUDREAUX: Richard figured out the show in the first two weeks. And then we spent several months watching him fuck around because he had us contracted for that time. But it was one of my favorite rehearsal rooms that I have ever been in. As every intern (who worked as hard as anyone on the official design team or in the cast) knows, being present for Richard's rehearsal process revealed more about his artistic ambition and intentions than the viewing of the final product ever could. The results reveal a great deal—his process is in there but Richard is incorrigibly talkative about himself and his process and thoughts, and to be a firsthand student is incomparable.

ROBERT CUCUZZA: It was the best of times. It was the worst of times. All told, I spent about one entire year in the rehearsal room with

Richard, working on four different shows—one as a production intern and three as a performer. It's so hard to sum up anything or come up with any kind of comprehensive take.

Tenacity—his unwavering search for, grasp of, and then hold on the slippery eel that is inspiration—was evident in the tiniest moments in rehearsal as it was in his decades-long pursuit of theatrical self-realization. In rehearsal, he would spend hours on moments, days on sequences, weeks and months on the whole shebang, digging and digging and digging. Digging for what? We never knew, nor did he. It wasn't like he had a clear picture in his mind of what he wanted. He never had that. He walks into a rehearsal room on day one, and then just touches one single solitary nerve over and over and over and over again until it manifests a three-dimensional, vibrating, visual and sonic hum that sustains over seventy-seven minutes. He just would try stuff. "What if there were discarded volleyball nets all over the stage?" "What if you came in with a gigantic devil mask perched on your head?" "What if you two roasted hot dogs over the giant vagina hats?" "What if you had baguettes as shoes?" (That one actually made it in.)

I was watching *Close Encounters of the Third Kind* again recently and it really struck me as being about the process for an artist like Richard. Richard Dreyfuss's character Roy has an encounter that he can't describe, but that obsesses him. A feeling. A sound. A hum. An inexplicable and unforgettable vision. Then, a lumpy pillow rings some distant bell. Then he forms a shape in a dollop of shaving cream. Then he sculpts a pile of mashed potatoes, getting closer. Then he makes a small clay sculpture ("What are you?" he says). Then he gets angry that it's not revealing itself, so he tears the top off and—boom—clarity. It begins to make not "sense," but *a sense*. Then he just makes the whole damn mountain in his living room. (Just like Richard used to do in his loft back in the 1980s.) Then Roy sees Devils Tower on TV, drives to it and becomes part of it; and it, part of him. To me, this movie is about the impossibly lonely pursuit of a vague artistic idea that no one, including yourself, can see . . . until you can.

Creating nontraditional theater like I do, and like Foreman does, requires the freedom to have an abstract and inexplicable idea and then the tenacity to try to bring it to life on stage, despite not knowing what in the name of sweet baby Thespis it is that you're trying to make. The moment of "that's it!"—when one finally sees a manifestation of that vision that first came to you—well, it's one of the most absolutely thrilling parts of being an artist. I learned it from him. I learned that tenacity from being the pillow, the shaving cream, the mashed potatoes, the clay, the yard waste, and, ultimately, the spaceship that arrives, the close encounter of the third kind.

When asked once if there was anything he'd like to achieve that he hadn't already, he said, "I'd like to be abducted by aliens." True story.

DAVID HERSKOVITS: In a conventional show you would take time out at the beginning of the rehearsal process to talk about the world of the play and the internal world of the acting. With Richard it began with a very outside-in physical direction for the actors but there would come a time in rehearsal where we wound up sitting around talking about the feeling he was interested in or what kind of world it was. There were those conversations, though we didn't start with that.

He would talk about other works that were touchstones. He talked about this movie called *Miracle in Milan* (dir. Vittorio De Sica, 1951) which he really loved. At the time, the Public Theater had an art-house movie theater. He got the Public Theater to rent the movie and screen it for us so one morning we came in and went to the cinema and they screened the goddamn movie for us. We watched it as part of rehearsal that day. It was amazing and that was just because Richard felt there was something about that movie and the kind of world the movie created that he wanted to remind the actors about.

So Richard would try to give us analogies or images to work with in order to understand this strange world. He would give conceptual direction like, "Everyone is your enemy and if you say the wrong thing everyone is going to kill you" or just imagine certain weird things about a particular environment and that would sometimes lead the conversation.

JOHN COLLINS: Being in those rehearsals felt like spending hours at a time inside Richard's brain. There was generally a kind of quiet intensity about the rehearsals. As a young director, I was delighted to get the opportunity to see this genius at work.

There was a kind of singularity of focus in rehearsals that was very different from what I do and what, say, Liz LeCompte does. We others go into the room looking for connections to appear between actors and set, actors and sound, actors and actors and then start to tease a show out of what we discover.

DENISE LUCCIONI: He always stimulated my awareness, focus, intelligence, practicality, and efficiency. It was a constant challenge to try and always keep up with his standards and expectations in rehearsal. I ADORED the rehearsal process, all three times. The first time felt like being thrown into the deep end of the pool and learning to swim by myself, feeling that this very human and respectful boss (a mensch) trusted me, somehow.

Attending rehearsals at the Public Theater for two months or so gave me distance from it that helped me get a broader picture of the work. Watching the work, it grew on me because of the physical space and the rhythm. It activated other parts of my brain, the ones that could register, clarify, analyze, and organize my thoughts, insights, and emotions about the work itself not only about its making.

JOHN OGLEVEE: It was a very manipulative, creative, land of fantastical id and ego battling each other. There is very little "drama" in a realistic sense in Richard's work.

I often felt I was watching a sculptor working with living clay.

DAVID PATRICK KELLY: It was like being in a living painting or collage. I always said it was very hard to build but, when finished, like inhabiting a luxury machine.

There were lots of laughs and discussions.

KARL FRANKLIN ALLEN: The rehearsal process was really satisfying. I enjoyed working with an artist whose work I respected and had been so influential for me.

ETHAN GOULD: The rehearsal process was something that was super interesting to me because it felt like a more human way of approaching text and objects. It really reverberated years later when I started doing more illustration and scene work. The iterating and accumulative process of addressing a moment from different angles is something I think about a lot these days with writing and art.

For a long time, my takeaway was my interest in the density and maximalism of Foreman's outcomes. And lately I've been thinking back on the kind of serene quality I was feeling at the time. It's hard to put into words but essentially it was validating to experience Foreman's transparent theater-making process. The process was creative in the moment and not something that had to be finished conceptually before rehearsal. He wouldn't hide or suppress his instincts and ideas. Instead, he would apply them with an immediacy that reflects how instincts and ideas are cognate to one another.

MIKE TAYLOR: [Rehearsals were] super fun and nerve-wracking. I came into a rehearsal of *My Head Was a Sledgehammer* one afternoon after they had been working all morning. They were running this one scene over and over again with variations each time, trying to get it right. I watched them do this for about half an hour. Then Richard, who had been saying, "Let's try it this way . . ." each time, said, "Alright, STOP." So they all stopped and looked at him, and he said, "Why isn't this funny anymore?" and Henry [Stram] said, "Because we've been doing it for 4 hours?" and Richard thought about that for a second and said, "No, that's not it."

FRANK BOUDREAUX: It was a bit frustrating to repeat the same actions for weeks and then have Richard throw everything out. It made me feel that he was toying with us rather than genuinely working out the right balance of the show. However, if I had not been in the underpaid position of "Stage Crew," it might not have even been frustrating—after all, that is what I was there for.

TRAVIS JUST: I loved it, though it was numbingly repetitive (particularly when the lights began to be added).

JOHN OGLEVEE: The repetition [was frustrating]. We were automatons meant to emote and bring his world to life. We were tools. We were learning to be a piece of a puzzle on which we could never really voice a perspective.

KEVIN HURLEY: It was hard work and very intense. You never knew where he wanted to go. You had to give up control to him, trust his process, and give over to his vision.

WILLEM DAFOE: Foreman is great for performers to work with because I think the level of engagement is always quite intense. There's no relaxing.

ROBERT CUCUZZA: Richard was the first taskmaster I ever worked with, the first true artist. Theater had always been mostly fun prior to that. It was the first time that I encountered that amount of drive and precision and seriousness. It was foreign to me. I'm a class clown and I don't like confrontation, so it was an adjustment to work with him. I couldn't slide by on making jokes, nor appeal to him in that regard. And his aesthetic is in many ways all about hostility and aggression. He's hostile toward theatrical traditions. His directing style is aggressively precise. He likes for his actors to menace each other and the audience. He doesn't suffer fools gladly and I was (and still am) a fool. He also has the ability to pierce to the core of your being and shine a flashlight on the darkest hidden corners of your soul. And then make you use it in performance. It was scary as all get out. I'd never felt intimidated in rehearsal until I worked with him. Intimidated by him, by his aesthetic, by his notoriety, by his intellectual rigor, by his brutal honesty, by the part of theatrical history that I was occupying, by the people who'd come see his shows.

T. RYDER SMITH: Rehearsing with Richard felt to me like doing the genuine work of theater artists for the first time in my career, and joining, in my small way, an obscure, disparate lineage. I loved it. It was exactly where I wanted to be, and exactly the work I wanted to be doing. I felt at ease, utterly engaged even when overwhelmed and confused or embarrassed, completely challenged, completely *called upon* in an existential, and even in what I would call a spiritual sense.

Nothing was easy [in rehearsal], nothing was coherent, things were impossible to articulate and yet it all seemed headed somewhere. Richard was searching for something, in the work itself—meaning in both the process of making the work and in the performance of it—but it was something which could not ultimately be fully found, which didn't fully exist to be found, which could never be arrived *at*, only moved *toward*—you could only ever evoke what the work was: you were *performing* what the work was *trying* to be—and it was that which made it so profound, for me, and so completely involving, and exciting. And so much fun, too. I was never happier—despite the dubious nature of that term—in my life or in my career than when working with Richard.

DAVID HERSKOVITS: *What Did He See?* at the Public Theater had a cast of three people. The actors did not have experience with Richard but I think they were interested in him. And they were kind of movie stars actually. It was Will Patton and Lili Taylor in that show who are mostly screen actors and they had a really hard time with Richard. I spent a lot of time just talking with them and trying to help them. Will Patton, a really nice guy, had a hard time with it. But nobody ever fought. Everyone was nice about it. Everyone was respectful but it was just hard for him to digest what was going on and find his own way into it. But eventually he did and he did a great job with the show. He did find a way to enter the strange world Richard was creating.

The actors that did best with him are the ones who would enjoy figuring it out for themselves. And they would even like it and then come back again and again. David Kelly leaps to mind. They worked together on many shows on and off over the years and David would just thrive in this world and he was the person I remember would say, "Don't tell me. Don't tell me." He didn't want you to try to explain to him what was going on. He wanted that space. He was one who could really embrace that.

DAVID PATRICK KELLY: In *The Cure,* after several weeks of rehearsal, Jack Coulter and I were struggling with the technique developed by Richard and Kate . . . one week all the actors had a day of exploding: first me, then Jack, then Kate. We were above the office of the Wooster Group and they heard us loudly expressing ourselves and were concerned. But it blew over and we all got back to work and won the Obie for best play.

FULYA PEKER: I remember being very nervous during the first few rehearsals. He would ask you to do something and would want you to do it right away. If he didn't like the way you did it the first time, he would drop it. Initially, that rush made me get frustrated; however, as time went by, and as I became familiar with his vocabulary, I developed a kind of promptness, a readiness, a keen responsiveness. In time, I even got to appreciate that rush. Such frustrations somehow help a performer be alert, more agile.

As far as rumors go, he was more aggressive and impatient with performers while giving directions in the past. However, during the shows that I was in, I remember him being respectful and kind. During one of the rehearsals, he told me, "Fulya, I am going to ask you to do something! But if you don't want to do it, I can understand." He wouldn't usually forewarn anyone, he would just directly tell you what he wanted. So we thought he was about to ask me to do something transgressive. And he said, "Can you dye your hair black?" And I said, "Are you sure you don't want me to do it naked?" We laughed. . . . Maybe he was choosing different approaches according to the personality of each performer so as to draw forth a necessary attitude. I don't know.

JAMES URBANIAK: The actors in Foreman's plays always have a wonderful, electric intensity, vocally and physically. Richard has various "rules" for the actors to achieve this. For example, he might say, "When you cross the stage, imagine that you're barefoot and walking on broken glass." What does that do to the act of crossing the stage? It makes your movements extremely careful, deliberate. Richard was full of very helpful mental images like that. Another "rule" was to imagine there was a string connected to your chest and the chest of your fellow actor. The idea was to keep the string taut. Again, this creates a tension and physical awareness as the actors warily circle each other. Another Foreman direction that I quite liked was, "Whatever you are saying, no matter how stupid it may sound, imagine that it is the smartest thing anyone's ever said." With these notes in mind, the performances start to take on that uniquely Foremanesque electricity (and danger).

ROBERT CUCUZZA: *Rules*—There were no rules for how to act in his shows but there were so many rules for how to act in his shows. You just learned them. Or you didn't. And then you'd be yelled at or embarrassed or threatened to be fired or maybe even fired. You could never relax on stage or stand up there like a normal person would stand. That was probably the biggest unspoken rule.

Stupidity—For being an incredibly intelligent, well-read guy who created heart-piercing theater, he really cherished stupidity in rehearsals. I mean, when you've got people walking around with swirly poop hats and baguettes as shoes, you kinda gotta have a sense of the stupidity of life. There were no intellectual discussions. A lot of his ideas were really inane and he'd be the first to admit it. And we'd try them and fail and look stupid and we'd all laugh and try something else that was maybe less stupid and worked or even MORE stupid and worked better. But we all learned to take the stupidity very seriously because it's the heart and soul of his work. He captures the utter absurdity of life better than anybody else.

Trying stuff—He would never give you a chance to learn how to do something. If he asked you to balance on one leg and touch your right eyebrow and you tried it once and failed, he'd cut the whole idea and try something else. He just wanted to see the idea in front of him, not an actor figuring out how to do the idea. He had no patience for that. And after a while we learned that this was a way to get him to cut some of the stupidest fucking ideas in the history of theater.

During *Permanent Brain Damage*, he had the brilliant idea that all of us should wear a short two-by-four on the bottom of one shoe. I'm not kidding. He was really excited about this idea—to have six actors who are running around a stage performing Foreman gymnastics suddenly do all that WEARING A BLOCK OF WOOD ON ONE FOOT. He had the TD cut short pieces of wood right there, got some tie-line and tied A BLOCK OF FUCKING WOOD TO THE BOTTOM OF OUR SHOES. D.J. [Mendel] and I knew just what to do, so we played up how hard it was to walk, how we couldn't figure out how we could manage, loudly trying to solve this problem, making it impossible for him to see what it would be like to watch his precious show WITH A BLOCK OF FUCKING WOOD TIED TO THE BOTTOM OF OUR FEET. He cut the whole idea.

CHRISTINA CAMPANELLA: It was often difficult to figure out how to embody the thing he wanted to see. Sometimes that led to struggles that put a real strain on things. I think my character was easier to handle than the two central characters [played by David Greenspan and Joanna P. Adler]; mine was even fun. Theirs were more complex and dark, and came with heavier burdens for the actors. I don't think Richard knew what he wanted out of those roles until several months in, so there was a lot of very taxing trial and error.

The work was hard and I felt like there was nothing I could do to help, which was foreign to me. It's not like in a regular play or film shoot, where the actors can work together off camera to try to come up with things that might help them get to where they need to be when they're on screen. Richard's process doesn't allow you to really connect with each other because it's so much about trying to find your way individually into manifesting the thing he wants to see. And when he is struggling or doesn't know what that is yet, and you certainly don't, it can be a terrible feeling. So it was every man for himself, and this was extremely hard on a personal level between us as colleagues and friends. It put a wedge between us. What's so hard about that dynamic is that in the end you still need to fire like pistons in a car engine to make the thing go. It was a difficult balance. I'd heard of struggles like this emerging between performers in other Foreman plays, especially between women— but I was still taken by surprise. I don't regret anything about my time on *Benita Canova*, everything about it was incredibly fruitful for me, except for that.

MIKE TAYLOR: Even if [performers] got it right there's a good chance it would change; especially if they got it right too early cause then it might not be taut or fresh by the time the performance took place. But of course he throws away his own great stuff as well. Script, props, anything that doesn't keep being the right thing, whatever that is. A lot of gaffer tape and foamcore went by the wayside, especially gaffer tape, vast rolls of the stuff.

As technical director there'd be a lot of figuring stuff out, which was fun as long as you didn't mind seeing twenty hours of work get put on the rubbish heap or immediately changed back to whatever it was before. I didn't really mind since the point was to get it wherever it had to go, which is probably why the whole set was moved four feet downstage a week before the show opened.

The learning curve was just to understand that he means what he says when he asks for something and it might change at any time. He might ask for twenty evenly spaced sticks poking out of a platform, or ask for a telephone that looked like a turkey. There was no one thing that was "right"; it all had to do with what happened with everyone and everything else onstage and in the house. It was synergistic, or maybe I should say *gestalt*.

Any frustration was basically when something was almost impossible to do without messing up something else, just on a practical level, like using invisible fishing line to get sixteen hanging lights at a specific matched angle from a 21-foot grid and then the next day having to change the stuff hanging between them without screwing them up or getting them tangled in an extension ladder.

JOHN OGLEVEE: There was an interesting hierarchy created among the cast and crew on many levels. The prop master, Ryan Bronz, bore the brunt of much of Richard's frustration and ire, as he was well aware of the fragile state of an actor's ego that he needed to both coddle and confuse his actors to keep them engaged. Ryan just needed to keep making new props that did or did not make it into the show. I do recall having drinks with Ryan after rehearsals when he was on the edge of trying to find out how he was going to fulfill yet another bizarre request for something that had to cost next to nothing but look great on stage and that might end up in garbage heap.

JOHN COLLINS: I was in a constant struggle to understand what was going on around me. There were usually others in the room who seemed to get it much better than I did, especially David Patrick Kelly and Henry Stram in *The Mind King*. They were both veterans of other Foreman shows. So it was a completely fascinating and intimidating atmosphere. I learned an awful lot from Richard's singular focus, his determination, and his rigor.

I came into the job with almost zero knowledge of professional audio. I realize now I was doing so much wrong! That is, I was doing things wrong technically speaking. But that didn't matter, Richard needed me to understand the delicate dynamics of the sound score that he was looking for. I had to learn how to hear the very bottom threshold of where sounds became audible and make sure that transitions and cross-fades were done seamlessly and, sometimes, almost subliminally. (These things would have been easier had I understood the gain structures of the analog mixing boards I was using). I also had to learn a lot of that technology on the fly. Why were we suddenly hearing taxi driver radio communications over the theater's speakers? (We accidentally built an antenna out of the speaker cable runs.) Why did that microphone suddenly sound like it was underwater? (There was a big drop of actor sweat on the mic element.) Why did the one actor's microphone suddenly stop working in the middle of a show? (We still don't know.)

KEN NINTZEL: I was hired as stage manager to run *I've Got the Shakes* in performance [not rehearsal] but this in no way prepared me for what was to come—actually stage managing Richard's rehearsals. I had taken stage management in college and had stage managed a main stage show there. That combined with things I had learned in directing classes like blocking, shorthand, and basic prompt book [master notes on the production] was all I knew. The first time I was stage managing in rehearsals, I remember asking Richard how the other stage managers did it, and he said he had no idea. I developed my own techniques: indentation in notation and shorthand for staging as a director but Foreman's plays were way beyond your normal play.

Change was the only constant in Richard's rehearsal process and keeping up with that change was a huge learning curve. Changes in scripts, changes in accents, changes in names, changes in where one would enter and exit, and changes in who would enter and exit with what prop and where props started and where they ended. Oh and not forgetting the sound and light effect cues that the stage manager also needed to perform because the sound operator was already overloaded. Let's not forget taking notes, constantly being at the ready to take note of a direction that Richard gives because in his famous words, "as soon as he says it, it's out of his head." Plus dealing with ten actors (four to five principal characters and four to five dwarfs depending on the production) all with unique personalities of their own.

Richard was not always the most communicative person so being expected to be a mind reader was always an issue.

Working for Richard was like Nietzsche and "the digging the hole"—excursive.

PATRICIA YBARRA: Doing technical work for Richard, even when you were redoing things or saw something you spent time on dismissed after fifteen seconds, was part of what you signed up for. What was harder was when I was actually trying to keep us on budget. When I was in that seat, seeing an idea I knew would be cut with a high price tag was stressful. The technical crew and I had a pretty good sense of when something was going to be cut, and we tried to delay him a bit at times to no avail. We waited two weeks for a giant fiberglass swordfish, and when he saw it live, he simply said, "That is stupid." We knew that. Also, [for me] as a scholar, Richard's deconstruction of his own models [of the set] made me crazy. They should have been in Lincoln Center, not in the trash.

JAN LESLIE HARDING: He generally would tell costume designers what he was thinking, they would come up with stuff, and then he would modify it or chuck it. But he would do the same with his contribution (the text).

I even made props for him like a duck with a ribbon coming out of his mouth and a golden egg coming out of his ass. I'm not sure. And the horse—oh my god, the horse. I borrowed the horse and somebody broke into my car that night and stole the horse so I had to recreate the horse, paint it, and get it back to him without him knowing it. It was a totally different horse. The horse he has in storage somewhere is not the original horse.

PAULA GORDON: It seems to me that Richard was trying to create a sensation in the audience (or maybe only in himself) that was almost always eluding him. The sensation would have to be intensely pleasurable and at the same time teetering on the edge of pain. This need not be a physical sensation only, but could be that precipice between enlightenment or nirvana and madness. A sense of astonishment—belief and disbelief. Or an oscillation between the two—I have the impression of buzzing, tremolo.

At the time, however, I was aware only that the precise effect he was going for was elusive and his methods were obscure. I could never predict when he would be invested in an idea and when he would toss it aside. As a technician and production manager, it was frustrating, because he would try different things; he would ask for props or effects that would take time to make and then be cut almost as soon as they appeared on stage. I remember when I finally figured out how to defeat these requests (sorry Richard, though I'm sure you knew what I was doing!)—or maybe it was just one request that I felt would take so much time to execute, I suggested something even more complicated and spun it out to an absurd extreme. It was a birthday cake or something, and by the end of my "what ifs," Richard just said, oh, never mind. But by then, I was so invested in my extrapolations, I actually wanted to try to make the thing!

I still believe that the giant carrot I made for *Miss Universal Happiness* from foam, muslin, hot glue, and large feathery ferny sticks I bought in the flower district, which took days to make and was cut almost immediately upon completion, and which Jim C. [Clayburgh] then hung from our sign outside, was years later the inspiration for the logo of The Gourmet Garage a bit further north on Wooster Street.

DAMON KIELY: I remember one time for *Benita Canova* Richard wanted some garden gnomes for the set. Pre-internet and pre-Uber and pre-cell phone I think. So we had to look in the phone book, find a place in Queens that sold garden gnomes, and send some interns way out on the train to buy them. They almost killed themselves getting them back because they were solid concrete and about 3 feet tall. They weighed, I don't know, 50 pounds each and they got three. It was an insane journey back on the train. He painted them pitch black and gave them little "nose rings" and "rings" made out of small fake jewels. Then he stuck them in the corners as set dressing. Was it worth it? Of course! Those kind of unexplained little Easter eggs all over the set did exactly what he said—made a reverberation box.

DAVID HERSKOVITS: One day, in rehearsal for *City of Amateurs*, he staged the whole thing and it wasn't satisfying. [In order to fix it] he was going to create a "bang" with a piece of wood and the actors would have to stop and react as if there'd been some kind of earthquake and then take a breath and continue. I was tracking where all the "bangs" went as he put them in based on his impulse as he watched the work.

Similarly, with *What Did He See?*, he was sitting in The Shiva at the Public Theater, the smallest theater there, and it was late; it was kind of like dress rehearsal time, and he was very unsatisfied and he said, "No. I have to change something." And in one day he said, "We're going to put in a wall of plexiglass panels between the stage and the audience." And it was the Public Theater so they have a lot of crew and resources and so they just did it like—boom. In came the plexiglass panels. They were not there one day and then the next day the actors came in and there were these panels. It was his willingness to look at the work he'd done and come at it from a totally different direction. At that time the panels were something he used repeatedly, not on every show, but many times.

FRANK BOUDREAUX: I was particularly struck by an ongoing attempt by Richard that he shared with us to have *Maria del Bosco* be a more minimalist design than his previous ten shows. He confessed to trying to minimize use of plexiglass and string, in particular, that had become signatures of his aesthetic expression, as anyone familiar with his work in the 1990s (and beyond, as it turned out) knew. By the time we got very close to the first public performances with very little of his typical visual interference involved, Richard added three taut strings cutting directly across the viewers' perspective in close, uneven latitudes. Some of us in the chorus appealed, "Why Richard, Why?! You worked so long and hard to cut the string." He replied simply—and I think with his profound and earned aesthetic philosophy—"To make it. Look. Better."

———

SHAUNA KELLY: *Why are the costumes, props, and set design so elaborate?*

RICHARD FOREMAN: *Somebody, I think it was Willem Dafoe that said he and his wife had been to some Orthodox Russian churches in Europe and he said, "Oh, it looks just like one of Richard's sets." Because those Orthodox Russian churches are so cluttered with icons and images that sort of create a sparkling jewel that will reflect maybe the activity of god in that space. I don't know.*

I start out with the sets and everything much simpler than how it ends up. And I remember for a number of years I would say, "Okay this year it is going to be simple" and then as we'd start to rehearse, I'd realize that the set especially was like an echo box for a violin and the more complex it was, the more different objects there were, the more facets there were, the more it suggested what was being said could have all kinds of multiple references. That's why it got so elaborate.

———

JOHN COLLINS: Something I remember well (because he said it more than once) was "I can't do the strings anymore." He would say that in an early rehearsal and, within days usually, he was running string all over the set.

KEN NINTZEL: Stage managing Richard's rehearsals was one of the most exhausting experiences I've ever had in my life. There were many days when I would come straight home and crash for two hours then get up and try to reinterpret the notes I had taken in rehearsal. Go to bed, get up, and do it all over again. I lived for the one day off a week. I remember I would go to central park to decompress and totally zone out.

I had a set of keys and was constantly at the theater. Richard really didn't have lots of employees per se. Performing Artservices did his bookkeeping and cut checks. It was really Sophie Haviland, me as Richard's stage manager, and the tech director who had the most access to the theater.

After making it through four months of rehearsals, opening night couldn't come soon enough. Running the show was a snap. I came in at six, reset the stage, checked the lights, gave time to the actors, ran the show, reset, and locked up. I was out by 9:30 p.m. or 10:00 p.m. This also gave me time for a day job.

So, come March, a month before we were going to close and enough time that I'd forgotten about all the stresses of the rehearsal, Richard asks me if I want to stage manage next year's show, and of course I'd say yes. Come September, the madness started all over again.

THERESA BUCHHEISTER: I remember coming home to my apartment on 148th and Broadway and telling my roommates about rehearsals. They were both beautiful musical theater actors who worked at a nice restaurant and made great money at the time. I would come home to sleep in my weird single bed on wheels in the living room and tell them that I slammed my body against walls, held balls aloft, tried not to fall asleep while I was "passed out" on the floor, and had fallen madly in love with one of the actors (of course . . . I was

From left to right: Temple Crocker and Stephanie Silver with strings obscuring the view of the stage action in *ZOMBOID!*, 2006. Photo by Paula Court.

twenty-two! and so impressed!). Then we would drink vodka with Crystal Lite and watch VHS tapes of *Sex and the City* or dating shows or *Most Extreme Elimination Challenge*. Then I would wake up super early so that I would never be late for a rehearsal. EVER.

STEPHANIE SILVER: He was always referencing writers, films, artists, and philosophers. Especially in the beginning, I would go to the performance library and Kim's Video on my day off and look everything up (this was pre-Wikipedia and ubiquity of Netflix). Rehearsals were very introspective in that way. Otherwise, staging was highly choreographed by Richard. By the second and third productions, he'd mercifully allow some of us to make suggestions.

DENISE LUCCIONI: Whenever Richard would say somebody was the only good whatever, I'd take his word for it and go ahead, whether it was a performance, playwright, philosopher, or film. For instance, he recommended the Wooster Group in 1984 when they made *L.S.D.* (. . . *Just the High Points* . . .) before he worked with them. I find this another token of his great generosity.

RYAN HOLSOPPLE: Our show was right after 9/11—so much going on in the world at that point and then my father passed away. Perhaps the OHT was the best distraction I could have had at that time in my life. Where the rehearsals can be really tough and labored, running the shows was really the most fun. Getting to live in that world for an hour almost every night of the week was the best escape from reality I could have, drugs included.

Foreman's Direction

DAVID COTE: As a director, he will give the actors simple micro-motivations: "Say this line like you have a painful throb in your stomach. Say this line like it's the most brilliant piece of wit since Oscar Wilde. Say this line like an idiot. Say this as if you're forgetting it as you say it." [This was all] to keep the performance constantly shifting, disruptive, de-centered, and elusive for an audience.

JAN LESLIE HARDING: He would give you [the actors] adverbs and adjectives about how he wanted you to go about the line or the movement. He never gave you a broad character description, only specific things that you were doing.

FRANK BOUDREAUX: Every day we showed up to essentially obey Richard's matter-of-fact directions—"Enter left quickly and then encircle the glitter-globe with your arms and stick your tongue out"—and revised directions—"now thrust your crotch at the globe, after a brief pause."

T. RYDER SMITH: In one rehearsal, Richard directed an actor to slowly raise a gun and point it straight out, "and everyone react," he said. One young actor asked "How?." Richard lightly gasped. "What?," he mumbled. "How should we react to the gun? What is the gun?," the actor said. The room was suddenly very quiet. Richard looked half appalled. He opened his mouth but couldn't speak for a moment, and then growled, "The gun is *Israel*." Which implied that he was working with a vast architecture none of us had any insight into. Nor did he need us to. He just needed us to "react" to the gun. So it was "Israel." And we reacted.

JULIANA FRANCIS KELLY: "Less Magoo; more Magritte." Apparently, RF gave this as a note to an actor, and it was repeated over the years among other companies of RF actors.

MIKE TAYLOR: "Now do everything with a French accent."

RICHARD FOREMAN: *I often gave my normal actors accents because I think they make you listen to the syntax and to the structure of what's being said as opposed to listening to the intention. "Oh I hate you and I'm going to shoot you." You're listening to the intention but if I say [with a Russian accent] "Oh I hate you and I'm going to shoot you" that interferes with listening only to the intention. When I [directed two plays with New York University students] I was already well-known downtown. It was different and I do think they were two of the best things I ever did. In many ways they were more like the early work because I was exploiting the fact that the actors weren't that good. It made me be very creative in other ways. I used to give them all accents and I liked very much doing that with these kids.*

MIKE TAYLOR: "How long do you think you can whistle?" "Maybe not that but something close to that." His instructions were always precise in some way even if they were weirdly general. "When you pick up this pencil, it is the most amazing thing anyone has ever done in the world." So some actors could run with it or enjoy it or find a way to be, others not so much. For my taste, his best work was with performers who had serious chops and many options. An actor or really any collaborator who can enjoy the game part—game is not really the word—people who know what they're doing and are not intimidated. They are people who are invested but not proprietary.

COLLEEN WERTHMANN: I remember him once saying to Henry [Stram] and David [Patrick Kelly], "You should be like two battling wizards, behind a filigree," and how hilarious it was to me.

DAVID PATRICK KELLY: "David, that's not as interesting as you think it is."

"Could you try not to point your toe like ballet?"

"Always complete the circle or turn. Don't turn back on yourself."

KARL FRANKLIN ALLEN: Richard's final direction to me was "neither smile nor be evil."

JAY SMITH: "Your character knows more than anyone else in the room. You know that the really important things are happening somewhere else, and what's happening here and now doesn't matter." RF said this more than once to describe either an approach to "tone" or to give the actors an idea of where and how their performance should land on the audience.

T. RYDER SMITH: Richard said an actor was too casual about how she opened a door. "That doorknob is a BOMB!" he called out. "If you open it wrong, it will BLOW UP!"

MARY EWALD: Foreman quotes from my rehearsal notes for *Eddie Goes to Poetry City* at New City Theater, 1990 (given in chronological order from within the rehearsal process):

"Trust that whatever you're feeling internally will get seen. Don't try to sell it to the audience."

"This play is brilliant, but over the heads of 90% of the audience. Play it subtly, with arrogance, to the three or four people who might get it."

General adjustment: "Whatever you're doing, try to hide it; try not to let the audience see it."

"Language is always problematic—is it really conveying my thoughts, or is it not? It's an effort, a mental cramp."

"Our task is to hide everything, not to show anything."

"Don't try to manipulate the other person with your words. Who you're really talking to is a memory—an archetypal situation, or nothingness, which hangs over your left eye like a storm cloud."

"Try as characters to attack the language in the way that I write, which is speed writing."

"A bemused quality to the language—notice what comes out—tasting the words."

"Think of trashing the text."

"Work against the tone of the voice on tape—an ironic reaction to listening to this self-important guy on tape."

"Go for a flat-footed performance style without dancerly resolutions."

"The universe is unknowable. Don't encourage the audience to reduce it to what's understandable. It's unreadable."

"It's as if there's one magic lozenge in town, and tonight you have it. You must keep it under your tongue and be on guard at all times. If you let down your guard and start trying to affect someone else, someone will sneak up on you and steal the lozenge of enlightenment out of your ear or nose."

"Make everything self-referential. Everything you're doing is trying to have an effect on your own intestines. . . . You're each your own chemical factory, trying to secrete the right juices to affect the organs in just the right way, which will lead to cosmic consciousness. . . . It's as though you have an aura cage surrounding your body, and you're noticing all the delightful color displays when you say or do something (which is much more interesting than anything Eddie is doing)."

"You were all dreadful. It needs to be much cooler. You don't need to work it so hard."

"It's as though every word has to be placed on a knife edge. On one side is the cosmos, and on the other side is the human. Think about the key words and place them carefully, so it doesn't tip over to either side. We're not trying to decide for anyone—keep it on the edge. True symbolism bridges the cosmic and the human. If I hear 'intention' [in your delivery] then it falls completely into the human side. It's not slow and searching. Throw it [the line] away. It's not that it's garbage, but more like a kid opening twenty Christmas presents. Open one, that's interesting, what's next?"

"All of you are too conscientious and working too hard. You need to smudge the edges, like on a charcoal drawing. More bemusement, lightness, childlike."

"All of the work should be aimed at the micro rhythmic structure. Not an emphasis on meaning, but on rhythm. Like a jazz musician enjoying the syncopation."

". . . like a Bible seller at her 50th doorbell. Jesus saves and you're a sinner, blah, blah, blah."

Actors' Experiences

CHARLOTTA MOHLIN: It was the greatest learning experience an actor can get—the constant line changes and stage instructions and not having a script until opening night. Nothing will ever be more difficult, although it didn't feel difficult as we went through the rehearsal process. We were part of Richard's process of creating his vision.

As a first time actor I had a lot of ideas as to how you create a character. Who am I? Why am I here? What do I want? I had to learn quickly that my ideas were not important and to put my ego aside. It was Richard's ideas that mattered. It was hard at first but once you allowed yourself to be what he wanted, it became easier. Richard was the creator and you ended up finding yourself in that character—whatever he had seen in us to begin with.

ROBERT CUCUZZA: Remembering. One of the hardest things about those rehearsals, that made them like some kind of fucked-up actor boot camp, was having to remember sequences of hundreds and hundreds of random and disconnected moves. With a traditional play, you have sequences of lines and movements that are based in cause-and-effect. I enter through the door, take off my hat, and say my line—"Hello, Diane." Sequences in Richard's shows were like "hot diggity—vagina hats—twirl thing—misfit club—club hit— row row row your boat." And then each of those sequences had dozens of disconnected moves that all had to be executed with the precision of a dancer next to Beyonce in the Super Bowl Halftime

Show. You're basically just doing what he tells you to do with little sense of how or why or if anything works. The actor compass of logic and story structure is shattered.

FULYA PEKER: He is very articulate and clear while directing actions or choreographing stage movements. Obviously, his shows are non-dramatic and do not require method acting. However, at times, his directions would resonate somewhere between Stanislavskian and Brechtian. But they were of course never story forming, linear directions; they were not connected. They were given to the performers, not as an answer to a "why" question, but rather to a "how" question, just to trigger a particular situation, a particular gesture, or attitude, at a particular moment. The next moment, another action would arise, provoked by an altogether different direction. *Short-circuiting impulses* . . . I always appreciated the way Foreman would trigger that hidden "shaker" within the performers, without letting the ice spill all over!

The rehearsal processes were long enough for the performers to belong to the ever-shifting reality he was creating, to own and refine the staged actions. By the time each show opened, we were each "someone" on stage—not a familiar someone from a familiar story, but a strange someone from a strange realm. Some people might think he uses actors as puppets because he directs every action a performer does on stage, even at times the minutest of actions. But for me, this approach gives actors/performers an immense freedom in terms of filling in whatever is hidden behind an action, as long as they can hide or contain it.

As far as I experienced, during Foreman's shows, it was crucial not to give in to typical acting flaws, such as the desire to be loved by the audience, or to be dramatic. During the period I was performing for Foreman, I was also attending physical theater workshops exploring and practicing Butoh. So, these two completely dissimilar performance approaches somehow got connected in my mental landscape and deeply affected my physicality.

MARY EWALD: Many of the things that we're taught about acting must be thrown out immediately, which is such a great challenge (intentions, clarity of action, etc.). Learning to let go of those

From left to right: Fulya Peker and Joel Israel in *Deep Trance Behavior in Potatoland*, 2008. Photo by Paula Court.

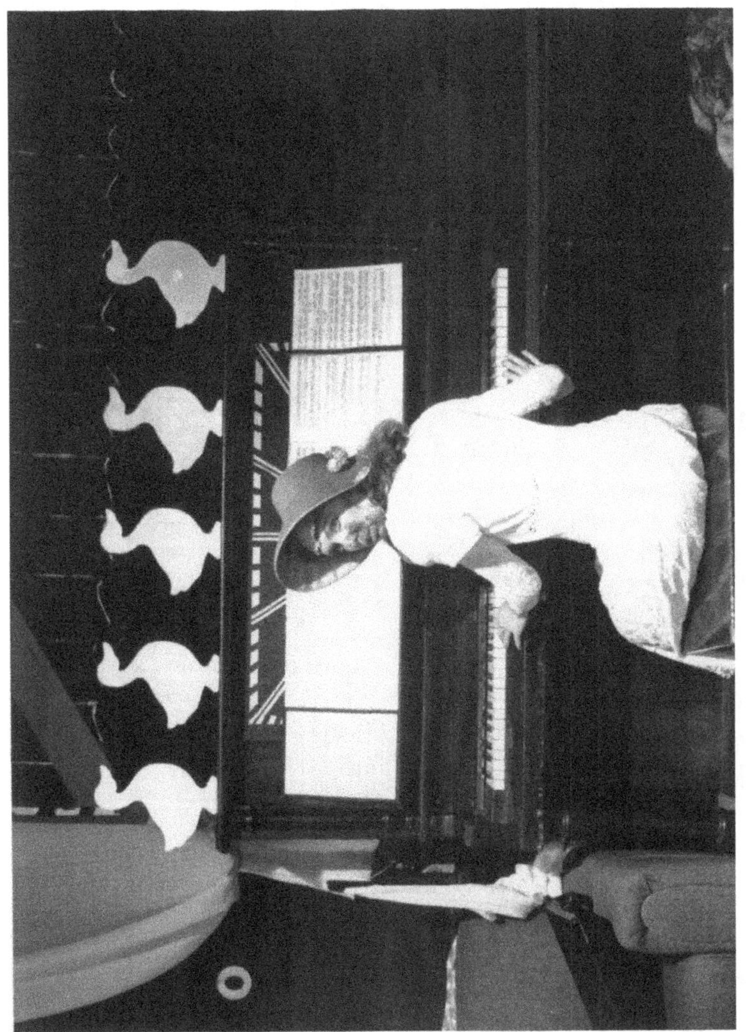

Mary Ewald, *Eddie Goes to Poetry City, Part 1* at the New City Theater, Seattle, 1990. Photo by John Kazanjian.

preconceptions has helped my work on other non-naturalistic texts like [Samuel] Beckett and [María Irene] Fornés.

It was very interesting to have to create a private internal landscape for myself that was very connected to my relationship to the audience. The sense of hiding what's really going on within myself is a very powerful tool to bring things to life in the present moment.

[The challenge was] finding that knife's edge that he talked about. Keeping things on the edge without "tilting into the human or the cosmic." Not full of intention, but not laden with symbolic weight either.

WILLEM DAFOE: He's an inquiring intellectual and sensually he's always looking for different things. So I love that I could never satisfy him and I could never satisfy myself. So if you take that [a need to satisfy] off the table it can be very liberating because you're motivated to find a level of engagement rather than that level of accomplishment. But, at the same time, I will say that because certain aspects of this theater are so frontal, so formal, you are always dealing with the execution [which demands] a certain kind of perfection. But I think internally to perform in his piece you have to be fresh, and you need to never quite complete a thought. It's a kind of—I keep on coming to the word *inquiry*, and that's very difficult to do as an actor sometimes because you're trained to do an action and complete it. In so much of his work, yes, externally you are doing very precise moments; your timing is very precise. But internally, your relationship to those movements is always unstable.

You either had dialogue to say or dialogue you were listening to that you were relating to but not necessarily in a psychological way. You weren't telling a story. You were just dealing with these kinds of psychic knots both physically and mentally. So it was a place of engagement that was very special. While Richard's work was very performed, very formal, and very scored, at the same time, it was very private and very personal and that combination appeals to me a great deal.

JAY SMITH: I primarily approached Richard Foreman's work from a technical angle (like trying to master a piano etude).

JOHN MATTURRI: I can't say that I, in any sense, was portraying a character. My role was simply to follow Foreman's instructions.

SHAUNA KELLY: The acting was physically driven and devoid of the emotional effort to embody a character.

STEPHANIE SILVER: It was very liberating not having to speak much.

CHRISTINA CAMPANELLA: I had to come up with an entirely different way of working—and was at a point in my development as an artist where I welcomed that kind of leap. I loved the constant rigor. It was grueling—very, very hard work—but it put me in the best shape I'd ever been in as an actor. So much was new to me; it was incredibly stimulating.

Finding a through line [a character's psychological arc] seemed impossible at first, but then he'd give me these really basic "soap opera intentions," as he called them—so I always knew exactly what I was doing from the inside, regardless of what my lines seemed to indicate. In fact, those two things were almost never in sync. This was revolutionary for me as a performer; the idea that what you're doing could have an inner logic that has nothing to do with what you're saying—and that when you speak, you're not trying to get anything from the others onstage. You hear each other and respond, but it's not really a dialogue. It's more like you lob your sentence over the fence and it just lands. Then they lob theirs back. I think this is why Foreman's characters, performed in his signature style, are so fascinating to watch. That disconnect—while giving me the grounding I needed to be super present moment to moment—was yet another thing that prevented me from internalizing anything, especially the darker tones of the play. I found it very freeing.

I also fully trusted him. I knew that the text was working on a level that I didn't totally comprehend, and my acceptance of that was also very freeing. I didn't need to totally know what was going on; I only needed to know what I was doing, and trust that I could continually return to that again and again. It was like being caught in a loop, but with no short-term memory to plague me. A continuous present.

———

RICHARD FOREMAN: *I was influenced by what I had read about Robert Bresson, the French filmmaker's use of actors—the way he'd work with them. He'd want them not to act. He'd erase any feeling of intention on their part. He also used non-actors. If you haven't seen any of his films, the best one to start with is* Pickpocket.

SHAUNA KELLY: *When did you read about his use of actors?*

RICHARD FOREMAN: *Early on because I had seen his films early on. When I first started, I thought of Brecht all the time.*

———

DAVID HERSKOVITS: Richard wouldn't naturally give the actors the kinds of things that some of them might need. Depending on the cast I would wind up working with the actors a lot mostly to just reassure and support them. I remember Richard saying in that very first project, "There are some actors who need to know their motivation and their character and they want to talk psychologically. But if I work with the Wooster group then they say, 'Oh shut up. Shut up. Where do I stand and how loud do I talk?'" The actors, of course, who thrived best and would come back more were the ones who kind of got what he was about and didn't need all that stuff. They were fine by themselves.

[As a theater director myself, I feel similar to Foreman in that] "I could give you a reason why we're doing what we're doing but I'd rather not. I'd rather you think about it for yourself." But I'm always ready if an actor or designer wants to talk more or get an explanation. I can do that but I always prefer to challenge them to have their own idea about it. I often say to the people I'm working with that it's more important *that* you choose than *what* you choose. If people have impulses or thoughts, I never need them to explain.

COLLEEN WERTHMANN: I was always worried that I wasn't sophisticated enough to understand how to be inside the text, so I relied a lot on my memories of what I'd seen other actors do in his plays, and on photos of Foreman's muse/wife, Kate Manheim. In fact, he would often call me Kate by mistake when directing me, not because I resembled her, but because I think he'd just worked with her for so long. I took it as a compliment.

FRANK BOUDREAUX: In a traditional play, an actor is trying to bring a writer's vision "to life," so to speak. But with Richard, it is all simple actions, and then he either accepted my way of doing it, or dismissed it as an unusable idea. I never felt it was the way I was doing the action; he just realized by asking me to do what he was asking me to do that, either, the action did not work in the overall *mise-en-scene* or that the direction needed a different presence than my own. Consequently, what was kept for final performance ended up feeling like entirely my own particular creation *left in* by the auteur of the whole. It is not necessarily that different from the performance that is brought out of an actor for a naturalistic play by a traditional director; it is just that I felt I was serving fewer masters. The goals were less layered—no writer's intent to intuit and interpret, per se.

Some felt that they wanted more of a role and more control to make choices. But for me, because Richard gives no motivation or actor's interior direction, I felt that my performance was one of my most self-generated and self-determined of my career.

ROBERT CUCUZZA: Rehearsals were very boring much of the time. It was a lot of just standing there waiting for him to have an idea. He didn't really welcome ideas from actors in the way that traditional directors do. That was one of the rules that new actors learned without anyone teaching them. In early rehearsals, you'd suggest something, he'd ignore you, and then you'd eventually realize that this was going to be the deal for the next three months. You were just a vessel for his ideas. No one was like, "Hey, what if we tried entering from stage right?" or "Ooh, I know, how about if I walk in with a cantaloupe on a sword?" We'd just wait.

Now, I understand why he did it and, in fact, I do it myself when I'm directing. It's not as much about control as it's about allowing actors to just be bored and at rest in front of you. It forces actors to stop performing, to stop people-pleasing, to stop trying to be correct. Once they get bored on stage, they shift their bodies, they chat with each other, they sit down, lie down . . . and it cleanses the room of "actors."

That being said, though, if you work with him enough, you realize that we actually had a lot more agency than I thought. D.J. and I were on our third show with him and we're both directors, so we started just doing our own thing. We soon realized that he either liked our ideas or couldn't remember if he told us to do it. "Did I tell you to do that? No? Oh, well, I like it. Keep it." A lot of our stuff made it into the show. I also could start to predict what he wanted—bent knees, long turns, hands engaged and touching something, menacing looks at other actors and at the audience, maintaining tension across the space, precision. The less he had to teach or demonstrate, the more freedom he gave you.

DENISE LUCCIONI: By the time I worked on *Faust ou la Fête électrique*, I think I "understood" what Richard was about, and into, and up to. All of that occurred almost unconsciously. I never had to "learn" anything, I acquired an experience and a kind of knowledge and know-how naturally, organically, and that is for me the best way to learn. I would say I observed the same kind of process with the actors. That is, as long as they were willing to accept the mold that Richard imagined them in, they would both get close to his vision and reach a type of freedom unknown to them till then. And they would be GRAND.

T. RYDER SMITH: I don't know how the other actors worked, or what structures they used to get through a performance. We didn't talk about such things, indeed there was no way to articulate them. (And even if there had been, Richard wouldn't have allowed it, as he loathed acting in general. He would speak blisteringly about actors discussing their "journey," or "motivations," and reserved a special contempt for any actor's attempt to be charming or emotionally persuasive or cute. "'Love me! Love me!' That's all actor's say!" he would snarl, and then turn to us. "Your job is to make the audience *hate* you.")

I also think actors talking about technique is akin to describing an elaborate dream; only the dreamer can make the emotional/ biographical associations the dream imagery holds. But for what it's worth, here is an attempt to evoke how I found a way to act in Foreman's plays.

I created a series of combined associations and tasks which led me through the action and dialogue of the play, but without any dramatic structure or cumulative emotional architecture. Nothing concluded or arrived; things just happened, and then stopped happening. The tasks I invented were usually physical— and as often concrete—"fling yourself against the wall" or "slowly shift your weight onto the ball of your left foot"—as they were abstracted and stylized—"let your skull melt" or "vomit through your ribs," and the associations could be sensual—"chew on foil," "fall onto grass"—or aesthetic—"gold light," "over-exposed film"— or emotional, sometimes using remembered episodes or moments from my life—"The first time I ever . . .," "That day when I . . . ." The tasks and associations were linked to dialogue, individual words, exchanged glances, props, sound cues, light cues, moments of silence, the facial or body expressions or emotional energies of audience members, and so on. And all were calibrated on scales of time, volume, and emotional intensity, as in feeling something at a high level of emotional intensity very quickly, or the high emotion very slowly and very loud, or low emotion very slowly and very loud, and so on.

And so the line of dialogue, to choose one at random, "Let's have a look," could be said "with" high emotion, low volume, and fast speed, while thinking of my skull melting quickly while looking at a slow cast of gold light pouring through the left wall of the set, and those things would combine, variously, night to night, to give a certain "quality" to the line, or rather an overlapping set of qualities, to reflect the different levels of meaning of the line. And

From left to right: Chris Mirto, Theresa Buchheister, and T. Ryder Smith (top). Tina Barney, *The Gods Are Pounding My Head (AKA Lumberjack Messiah)*, Richard Foreman (photo originally in color), 2005. © Tina Barney. Courtesy of the artist and Kasmin, New York.

that moment of the line would be immediately followed, perhaps, by the simple task of gripping a pole with my right hand, tightly, so as much of my palm was pressing on the pole as I could manage, followed by the idea of my elbow becoming fused with my knee through the air and both vibrating, without me being allowed to show the vibration, which would continue until I let go of the pole, which I only could when another actor said a certain word, and while letting go of the pole I had to run as fast as I could but not move at all, and then there was a sudden sound cue which was "yellow" and "dry," at which point I knew something awful (some remembered biographical moment) was going to come through the ceiling but I had to look at it very slowly to prevent it from falling on me, but then was suddenly tasked with rushing to the other side of the stage while inhaling as quickly as I could and saying a certain word so it made a sound like a stone dropping into a well, which I hoped would affect that audience member right there in a certain way and I had to look to see if it had, but then my bare foot was in ice water inside my boot and I had to put that feeling into my next word.

Again, not interesting except to the performer, but it was a way, for me, to keep every moment onstage charged. I did not contrive the associations, they just arose and "magnetized" themselves, nor could I make any effort to invoke or apply them each night; they simply arose or did not, returned the next night or did not. And I did not construct a narrative or contrive any sort of climax to the events, they simply varied in intensity and pace from night to night, I simply kept part of myself open to the energy of the room, and tried to be aware of everything that was "happening," inside my body, my mind, the body and mind of my "character," the other actors, the audience, Richard sitting in the second row. [Sometimes] I did something learned long ago as an actor: stop acting. Grip the floor with your feet, stand up straight, relax your jaw, your neck, your brow, and breathe in slowly through your nose: place yourself right there where you were, without acting, without any defenses, and just receive what is going on around you, and what is passing through you.

Here was another challenge in dealing with Richard's text: At one point in *Gods*, a character rushed on stage holding up two stone tablets, clearly the cartoonish convention of The Ten

Commandments. The lumberjacks Dutch and Frenchie looked at the tablets and then at each other, and Frenchie says to Dutch: "Don't even think about it."

The line could mean:

- The Ten Commandments could be summarized as saying: don't do these certain things.
- The meaning of The Ten Commandments is that *thinking* of committing a sin is as bad as committing it.
- Don't quote or invoke The Ten Commandments.
- Don't even consider reproaching me with these Ten Commandments of yours.
- Don't you dare write the The Commandments.
- Don't rewrite The Ten Commandments.
- Don't you dare write some manifesto like The Ten Commandments.
- Don't you dare violate The Commandments.
- Don't desecrate the tablets of The Ten Commandments.
- Don't steal, sell, or hide the tablets of The Ten Commandments. Like I am thinking of doing.
- You have broken some of The Ten Commandments but don't let that trouble you.
- Ignore The Ten Commandments.

Those are some of the obvious readings. There are surely more.

And so, as an actor, how do you say the line so that all those meanings are simultaneously there?

Associating them with any sort of image or emotion, as mentioned above, would color the line too strongly, and limit its range of meaning.

I think the only solution is to say the line as simply and blankly as possible, as "blankly" as text on a page; disembodied.

So those two methods overlapped or combined or displaced each other for me: linking the action to associations and tasks, and erasing any coloration and being "blank."

JAY SMITH: I did have a frustrating time in *Now that Communism Is Dead My Life Feels Empty*, when Richard decided that he hated my character about two-thirds of the way through rehearsal. I offered to quit but he said it was too late for that. I was saved when Diane White stopped by and told Richard to cut the American Southern and Russian accents that Tony Torn and I were respectively using. Fred became a completely different character as I struggled to ditch the dialect. Thankfully, Richard liked it.

ROBERT CUCUZZA: Developing the character Umberto in *Panic! (How to be Happy!)* was by far the most frustrating and physically challenging rehearsal process I've ever encountered. Richard had a very clear image of what he wanted from me from the very beginning—which was odd for him. On the first day, he said he wanted my thumbs hooked in my armpits, eyes wide open, and a big toothy grin on my face the entire time. The thumbs were fine but as the rehearsals dragged on, I gave up on the grin. Then he'd ask me again and demonstrate, which turned my stomach. I resisted because I hated to do it, felt stupid, and felt like it was torturous to ask an actor to have a smile on their face for six-hour rehearsals. Then, he wondered out loud if I could get an operation on my mouth. Knowing him well, I knew that he was only half-kidding. As rehearsals wore on and I did it less and less, he'd get angrier and angrier at me. I was unhappy because I knew that I was letting him down every second I was on stage. One day he told me that he had a dream about me—that I had ruined the show. I had a nightmare that I remember clear as a bell to this very day. I was on stage in the middle of the show and I could see a figure in a dark corner of the set. The figure hunched and whipped around fast and looked right at me. It was me, in costume and character, with wild murderous eyes and a demonic saber-toothed grin that stretched my face from side-to-side. I screamed, "Heeeeeere's Johnny!" The real me was ripped from sleep in a way that you only see in movies—I sat straight up, screaming, tears gushing. To this day, it's one of the scariest fucking things I've ever experienced. As we went into dress rehearsals and everything was coming together, I was crestfallen that my biggest role yet had turned out so disappointing. Then, one night as I was getting ready for one of the final dresses, Richard walks into the dressing room, all excited. "Bob! Kate had an idea last night for how to solve this problem with the smiling. Look!" He pulled out a pencil wrapped in black gaffe tape and put it in between his bared teeth, looking around like a maniacal W. C. Fields. I put it in my mouth just like him, looked in the mirror, and saw myself. And I saw the character. And we finally became one. I called the pencil "my bit"—like a horse's bit, for it controlled me. It helped me keep my face in that garish mask for the entire seventy-seven minutes. I'm an extremely technical performer and it became an element of mastery to figure out the choreography and timing when I would rip my bit out from between my teeth to swallow (often when I turned upstage, to maintain the illusion that that was really my face), or say a line. Whether my bit was in or out, my face was frozen in that mask. He never once mentioned it to me again through the course of a three-month run. It became such an integrated and seamless part of my physicality that no one, and I mean no one, even noticed that I had a big black thing sticking straight out of my mouth. He put me through absolute hell but it was worth it in the end because, jesus christ almighty, was that one weird and unforgettable character, and he cast the exact right freak to play him.

JULIANA FRANCIS KELLY: [My role as] Julia Jacobson in *Paradise Hotel* was my first play for Richard, and even though I felt very much at home in non-narrative performance, I was very confused by what he wanted me to do. Every time I thought we were getting somewhere, he'd give us terrible notes, saying our work was something like an awful cabaret performance (paraphrasing here).

I secretly pretended that Julia Jacobson was someone with profound temporal lobe brain damage. To my unscientific mind, this allowed her to be present in a world she could try to navigate but could never understand.

[My role as] the Beautiful Woman in *Bad Boy Nietzsche* was right after *Paradise Hotel*. Richard warned me that the Beautiful Woman would not be such a big part, but I thought that might be a good thing, that a smaller part would give me more of a chance to figure out how to work for him. But I soon discovered that, for

From left to right: Robert Cucuzza and D.J. Mendel in *Panic! (How to Be Happy!)*, 2003. Photo by Paula Court.

me at least, not such a big part in Richard's work did not offer any of the pleasures of a small role in almost any other kind of play or performance. Excluding one speech, my small part meant that I functioned almost entirely as a kind of human special effect. I could not imagine a supporting role in a Foreman play existing outside of their relationship to the central character. They are literally supporting. You are less of a character and more of an element that opposes the central character. They exist only to affect the central character. They are switches on a track, but imagistic. A topless woman with a bag over her head wheeled out on a hand truck (Julia Jacobson in *Paradise Hotel*). You do the same kinds of things any other character might do in a play but far removed from the appearance of realistic psychological development traditional plays require. I did create my own secret narrative to get me through three months of performances, but it was harder, because the character was not designed by Foreman to be psychologically complete.

The Beautiful Woman did get to speak one of my favorite ever Richard Foreman speeches—the "jewels in my bread," in which I mistook jewels for jews in the bread. And it offered up this discovery: as I made a very late entrance in the show, but was required to attend every minute of rehearsal nonetheless, I found myself sitting with the interns watching Richard work for about three full weeks. To occupy the time, I started trying to guess what Richard would do next —"Oh, he will cut that." "He will make that performer spin more, or slam herself into the wall one more time before she exits." I found that I often guessed correctly. I couldn't explain *why* Richard directed things the way he did, and still cannot speak to the philosophies that guided his work—but guessing his next moves correctly felt hopeful for me. I felt I learned some things about theatrical timing and rhythm that I wouldn't have any other way. I'm a person whose education was disrupted by family violence and instability from a very young age, so to discover that I could intuitively respond to work that had previously seemed like a secret language for rich eggheads was exciting.

JAN LESLIE HARDING: He was telling me how to do a line over and over: "Try it this way. Try it that way. No." And it just kept going on. He would obsess about this stuff until he got it right. And then the next day he would cut it and whatever. Finally, I just looked at him and said, "Richard just come up here and show me what you want me to do." So him coming up doing me doing the part, and showing me, and acting, and saying the line was so informative in so many different ways. We had such a good time with that way of working.

COLLEEN WERTHMANN: [During rehearsal] he'd kind of lie on one of the risers, limbs splayed, utterly relaxed, and then calmly spring up to occasionally demonstrate how he wanted a bit to look physically.

MANNY IGREJAS: One of my favorite memories was watching Richard show a beautiful actress how to be sexy. It was brilliant and hilarious.

T. RYDER SMITH: Richard was a remarkable performer, with a unique style. You could hear some of his vocal "acting" in the shows, of course his voice often on tape. [You would also see] flashes of him "acting" when he told a story in rehearsal, imitating someone or re-enacting an event from his life, but on some rare occasions he would come onto the stage to demonstrate a bit of business or explore an action and briefly, fully, perform. At those moments he was like a wizard crawling out of a hollow tree, extricating himself from the cramped small desk-arm chair he'd been sitting in for hours, and trundling down to the stage. His eyes would be bright and mouth open in a half-smile, like a child about to play a trick, and he would begin to explore with an exceptionally fluid physical grace and deep wit. It was like watching Buster Keaton or W. C. Fields. He would pick up a prop or stand in a certain place and start to "fill" it with explorations, deft, weird, frightening, hilarious, like sketching behavior in the air. Sometimes he would find the perfect gesture and say, "Do that," but other times he would suddenly fade in mid-gesture, his face falling in a frown and eyes darkening. He would hand the prop back to the actor and mumble, "I don't know, do something with it" and move slowly back to his chair. It was impossible to say what happened in those darkening moments, but the explorations before them were ingenious. He could have been a great tragi-comic performer. But I imagine he found such things silly.

DENISE LUCCIONI: He made me laugh with his brilliant way to get actors to do whatever he wanted. He was always ready to invent an explanation, a motive, and provide them with what they needed to nourish their part; and how he physically showed them what he wanted. His intensity was contagious.

MIKE TAYLOR: Richard is an amazing actor and raconteur. Great stories. If an actor said, "How can I do that?" sometimes he'd get onstage and try something out, not knowing how he'd do it exactly till he did it, and it was always compelling which I reckon was hard on the actors in some way, though some found it inspiring. But also exasperating.

WILLEM DAFOE: He does a lot of work with making little dances because there's those breaks that he has. So you're making the dances and he would get up and show you something. Richard Foreman is one of the best dancers in the world. You wouldn't think it to look at him but he's a beautiful dancer. He'd get up and do something with you then you would copy him. Or you would try to find your equivalent of what he was doing. That's often the way you would find these little dances, gestures, or movements. Particularly for the chorus people, I think he would often show by doing and I loved watching him move.

————

RICHARD FOREMAN: *I'd like to think that I was pleasant enough. Some directors can be really vicious and nasty. I think I was rather aloof. I've tried to be friendly and open but I was pretty inner directed when I was working because the actors, you know, I didn't want to mold the actors and make them do things that they couldn't do or they'd never done before. I wanted to use the actors sort of as the found objects of their personality. Now, of course sometimes I'd say do it more this way or that way. But I was not interested, as so many* *directors are these days, in getting in there and intimately working with the actors to help pull a character out of them or something like that. That was not my theater. I wanted to use them pretty much as they were. I was satisfied with everything everybody did because I used people who I thought were interesting people and I tried to just use their qualities. My job was to make a composition surrounding them including set, costumes, lights, and everything, but setting them in a composition that they, as they were, would make sense in, would reverberate in, sort of like a jeweler has a diamond that he thinks is good and he puts it into a setting of a ring. So I was putting the jewels of each of these personalities into the setting of the ring—that was my piece. But I'm aware of the fact that I was rather distant because there are directors who are always over their actors saying, "Oh yeah Shauna! Oh that was so great what you did!" And I was never able to rouse myself to do that.* [Laughter]

TRAVIS JUST: Foreman had an ability to draw out qualities from his performers, cajoling them in myriad ways. He could effortlessly alternate between utter inanity and stupid jokes to rapturous, intellectual, and visceral moments.

DAVID COTE: His actors can be encouraged to vacillate between states of stony incomprehension and gooey chaotic emotionalism.

DAVID HERSKOVITS: For many people, not me, rehearsal was really hard. They didn't know how to take it. They found Richard very forbidding. My experience at the beginning is that Richard would tell people very directly what he wanted them to do (not mean, not hard, just upfront about that). I remember him even saying, "I am going to control your body but I'm not going to control your mind or your soul. I want you to live inside it however you live inside it. But I'll tell you what to do." So it would be very choreographic.

T. RYDER SMITH: During the early rehearsals of the first show I did, Richard asked me to perform a certain moment faster. I did so. The next day he told me to slow it down. I did. A few days later he said I needed to do it fast. This kept on for a bit, back and forth, and I privately confessed my confusion to the remarkable performer Juliana Francis Kelly, a veteran of several Foreman shows as well as those of the exceptional Reza Abdoh. "Does he want me to do it slow or fast?," I asked. Juliana laughed. "He wants you to be slow and fast *at the same time*," she said. I felt an entire lobe of my brain light up. It took me months to get even close to performing the moment properly, but I got a glimpse of a whole new way of living and acting when Juliana said that.

JOHN OGLEVEE: As Large Male Dwarfs, we were given contradictory direction for the same movement on nearly all of our blocking. The result was an amalgam of emotions and confusion in our heads as we performed our duties. Whether this was his intention or not, it was very effective in flattening our expressions, but keeping us fully engaged and engaging onstage.

I would watch Richard as he would pull actors aside in between scenes to talk to them privately and then say, "Let's do this again" to everyone. On the one hand, it was Richard revealing his dark secrets to that actor about what that beat was about, on the other it created an atmosphere of paranoia onstage that was palpable. "What had he said? What was the direction?" All of that helped maintain a buzz of engagement with the work beyond the text itself.

STEPHANIE SILVER: I remember T. Ryder and Jay Smith going into the office with Richard to discuss *Lumberjack Messiah* and airing their frustrations with the staging or script or their roles, stifled actor instincts, who knows. It frustrated me that I never felt powerful enough to have that conversation with him. I think I was too young to question him in any meaningful way. Or maybe I was too content to live in that world where art meets philosophy and social disruption that I didn't really care what my role was.

JAY SMITH: It was sometimes hard to know if you were up to snuff. I finally learned that no news was good news: you were fine if he said nothing.

———

RICHARD FOREMAN: *One of my first actors in my first plays was a guy who was not an actor. He was in my first five plays. A friend of ours said, "Oh Bob told me that you never told him he was any good. You never praised him and he was very upset about that." And I thought, well I'm sorry about that. Yeah, but I never told the actors much of anything. I mean we were all in there working together and we were doing this thing. I was not effusive like most directors who deal with actors by telling them, "Oh, honey you were great. Oh, that's wonderful." I never could bring myself to do that for anybody involved in art or anything.*

I used to tell my actors, "Look, I'll be changing things and you'll hear me saying, 'Oh stupid stupid!' and it is never to the performers. I'm referring my own stupid choices, my own stupid inventions."

My first task as an artist is to find a way to use so and so. I did Don Juan by Molière—there was a well-known actor who was really talented who had one little scene playing the tailor and I didn't understand the scene (why it was in the play) but I couldn't make the scene work. And I had to let that actor go because even though he was great, you know he was very good, but I couldn't make the scene work.

I sort of knew who the actors were, and I knew what I would get. I was always looking for whatever was the idiosyncratic nature of any particular actor and just trying to exploit that. That's why if an actor started to do something and I thought it didn't work, they would say, "No, no, no. I'll work on it." I don't want that; it's not the idiosyncratic you.

———

THERESA BUCHHEISTER: I wanted him to like me, which I think I got over. I learned how to observe without fixating on "getting it." I am very grateful that Patricia Ybarra told me to be ready to listen. She told me that it was not my job or in my best interest to try to impress Foreman or teach him anything. That if I could move through my

From left to right: Jay Smith and Tony Torn in *Now That Communism Is Dead My Life Feels Empty*, 2001. Photo by Paula Court.

ego and really listen, I would learn a lot. I did not always succeed at being without ego, but I listened and learned so much. I feel like I never stop learning from that experience and from Richard. I also feel like I developed a weird sense of how things could and should happen to create complex, fascinating shows.

DAVID COTE: During one rehearsal in Hartford or New York City, I remember Richard said something offhand like, "Well it works because you have an actor as good as David doing it," or something like that and I couldn't believe my ears. He praised my acting! But the more I thought about it later, I realized that being "good" isn't necessarily a virtue, or prerequisite for making great art. It was all an ego dance.

JULIANA FRANCIS KELLY: Richard gave me the best worst note I've ever gotten! During the first week of rehearsal of *Paradise Hotel*, we were attempting a sequence called "the coat scene" that I believe had almost made it into several other plays, but after hours of painstaking rehearsal, always got cut. I was trying to figure out a new way of putting on one of seven coats that were scattered across the stage. Richard looked at me, and said, "Oh, I know what kind of actress you are. You are the kind of actress who gets what she thinks is a good idea and then tries much too hard to enact it." Yikes! The coat scene did not make it into *Paradise Hotel*.

SOPHIA SKILES: It felt so mysterious what he liked or didn't, what worked or didn't. It was impossible to know and not feel somewhat anxious about it. I very much loved watching both the actors in *Bad Boy Nietzsche* and *Now that Communism Is Dead My Life Feels Empty* up close as they sharpened and shined their roles.

MARY EWALD: It was one of the most challenging things I've done in my thirty-five years of acting. Finding the right attack to both the physicality and the language was very tricky. After one rehearsal, his feedback led me to think I was finding it. The next rehearsal started with him saying that we were all dreadful. I think part of what made it suddenly dreadful was a sense that maybe I knew what I was doing and started feeling confident. That probably led to an actorly sureness that Richard hates.

JAMES URBANIAK: I remember after a run-through of the whole play, probably in the third week of the four-week rehearsal period, Richard said to us (in his gentle but pointed manner) "Well, that was really terrible. I can't tell you how bad my plays are if they're not performed correctly." I remember in that particular rehearsal I was experimenting with a somewhat bombastic voice for my character. Looking back, I can see what was probably wrong with it: it was presentational without the inner deliberation that's so essential to Foreman. In the last week of rehearsal I hit on a new voice: a slight New York accent delivered with a kind of guarded intensity. It felt right. I also felt I was owning the physicality more. No longer forgetting my blocking, I was more confident and grounded. After that rehearsal Richard said, "James, I really love what you're doing." I mention this not to boast but to show how it all came together quite literally at the end of the last week of rehearsal. Richard was self-critical as well. Once after staging a sequence he shook his head and said, "Too arty." There was another long scene between Mary [McBride] and I that we rehearsed several times before he finally said, "Dammit, I've tried to put this scene in a couple other plays and it never works." He blamed himself and cut it again.

WILLEM DAFOE: Richard is so much fun to work with and so inventive and inquisitive. Often you'll do a performance (particularly in *Idiot Savant* where I was kind of the engine of the play) and sometimes you judge a performance. By the end you think that was a good one or that wasn't so good. He was always hard to read and he'd come back and sometimes I'd feel very good about a performance and he would despise it. [*Laughter*] Sometimes I'd feel not so good about a performance and he would love it. I think that's because he didn't like stuff to settle. He didn't want an actor to be too in control and he didn't want an actor to be too sure. He liked tension; he liked things off balance (as I do in theory) but when you're actually doing it sometimes you crave a little satisfaction of him saying, "Oh you really put that together well." I seldom got that kind of encouragement from him. But I got to appreciate even his often negative feedback.

Miss Universal Happiness was a really good experience and really fun and I enjoyed it so much, but I was kind of buffered by the fact that I was one of the ensemble and there were many of my colleagues there. Therefore, my experience of Richard was a little more muted than it was in *Idiot Savant* where I was his guy. There were other performers but I had to be the motor.

JAN LESLIE HARDING: His idea of what was a good show or a bad show was a total mystery to everyone. I think when you're doing a standard play and you had a good night you know it, the director knows it. With Richard Foreman you just have to stay focused and hope to god it's gonna hit that night.

FULYA PEKER: By the time I started performing in his shows, I was already quite familiar with his production process and his backstage because while interning for him I was part of the team that was constructing the ever-changing [set] design after each rehearsal. Hence, as a performer, I was able to relate to his sets, costumes, and props rather quickly. But receiving direction from him as a performer, was undoubtedly an entirely different thing. Because, in that realm, it felt like even the subtlest actions could cause immense differences. He was sharp in disapproving his own choices as well. "Ah well, forget it! That's stupid," was a recurring phrase he would utter after watching some of his ideas. Sometimes we would work on a very brief segment of the show for hours, repeating it over and over again; and sometimes he would come the next day, watch us run it, and then decide to drop everything we had worked on. But, all those erasures would leave a residue, and those residues would create layers over layers. For me, the rehearsals always felt like being in a playwright's mind; as if he was sitting in his room alone, and we were some figures in his imagination. He would write a line, he wouldn't like it, and he would crumple up the paper and throw it away. Then he would write another line, and so on. . . .

Sometimes he would pick up on a certain thing that a performer would do while casually waiting on stage and add that to the show. He would ask you to do something, but if you liked doing that thing too much, he would sniff that out real quick and eliminate it. We were always joking about that: if you liked something you did and wanted to keep doing it, you had to conceal your feelings, or look uninterested. I guess that was feeding the usual Foremanesque, "I have a secret but I won't tell it!" type of enigmatic performer disposition.

BRENDAN REGIMBAL: It was a lot of work and he would demand a lot with a short turnaround. Maybe he would say to an actor, "Here's two pages of new stuff and we're going to do this tomorrow so I expect you to go home and learn it." Or, "We're going to paint the entire set black tonight and then put stripes on it and we need that done by tomorrow." Everyone is constantly working hard. But it always went somewhere; it always felt like it was going somewhere even though it's circling in on itself. But he was a good leader so you never felt like it was not worth it.

JAN LESLIE HARDING: I am just an actor. I really respond to strong directors who know what and why they are doing what they are doing. Richard is authentic. That means a lot to me and I can give over to him easily and confidently even if I don't understand completely. I was always allowed to ask sincere questions without being judged or misunderstood. There was no ego. Just an innocent quest to bring the piece to its true fulfillment. With a new piece [an original script and world premiere], when I have the director right there, I am not shy to ask, "Where did this come from?" That's where all the really interesting stuff came from about the insights into how he worked and how he wrote. You would ask him a question about a simple thing like the color of something or a gesture and he would answer, "Well in the third grade I was on the bus and I looked out the window and I saw this . . ."—knowing exactly.

I later worked with a big fan of his and he said when he asked Richard, "How do you direct?" Richard gave his little laugh and said, "Well I just tell them where to go." Which is not true. He did so much more than that. But the new person I was working with was a real dick and said, "Just do what I say. I don't have to answer your questions." And I said, "I have to get your ideas out to 600 people. I should understand your ideas."

Richard would always have a bunch of interns and by the third week of three months of rehearsal they'd all be falling asleep on the risers. I remember this one time in *Sledgehammer,* we had these potatoes on sticks and we had to go up the walls with potatoes on sticks. And then we had this other thing where we came in with plates with babies' heads on them and you've been doing this stuff and you're really serious about it and you're on your hands and knees with the potatoes on sticks and the plates with babies' heads on it. Henry [Stram's] had fallen off the plate and we got the worst case of giggles. We could not stop laughing! Every time we stopped laughing it would come up again and then Richard started laughing. The four of us were beside ourselves. It went on for a while. Some of the interns woke up and started laughing. They didn't even know what had happened. It was a stupid thing. But to see Richard lose it and not be able to stop laughing! It would subside and then it would bubble up again so we had those really close moments where you are just on the same plane and it hits everybody in the same way. I love stuff like that.

Foreman's Iterations

PAULA GORDON: One of my favorite expressions, which I attribute to Jim Clayburgh, Wooster Group designer, is "Do it once, then do it right."

FRANK BOUDREAUX [QUOTING MAC WELLMAN]: "Go with your third idea."

KARL FRANKLIN ALLEN: I liked that the work was always changing. Day to day we got new direction, new movement, new additions to the show.

CHARLOTTA MOHLIN: It was like being part of a painting. Richard creates and then erases part or all of the picture. Then you start from scratch. You had to stay on your toes and trust his vision. As an actor you had to stay open to anything and everything. It was an amazing learning experience. And a lot of fun!

COLLEEN WERTHMANN: I remember that huge chunks of the play were being reblocked every single day—often six, sometimes as many as ten pages. The actors were total thoroughbreds, extremely athletic and game for whatever he asked, and he worked them until they were absolutely exhausted.

JOHN OGLEVEE: Richard would block the whole show and then revise and revise and revise. Revise and repeat. Then he'd whisper to someone and repeat.

SHAUNA KELLY: Working with Foreman was a good mental exercise in embracing impermanence. He reinvented the play five to ten times over during the rehearsal process. What had been a "complete," hour-long play was slowly chiseled away in rehearsal until nothing of its original piece remained. It was a lesson in taking risk and not holding on to a creation for fear of not being able to create something better.

DAVID COTE: He works like a painter. Sketching, throwing color on the canvas. Doing a sketch, shading it in, throwing it out, starting over. He works with as much of the set, costumes, and sound as possible to stage the possibilities that arise out of associations with the text. And so, during a seven or eight hour rehearsal, he will go through innumerable combinations of sound loops, movement ideas, use of props, vocal delivery of lines, sound FX, moving around of furniture, and so on, until he achieves the right symphonic, kinesthetic machine he wants.

MANNY IGREJAS: [Richard's process] was very pure and organic. He would work a notion every which way until it suited him and you understood why.

MIKE TAYLOR: The lights and set and props changed constantly. The script changed a lot. There are changes every day. Sometimes for the actors there'd be really really small changes that were very difficult—like, "Where you used to say the word 'the', change it to 'a.'"

T. RYDER SMITH: For the actors, there were an enormous number of daily small changes to take note of and precisely remember. This was a result of the rehearsal method in which Richard would talk as he worked, sometimes explaining what he was searching for, sometimes merely honing physical behaviors, sometimes telling jokes or stories, but it was all following trains of thought, links, associations.

Given the actor's union rule—which Richard despised but obeyed—performers had to be given a ten-minute break after one hour and twenty minutes of work, and so his system was to work for an hour and *ten* minutes and then all sit for the next ten minutes and collectively review and write down all the changes in text and movement which had occurred during the preceding session—and here the stage manager had a daunting task of keeping up with this endless number of miniscule changes—after which the actors had their ten-minute break and returned to run the new material and the changes, off-book. So you were rehearsing during the break, really, if only in your head, because you weren't supposed to have your script in hand once you came back. It was a lot to keep up with, and it never stopped. Every day generated new material, new variations, choreographies. The scripts were quickly filled with notes, cross outs, new dialogue to the point where they were unintelligible and new copies had to be printed. We went through eleven new copies of the script on one show.

DAVID PATRICK KELLY: Short breaks during rehearsal would often be signaled by Richard saying, "Okay. Write." We would have to get down on paper as many of his ever-changing specific directions as possible. I really admired the way Kate's scripts would look at the end of the rehearsal period. It would be covered with glued-on rewrites and notation for movements and directions. It would be thick.

I always thought of it as kind of "ghost ads." Like when you see a building with layers of vanishing advertisements on the outer walls peeking through. Like archaeology. If you didn't remember a change sometimes Richard would occasionally like what you remembered better and change it again.

SOPHIA SKILES: I loved the "stop and writes" and wish other directors would integrate them into rehearsals—just the idea of building in time when everyone can catch up on the changes and record them in the scripts. I am also wondering if these were breaks for him to be released from the pressure of carrying the production energy, providing the logic, direction, and dynamic of the piece. [There were no] conversations or collaboration in generating ideas. Here rather, it was just remaining open to and taking on ideas he came up with. I do remember once playing with the dog tails and chasing myself in circles on break, which he observed and put in the play. Several folks remarked that rarely happens.

We managed to do a full-length run-through within the first week but that show was never performed as the rewrites were so frequent.

JAN LESLIE HARDING: In rehearsal Richard would go through the play bit by bit to the end so you didn't get back to a part of the play for three weeks and he would work chronologically so by the time you got to the end of the play you had not done the first five minutes of the play for three weeks so I would be like, "Shit. What were we doing again?" So we kept these little notes. I would start off with a sheet of paper and I folded it up into sixteen so it was the size of a credit card. I still have one. I found it when I was cleaning out my car and I kept it because they we're just so perfectly Richard Foreman: stick with potato; just cross upstage to roulette wheel; wink at audience; shake your bum. It was just all these bizarre crosses and I would use the note, fold it, and go to the next thing.

RYAN HOLSOPPLE: There was so much blocking, I kept notes and had cheat sheets till I learned it by rote.

FULYA PEKER: During each break we would gather on stage and Brendan Regimbal, the stage manager of the shows I was in, would give us notes from a huge script on which each and every cue was marked with various colored dots.

FRANK BOUDREAUX: Time discipline was complete. We were absolutely on Richard's time, second-to-second, of working time. Breaks were exact. Most Equity productions, of course, can feel similar depending on the stage manager's time management. But there is typically some rehearsal set aside for rumination, discussion, script analysis. In a Foreman process, breaks and lunch were the only time for discussion and wandering focus. Rehearsal time was Richard's time: we acted out his instructions and his imagination. Otherwise we were offstage, and reading silently.

KARL FRANKLIN ALLEN: Some of my favorite moments were at the end of every break going over with my fellow performers each of our distinct choreographies and how we interacted with each other. I still have the notebooks that I wrote all of that movement down in.

SUSAN LATHAM: Though I wasn't present at the rehearsals I know that they were a very intensive and immersive process and that Richard changed things up quite a bit. One year I had a cartoonist for *The New Yorker* who was creating a cartoon for the "On the Town" section. I brought him over to rehearsal and all of the women in the show were wearing elaborate dresses. He spent about an hour creating the cartoon and asked to return several days later to put the finishing touches on his drawing, so I brought him back to rehearsal—he was very dismayed to see that Richard had completely changed all of the costumes, no more elaborate dresses. Needless to say, there was no cartoon in "On the Town" that week.

———

RICHARD FOREMAN: *It's just examining again and again and again to see what's really underlying and what might be discovered that is definitely not visible and self-evident on the first look or the second look or the third look. I don't know if polishing and polishing to see what's really there is creating or if that's just not being satisfied with what appears the first time you look at it. You've got to look at it again and again and again and again and again. So it has a big critical aspect also. Not that I'm making the decisions as a critic but I'm just making decisions as somebody who's totally dissatisfied.*

I used to make the analogy—an old prospector panning for gold. In other words, you pick all this mud up that's coming down the river and you have your little screen and you keep sifting and sifting and sifting, seeing if any gold nuggets appear, and it has that aspect also.

I'm convinced that whatever material you take if you sift often enough, something will appear. Now of course you also have to be a person that can recognize what is useful when it appears. What is gold? I think I can recognize what is gold. I think a lot of other people wouldn't but of course there are people who would disagree with me.

Doing this in the theater and now in film, is similar but it's radicalized working in film because I'm no longer dealing with having to take account of the performers and their real needs (even if people thought I wasn't paying much attention to them). And also having a certain date that I have to get ready for in time—all kinds of practical things in the theater. I have none of those constraints now, working in film. It's going to be ready when I think it's ready.

And much more than in the theater, I'm amazed at how I'll think, well it's done, and then I go back to look at it one last time— It's terrible and I have got to make so many changes. And that process repeated again and again and again. Now it could be that that's because on different days you're a different person and you're looking at it from a slightly different perspective. However, that's okay. You reach a point where you can look at it several days in a row and it still looks right and acceptable. I don't think that was the case so much in the theater.

I think, vaguely, I knew what I wanted to achieve in the theater much more than I do in film because in the theater when I would look at my text before we started rehearsing, I would look at it very quickly and I would have a feeling of, "Oh the play is going to be like this." And then in rehearsal as we worked on it, it would start to go this direction, that direction, god knows what. And then at the end, finally I think that it sort of recaptured what I had originally intuited from that first, fast, casual reading—the feelings I got from that. Of course that's not the case with film because I don't start out with any text that's given me an impression that I then, well, realize. So it is a different process. It's a different trajectory.

KARL FRANKLIN ALLEN: You had to be good at letting things go. Sometimes you'd have a particular movement or action that you really loved and he would cut it or give it to someone else and you just had to be good with it.

THERESA BUCHHEISTER: If [Foreman] liked a line too much it would get cut. He also needed to see things to understand if they would work. One day he couldn't continue without seeing what it would look like to cover the floor with astroturf, so we were all released and I went to see a movie at Sunshine Cinema with Chris Mirto. He would usually only give one chance for something to work . . . I think he just knew very quickly if it was an idea he wanted to carry forth or one for the scrap heap. I learned to update my script in pencil and only at the end of a day, as it would change a lot. Whatever was published in *American Theater Magazine* was not the script we actually performed. I definitely made an effort to not get attached to anything.

PATRICIA YBARRA: The one thing that was fascinating was Richard always directed shows twice. Because of the long rehearsal periods, he would complete a version of the show about halfway through and then tear it apart. It would be better the second time, but there was always the ghost of the other show in the room. I think that Richard was never afraid to throw things away—which is something that is hard to do as a writer and a director. He made difficult choices.

WILLEM DAFOE: Sometimes Richard would do things for a very long time and then get tired of it and just drop it. He's very restless in the rehearsal process. While there's a kind of playfulness, he always has a kind of dour mask of dissatisfaction. And sometimes while he has a great sense of play, sometimes he would just do something that made him laugh and he really enjoyed it but then it would sort of complete itself and he would just cut it. I remember one sequence in *Miss Universal Happiness*—I was in a catcher's outfit and I was naked from the waist down and he had me do this little dance and we did that forever and he'd laugh and he'd enjoy it and he'd start adding elements and we started to build this thing. And then one day he just said, no, you know, we're not going to do that.

T. RYDER SMITH: One consequence of Richard revising so frequently was that many wonderful scenes and sequences would get cut, to everyone's distress, because we felt they worked so well and were so much fun to perform. There was a long sequence we rehearsed for *Gods*, a combination prayer-cycle sex-ritual as if written by Brecht, wherein we sang of the hours of the day while feeding loaves of French bread into the "mighty engine" of a small train. We worked on it for two weeks and had honed it into a precise and very funny and strange sequence and then one day Richard announced it was cut. We all exclaimed "No!" and tried to convince him to put it back, but he was insistent. I asked him, finally, why, and he said it only had two layers of meaning, but everything that wound up in the show had to have at least four.

Later, he explained more: "I have no desire to mystify anybody, I just have a desire to tell the truth, and the truth contains contradiction. I cut things because clarity is not true to the clear contradictions. To eliminate the contradictions eliminates the life."

DAVID HERSKOVITS: Richard is ruthless about cutting his ideas in rehearsal. He is completely harsh and unsentimental. He'll cut anything. He'll work on something very hard and bring it up to a very high level and then he'll have a look at it and if it's not working or he doesn't like it, he'll cut it. There's no sentimentality; he's just a disciplined and mature artist in that way and I think that's really inspiring.

ROBERT CUCUZZA: Richard would stage these complex and theatrical sequences of absolute idiocy, with babbling voices and goofy choreography and crazy music—like some of the most unhinged and brilliant sequences of theater I've ever been in or witnessed. We'd work for hours and sometimes days on these. Then we'd run them, knowing that we were in something spectacular . . . and he'd cut the entire thing. You know why? Because it was too good. Because he knew that the audience would watch it and would collectively agree that it was gold-plated crowd-pleasing THEATER. The only show that I ever saw where it looked like he left all of those scenes in was *Paradise Hotel*. I remember watching that show and just being 100 percent jealous. I mean, the real title of that show was *Hotel Fuck* and it was all about the absurdity and necessity of fucking. And it was just flat-out glorious vaudeville.

Rigor—We started *Permanent Brain Damage* with an entire script of unassigned lines. We took months and staged the whole thing, from beginning to end. He watched a run-through and then threw out the entire play and started over. It was infuriating. The show that we built was fun. But it wasn't what he wanted.

JAN LESLIE HARDING: I don't find he made a lot of cuts. A couple of things always happened. You'd be coming in [into rehearsal] being off-book and the text sounds like some sort of stream of consciousness that he's written on the page (it was a lesson in memorization). Then you come in and start working on it and there are so many things to hang your hat on; it becomes easier. He might change a word or two or a line here and there on the spot but I didn't find he did a lot of cuts. One cut he always made in every production though is he would work a big monologue. Oh, I remember Mary McBride had this big monologue and she was excited because she was one of the chorus. She had this monologue and I was shaking my head going, "This is going to get cut," and of course three days before the performance he cut it. And I was just like, "Welcome to Richard Foreman." But he always does that. He likes to keep the show at a certain [running] time.

Performing the Show

JULIANA FRANCIS KELLY (QUOTING REZA ABDOH): "No matter how harsh the creation is, you must give it as a gift."

DAVID COTE: The final result [the performance] is, in many ways, radically meaningless. No single interpretation of a Foreman play has any more validity than another. It has truly open-ended meaning. So in a sense he stages a demolition of theatrical realism, obviously—but also creates a radical space of sexual and moral anarchy. There's a terminality to the work that is still bracing, and a look and style that is completely unique. In 100 years, Foreman will still be weird. You can probably only say the same for Balinese ritual and ancient Greek tragedy. And maybe early [Philip] Glass opera.

In performance, I really luxuriated in the Zen state of being one with the chair, the poles, my padded butt, the sound loops, the flashing lights, the whole whirling madman circus of it. It was like dance, I suppose. You're just in your body, moving and counting, not worrying about psychology or pleasing the audience. While at the same time, imaginatively, having emotional flashes that are purely fictive—feelings of elation or anger, that are randomly generated by being in the performance. Very trance like and meditative. It was good for the actor's ego.

THERESA BUCHHEISTER: I loved [performing the shows]. I recall. But I probably didn't love it every night. . . . I know I got very depressed during stretches. But every night I would stand out in the lobby and look out the window as Jay Smith stretched his long, long legs on the window sill and watched the graveyard activity [outside St. Mark's]. Foreman would come out and chat about wondering who would come and an idea that he had about a project that revolved around not knowing he was Jewish and adopted until he was in his thirties . . . he was very funny. He would sometimes wear this nice scarf to complement his gray and black uniform he claimed to have purchased at Urban Outfitters. Then, we would go inside when the lobby opened and Jay and I would look through the curtains of the moving castle and spot the older queer couples who dressed alike. Then we would do the show! And maybe some of us would go to Grassroots or Telephone Bar or Cosmic Cantina after.

Sometimes I thought it was unreasonable to give notes after each night of performance, but he was there every night and he cared about continuing to work on the show, regardless of it being open. I respected it but also it was hard, because it made one feel like a failure more often than my heart and mind liked.

JOHN MATTURRI: Once the final form took place, performance was ideally identical, night after night for the run of the show. Small adjustments might need to be made as things inevitably went wrong but there was little room for development and improvisation. This might sound boring but in fact there was something relaxing about knowing that you would be doing the same thing each night for the next several weeks.

This sameness would be balanced by interactions and short conversations—and with one fellow performer, occasional surreptitious sips from a pint bottle backstage. There was a moment in *Rhoda in Potatoland* when I would pass by Phillip Johnston in a narrow backstage corridor. Each night we would improvise some novel and humorous way of getting past each other. For me, as performer, this became an essential element of the show, albeit one hidden from the audience and unknown to anyone else but Phillip and myself.

Each night at a certain point Foreman would shout, "Cue!" and the audience would react the same each night. But the audience reaction [to the play overall] would be different and one would pay attention to that. I remember looking at the reservation list each night to see what friends or celebrities would be present.

JOHN OGLEVEE: Our show was a little different than others as we had our first major run at Hartford Stage. This was a bold move on Jed Wheeler and Mark Lamos's part. Richard's work is a challenge for the 100+ who would gather in the East Village but a subscription audience in a dying insurance town of conservative Connecticut? Well, it went over like a ton of bricks.

In that first run, my favorite story was of a woman in the very front row who answered the seemingly rhetorical question, "When is enough, enough?" When DPK [David Patrick Kelly] was in the middle of a monologue, one of his most salaciously delivered lines was ". . . and I bleed my own birth." It was at that point that the woman in the front row, of Hartford's thrust stage mind you, stood up and said, "All right, that's enough." She grabbed her mortified husband's hand and dragged him right across the stage and out of the room. Richard seemed to revel in that. He said that if the audience was not fleeing the theater, we were not doing our job. He stated on a number of occasions that we were performing to 2 percent of the audience.

T. RYDER SMITH: He said if a few people didn't walk out mid-show, he felt he had failed.

ROBERT CUCUZZA: Oddly enough, I never really considered myself a serious actor or pursued it as a career. I don't know if I was conscious of it at the time, but I mostly just wanted to be in the rehearsal room with him as a director, to be inside his creative process. So, it was always a bit disappointing when rehearsals ended and the performances began. Performances 1–10 were kind of exciting but then 10 through 90 were a struggle for me to stay focused. I had no lines in my first two and then in my third I repeated the same line like six times ("Let's all join . . . the Misfit Club!"). You know, it's not exactly playing Stanley Kowalski. I was basically just a puppet and not riding on the same kind of effervescence that you get with a traditional show. I recall during *Permanent Brain Damage* that I would spend entire performances thinking of other things while still doing my job. I mean, he was at every single show, watching as closely as he did in rehearsals. If he had noticed that I was disconnected, he certainly would've said something . . . possibly even in front of the audience during a performance.

CHRISTINA CAMPANELLA: I loved the long run—when do you ever get that in downtown theater? The work was so detailed and specific that it never became boring to me. Things could always be further refined. It was also amazing to have full houses almost every night, especially when you spend most of the performance staring at the audience.

JAMES URBANIAK: Once you're up and running it's exhilarating, but his shows are so dense, you're glad they're over in an hour. It takes a lot of energy!

KEVIN HURLEY: [Performing is] a lot of fun because he's in it with us. We become a real ensemble.

COLLEEN WERTHMANN: [Performing] got very hypnotic. Because I was in the show for about a total of two minutes, I would be backstage in one of the hidey-holes, listening to the alpha-state-inducing text, and having to kind of pinch myself so as not to get lulled into unconsciousness. I was a visitor in his world at best. It was super exciting to be a part of the play, and an honor and massive privilege to be in the work of one of the twentieth century's greatest avant-garde minds. He was and is a genius.

WILLEM DAFOE: I loved performing [in Richard's shows] because it was so demanding. He gave you this very strong physical score. So much of my approach to performing was formed at the Wooster Group. Basically it was a very task-oriented approach and then, adding on to that, was this kind of enigmatic text that Richard would have.

SOPHIA SKILES: [Performing the show] became about who was coming to see it, the brightness of the light, the distant nearness of the witnesses, and the darkness behind the stages. It really was a dense, disciplined machine with all of these layers, some of which were visible in remembered earlier versions.

JAY SMITH: Performing the shows felt a bit like climbing Mount Everest every night. Though the run time was always about eighty minutes, it felt longer. I attribute this to the physical tension one was required to maintain throughout the performance; you could never go slack or let your guard down. The heat in the theater and the bright white lighting were occasionally headache-inducing, as well. And the audience response was inconsistent, so you never knew at the outset whether you were going to get hostility or enthusiasm coming back at you.

MANNY IGREJAS: We were always after that all-important *New York Times* review from Ben Brantley and got it 99 percent of the time. One terrible year with the gorgeous *Pearls for Pigs*, Brantley was sick and we got the third string critic who didn't understand the show and wrote a listless review. It was heartbreaking. I do wish we could have gotten some more mainstream coverage but it might have disrupted the delicate world Richard created and the purity of it (I have to use the idea of purity again).

———

RICHARD FOREMAN: *One of the reasons I gave up the theater—I always used to be very tense, you know, especially for what kind of review I would get in* The New York Times. *Fortunately, I got pretty good reviews down through the years, but the day I knew that the review was coming out I had a hard time sleeping and in the morning I'd run out and get the newspaper very early. I'd open it. There was a review. It was generally good. Ah wow, great, oh everyone is going to read this. I'm going to be so successful. It's going to change my life but of course it never did. But I kept having that relationship to it. But a couple years before I stopped making theater I still got very nervous.*

I went and got the newspapers but I realized I was no longer seeing a good review and thinking, "Oh boy this is great!" No. I was opening it, seeing a good review—"Thank god they didn't hate it." And that's the difference and I think it meant that some of that drive and lust to make theater that was going to change peoples heads maybe had stopped for me.

———

FULYA PEKER: *Deep Trance Behavior* was a quiet and contemplative show, not aggressive. Some found it "mesmerizing," some found it "not Foreman enough." There were many moments of silence and stillness, along with long stares, elegant stabbings; not to mention giant "Lacanian knots," and a huge humming bird. "Trance" was the key word. In the show, I was constantly ingesting pills in an extremely gradual manner, slowly retracting them on my tongue. A pill that "let you know things," or what have you. There was a sense of being filled with the void. . . . Rather, of meditating. I remember that one day, at the end of a show, as the audience was clapping, I was lying on the floor and saw the red velvet fabric draped right beside me. I couldn't feel a difference between that object and myself. I couldn't feel anything. I was de-subjectified, momentarily. And it gave me so much freedom. Capturing stillness in that ever-shifting present moment. . . that moment of disinterestedness. . . . An emptiness that is full of "reality." During that period, Foreman frequently mentioned Peter Kingsley's *Reality*, and during the rehearsals we had some delightful conversations about that book on Empedocles and Parmenides.

In *Deep Trance Behavior* there were also two large screens covering the upstage wall, films that Foreman shot in Japan and the UK with the Bridge Project. So, even when staring at the audience, I felt like I had another eye on the back of my head, staring at the screens. It helped me constantly shift my awareness on stage back and forth, existing in between two layers of consciousness. It wasn't until the show closed that I saw the whole film. Yet still, I remember only the fragments I saw when I was facing the screen as part of my actions. That feeling of knowing but not knowing helped me practice that unnerving and "penetrating" stare, as if I was *seeing through* but not *looking at.*

Astronome was a collaboration between John Zorn and Foreman. It was an extremely aggressive show. The set was crammed with many objects. There was a giant nose and a huge pendulum on stage . . . "alchemy" was the key word. The relation, if I may call it that, which the performers had with the movement on the film screens during *Deep Trance Behavior* was replaced with Zorn's music during *Astronome.* Because of the intensity of the volume, we were allowed to wear earplugs during that show, as was the audience. I chose not to wear them because I wanted to somehow test how well I could retain my inner silence under such violent aural circumstances. I particularly enjoyed the moments when I got to move against the pace of the music that continuously filled the air all around us. We were kind of encapsulated by it. Hence, I tried to expand my awareness toward the entire space, toward every direction. While performing, I felt somewhat synesthetic at times. Seeing a sound or hearing an image. . . . As if there were two parallel worlds, an aural and a visual one, sometimes touching but never intersecting one another; and I was hovering over those tangent points.

In both shows, almost every action on stage was linked to cues: light bulb cues, screen cues, sound cues, cues taken from another performer's movement, etc. In *Deep Trance Behavior,* we had the film sections whereas in *Astronome* we had the musical sections, scripted as our time score, our framework for the live stage action. The performers had to be continuously alert to hold pace with those scored and cued durations. It was a great test for a performer to improve their concentration and time-keeping skills.

From left to right: Deborah Wallace, Fulya Peker, Karl Franklin Allen, Morgan von Prelle Pecelli, Jamie Peterson, and Benjamin Forster in *Astronome: A Night at the Opera*, 2009. Photo by Paula Court.

T. RYDER SMITH: Performances were an extension of rehearsals. Once the show officially "opened" there would be more people in the room watching, and a bit of vaudeville added, but it would be no different from what we were doing each day. That's what Richard's rehearsals uniquely were: an ongoing performance; not a rehearsal but the thing itself. The work was fully there at every moment, the "result" was already achieved, and yet could never be fully discovered, or known, or expressed; it was simply entered into, and given away. It passed *through* us. And so it all felt infinite. Artistically, intellectually, emotionally infinite. Hence otherworldly. Working on Richard's plays was, in all senses, to live in a different world.

There was a high tension in the room during a performance, which you could not escape from, only find ways to deal with. The action of the play was odd, the language dense or obscure, and there was a deep and penetrating silence beneath it all, which spread out into the room like a solid object between sound cues. That silence was an invention of Richard's, somehow, it was crafted by him as a counterpoint to the frequent volleys of noise and music and language onstage. I've never heard the same sort of quiet in other shows or anywhere outside of real-life crisis; it was provocative quiet, a *noise of silence*, heavy, occult.

Audiences sometimes said they felt something was *expected* of them, sitting there, and they didn't know what it was or how to give it. Some would laugh at certain moments, some stay resolutely or disapprovingly silent; some would glare at us, affronted, hostile, disdainful, some watch in fear, some with an awed hilarity or fascination, many with puzzlement, and some simply drift off.

But the collective energy was focused more intensely than any I have ever experienced, and it gave the actors, from their own point of view, nowhere to "hide." You weren't acting in the conventional sense and so you couldn't "vanish" into your character or characterization. But you weren't merely yourself either, and none of your potential social or personal or theatrical skills had any place in the work, or the room. And yet the work utterly depended on your energy and precision in performing it; nothing could be sloppy, casual, sardonic; nothing could "comment" on your performance as an actor, or distance you from your part in the unfolding event; you couldn't indicate to the audience that you weren't fully there, or seek some sort of complicity with them, as if you were holding something of yourself in disdainful or mocking reserve from the action; you had to find a way to be *fully* there, yet without being yourself and without acting. And any failure to do that, any wavering in your "presence" in or commitment to the action, would be instantly seen by the audience, and would poison the event. And so even though the audience may not have understood what you were doing, or "liked" what you were doing, the event needed you to do it. The event needed your complete and utter presence, as if enormous things were dependent on it. As they, in an aesthetic, and an existential, and indeed perhaps in an ontological, sense, did. So, how, as actor, do you achieve that? And *if* you do, what you do *with* it?

Performing the work changed me. Theater was a crucible, for me, for the things I was dealing with and thinking about in my life and a correlate for what I believed philosophers and psychologists and anthropologists and activists and mystics were doing in their different ways. And that larger or broader endeavor, which had nothing at all to do with a career, or, indeed, with a "self," found expression and definition, for me, in my interactions with the audience in Richard's plays.

The Performers and the Audience

T. RYDER SMITH (QUOTING HENRI MICHAUX): "All is translation, at every level."

CHRISTINA CAMPANELLA: I'd say Richard's style of theater puts the performer in a very powerful relationship to the audience, hierarchically. This is one of the baselines of his performance style. The performers tend to stare directly at the audience for long periods of time. And then there's the big element of the plexi. In *Benita Canova* (as in a lot of his shows), there was a wall of clear plexiglass installed at the edge of the stage, dividing the performers from the audience. In some shows it's a continuous wall; others, there are gaps in it, where the view is unmediated. The house lights are generally kept on, so the audience is visible, and as a result, the audience can see its own reflection in the plexi; a continuous reminder of their own spectatorship.

Concurrently, the performers are watching the audience from the other side of the plexi—and we can see our reflections too. Watching the audience watch me made me feel very powerful, like I was in control of them. Seeing my own reflection simultaneously—watching myself perform for them—became a perverse kind of narcissism: I (the performer) know what's going on and you (the audience) usually do not. One of my recurring lines in *Benita*

Canova (spoken in my valley-girl accent, with increasing volume to be heard over a maniacal sound loop) was: ". . . get it? . . . Get It?? . . . GET IT???!!!"

SOPHIA SKILES: I felt like I was spying on the audience watching—the sense of asking and wondering on their faces.

WILLEM DAFOE: I remember that because of the lights you couldn't always see people. Sometimes you could. I never liked being able to see the audience too much because then you get suckered into performing specifically for an individual or you get more self-conscious. But I remember he always loved the idea of kind of seducing the audience and kind of teasing them.

JOHN OGLEVEE: That wee black space of columns and cramped seating called the St. Mark's Church was a magical temple to the cogs of Richard's brain, I think. I feel Richard's work succeeded best for me there. With the use of the plexiglass and the bright lights on stage we can feel them seeing us and themselves at the same time. There is an intimacy that is lost in larger venues that disperses the energy of the work.

T. RYDER SMITH: I realized, from the first performance in front of one of Richard's audiences, that any attempt to act, to impose an acted "performance" between the audience's intense collective gaze and myself would be a cowardice, and a betrayal of the work. I had to let myself be seen, fully seen: all my flaws, all my compensations, all my history had to just be there. They would see it all anyway: *it couldn't be hidden*. And: *nor could they*. Since so much of the performances were spoken directly to the audience, or played directly out to them, the audience was as exposed to the actors as the actors were to them. I made a point of trying to connect, each night, with every audience member at least once during the show. And by "connect" I meant to just look at them, not acting, not asking anything, to just see them. And what you see is everyone's "performance": everyone's costume, characterization, routine, and also their history, and also everything they are trying to hide, and deny. The only answer to that moment of seeing, that mutual exposure of everything we were both attempting to hide, was compassion. The only way I could have the right to perform the work, the right to answer the audience's attention, and the right to be a conduit for what Richard was searching for, was to erase judgment, egoism, vanity, the "self." We were remembering it all; remembering without judgment what we did, however foolish, harmful, heroic, kind, awful, useful, destructive it was at the time; now it was just acknowledged. Yes, this happened, yes, that happened, yes, look what's happening now. It was, in a way, like spending the entire event just saying "yes." Yes, look at you inside all those choices you've made and choices you never made, look at all that you've survived. Look at what I'm doing now. Look at what they're doing now over there. What do you think of that? That sound, what is that sound? Oh yes, it's a terrible sound, it means terrible things are going to happen. And now what's this prop about? Look at that. And look at you there, looking at it. And now what's this . . .

There was an integrity in it, in the attempt to be merely present, and that meant selfless, somehow, and also completely compassionate. After each show, walking from the theater, I would wonder: "Was I accurate?" Meaning did I give each moment the weight—light or heavy—which it deserved? Did I see each audience member clearly, did I see all the routines and just say yes? Was I present during it all, or did I start to "act," to persuade, to embellish, to perform, to evade, persuade, charm, to judge, to ask for anything, to hide who I was: to lie.

THERESA BUCHHEISTER: T. Ryder would look each audience member in the eyes at least once. I found and find that to be powerful. And wildly generous and exhausting. And only possible in a small enough house. The audience always mattered while also not mattering at all. That balance was gorgeous. We could see if they got up and left; we could see if they made out with their date the whole time; we could see if they were sick or tired or amazed. And that affected us on stage. But also, the audience could not throw the train off the tracks, really. It felt different every night, but also not because of a looseness. It was maybe because of an awareness?

JAN LESLIE HARDING: You were speaking directly at the audience and you could see them. One time this woman was knitting through the whole thing with metal knitting needles and I was like, I'm going to lose my mind and I was like, [addressing her] "Stop that" and Richard was like, "That was great. I could tell you were going crazy. It was great," and I was like, "Thank you." Torment! When the actors were in torment it added to the enjoyment for him to some extent, I think.

FRANK BOUDREAUX: Engagement. Presence. Disruption. Aggression.

Many of Richard's "characters" project neuroses and insecurity, of course. But the unexpected, abrupt actions and shifts inside any performance in a Foreman piece suggests the inherent danger of uncertainty. And, frankly, there is an intentionally frightening presence. So the audience might well be scared of the performers. Unsettled at a minimum, I would think. I certainly was by many a performance I saw as an audience member.

The separation of performer and performance seems much narrower in a Foreman piece. It is not that I believe, say, T. Ryder Smith himself *is* a loony, lascivious embodiment of id outside of the Ontological-Hysteric Theater (in fact, I know him not be). But the performers in Foreman pieces collapse the distance between action and person. The anger that might instantly manifest in a gesture, vocalization, or rushed entrance often felt unhinged. Like the performer might just chuck the prop they were holding directly at your face at any moment.

JAY SMITH: The performer's relationship to the audience in a Foreman play ranges widely from entertaining clown to tour guide to teacher to sadist. I'm not proud of it, but if audience response was tepid I would sometimes slow down a bit to torture them even more in retaliation.

CHARLOTTA MOHLIN: It is very close since the lights are aimed at the audience and you can see every face out there. At first it was daunting. Seeing someone yawn or look at the clock. Then it became part of the play and we would use the people out in the audience as part of the performance. It almost turned into a game making the people who made you uncomfortable out in the audience more uncomfortable than yourself. And to give the enthusiasts an extra rewarding interactive experience.

JOHN MATTURRI: In much traditional theater the point is to create a participatory sense in the audience, a bracketing of disbelief, of empathy, etc. [Foreman's work] with its lack of clear narrative, its Brechtian distancing devices (strings or plexiglass set up in front of the audience), and aggressiveness (bright lights into audiences' eyes, loud noises, taped dialogue, broad pronouncements on tape in the voice of Foreman, presence of Foreman at the controls in front of the audience during the early plays I was in, etc.) the audience is encouraged to attend carefully and in a less involved manner. At times the relationship was confrontational, as with Foreman's instruction to pick out an audience member and stare when on stage.

The audience changed during the course of the three productions I was involved in. I don't remember the audiences being large for *Vertical Mobility* and I think there were still a good many walk-outs. By *Rhoda in Potatoland* shows were sold out.

FULYA PEKER: There were many things happening on stage during Foreman's shows. The stage was like a maze or a net with precisely designed yet constantly shifting focal points. As far as I experienced, during the shows, triggered by the performers' actions or behaviors along with the light design, the audience's eyes and ears would meander toward those focal points.

While performing in his shows, I always tried to sustain tension on stage and to hover over that unsettling feeling—keeping a distance from the audience while performing the actions in a myriad of manners such as possessed, panicked, curious, otherworldly, weird, mysterious, seductive, sinister, etc.

Oftentimes I saw audience members responding in completely different ways. Some of them got angry, some got shocked, bored, laughed, or even cried.

The work was not imposing a message; it was just opening a door through which one can enter a realm with a hidden system, in which anything could happen at any time. I always enjoyed seeing that curiosity, that uncertainty, in the house. The audience's desire to figure out the secret system, to find a crack to fuse into that realm, was always evident. And it was fun to tickle that desire, to flirt with that. Whatever was happening on stage was not an invitation for a collective response. Shaped by their own selective perceptions, audience members were giving rather personal responses during the shows.

PAULA GORDON: The performers are guides. I see them as characters, but the characters seem to be trying to communicate something to me in addition to interacting with each other. These characters are aware of the audience, maybe not all the time, if they are carried away, but there is always some intimation that the audience is observing some private matters and the characters kind of like being watched, are turned on by it, and are playing with us, but they have earnest motives, too.

RYAN HOLSOPPLE: I saw [the band] Throbbing Gristle once and they kept the lights on the audience as they played. Fugazi would do that as well. This made the audience and the artists on equal footing . . . sharing a space. I never really felt that watching a Foreman show. There was something different, like a Francis Bacon painting behind glass, keeping its distance on purpose . . . but still very close.

JOHN COLLINS: I think the performers' assignment was to coax the audience into some kind of deep trance where they would reach some kind of intuitive (if not intellectual) understanding of some kind of indescribable magic that was transpiring between the people and between the people and the objects on stage.

JOHN OGLEVEE: Richard said his work is like a child's metal toy top that has the plunger in the middle. When the top is at rest, the pictures on top can be seen clearly, but when you push down the plunger the top spins and spins and the image becomes a blur, oscillating meaning and spreading energy. So when the show's machinations are in full swing, the space has the power to feel like it's hovering off the ground and everyone along with it.

BRENDAN REGIMBAL: The performers in a Foreman show are not only acting out whatever is trying to be displayed on stage but they are almost like spiritual conduits or invitees because they're very present. They're not pretending they're not there. There's a lot of staring and speaking directly to people and all that. In many ways it is meant to draw them into something that, in general, is pushing out with everything else. I think of them as the gateway into that world.

————

RICHARD FOREMAN: *For me it was just the actors' idiosyncratic nature as another color to put on the canvas. That's why I always hated videotapes of my work, for instance, because I always knew that so many aspects of my work were sort of cold but on the videotape the actors no longer had the warmth and the sweatiness and the reality of the actor with their real texture.*

SHAUNA KELLY: *Have you accomplished that warmth with film?*

RICHARD FOREMAN: *I don't think so. I think it's different because the essence is not narrative. You're not identifying with people in quite that way. It's different because in the editing and the way you're treating the footage, you're able to introduce some of that stumblingness that I always thought was so important from the actor.*

SHAUNA KELLY: *Stumblingness?*

RICHARD FOREMAN: *Stumbling from the actors—the fact that they're human beings and they could stumble or they could sweat. You were aware of their palpitating, stumbling nature. Even method actors would claim they want to present people in their fallible, real nature. Maybe there are schools of classical theater that don't want to do that. Yeah probably a classically trained English actor who can be a* *virtuoso—any virtuoso doesn't want to present that [fallibility] really in opera or classical theater.*

————

JULIANA FRANCIS KELLY: The performer is combative, remote, disdainful, and secretly generous toward the audience.

COLLEEN WERTHMANN: "Fuck you," "Lemme let you in on a little secret," and "Get a load of this."

STEPHANIE SILVER: Hostile. Challenging. Very direct and sometimes completely detached and aloof. Occasionally loving.

SHAUNA KELLY: The characters seem skittish and confined; infantile and alien; ritualistic and formal. They are not unfriendly but they can live without you. Performers create continuous stage pictures and their presence is loud and close. When they do something joyful, it all comes crashing down.

PATRICIA YBARRA: There is mild antagonism [toward the audience] if the actor is doing it right.

MANUEL IGREJAS: Richard's performers were uniformly fearless and didn't really give a fuck about the audience. They were in their own remarkable world.

DAVID COTE: There is an undercurrent of cool, appraising hostility. Maybe fear. Never love.

KARL FRANKLIN ALLEN: For me the audience was very present but I never felt like I was performing for them in the traditional way an actor might. *Astronome,* in particular, was a bit assaulting because of John Zorn's music, which made the show feel like a ritual or incantation, performed on behalf of the audience but not necessarily for their entertainment or amusement.

From left to right: Joel Israel, Stefanie Neukirch, Christ Mirto, and Stephanie Silver in *Wake Up Mr. Sleepy! Your Unconscious Mind Is Dead!*, 2007. Photo by Paula Court.

KEVIN HURLEY: [Performers were] aware of them but not pandering to them.

ROBERT CUCUZZA: The relationship with the audience was either hostile or flirtatious and often both. It was my least favorite part of performing in his shows. I really don't like any kind of direct audience interaction in theater. The theater was tiny and you were sometimes about two feet from them. He demanded that you look them in the eyes and think the most disgusting, depraved thoughts about them. That was his direction. When we were deep in the run of *Permanent Brain Damage*, we were warming up on stage before the house opened, and he'd walk around the space saying things like, "Think dark, awful thoughts! Think the most depraved, horrible things about the audience!" And then if we had put in a bad performance the night before: "Look. You need to be thinking the most disgusting, horrible, depraved sexual thoughts about the audience every moment of the play." Okay, Stanislavsky.

FULYA PEKER: The way he handled the director–performer relationship undoubtedly created the basis for the performer–audience relationship. His directions helped us develop that "anything can happen anytime" attitude during the rehearsals, and the audience was seized or tickled by that attitude during the shows. [Based on his direction in the shows] we were pointing at things as if signifying a vital secret, gesticulating as if concealing some important knowledge; pausing as if receiving some enigmatic information delivered through the speakers by some peculiar voices and sound loops.

T. RYDER SMITH: Richard once said to think of sending your performance as giant beams of energy into outer space, to an alien planet. He needed you to act *through* the back wall, and yet to appear that you weren't acting at all. The way you moved your gaze two inches had to go through the wall. The way you stood still watching another performer do something had to go through the wall. And it all had to be, somehow, utterly real, uninflected, selfless. Like you weren't doing anything. Like you weren't even there.

DAVID PATRICK KELLY: In *The Cure* my character entered the stage first and made a slow cross, making eye contact with every member of the audience (about 100 people) with a kind, benign, but serious mystic ritualism.

In *Pearls For Pigs* when we were trying it out in Hartford we were supposed to look at the audience with contempt. The ultimate affect was very funny but some audience members took offense and thought we were insulting them . . . not realizing that the whole show was about this artist sacrificing himself for their benefit (also very funny).

JAMES URBANIAK: In *The Universe* there was a moment when my character wore sunglasses and looked out at the audience, so I had a chance to watch the people watching. One night I saw Lou Reed and Laurie Anderson sitting together. She had a big smile on her face and he had his eyes shut, which struck me as perfect.

KEN NINTZEL: Usually, I think Richard instructed the performers to ignore the audience, except when he told them to stare directly at them.

FULYA PEKER: Once, during *Deep Trance Behavior*, I was staring at an audience member in the first row and she suddenly began throwing up! It wasn't because we were disgusting, but perhaps because she was over-stimulated. She waited in the lobby till the end of the show to apologize and explain her experience. I represented a darker side in the show. After devouring "a pomegranate that looks like a sick vagina," or "violently stabbing a giant Lacanian knot," it was inevitable to receive audience comments like, "I'm glad to see that you are actually a kind and nice person in real life."

"Foremanesque"

FULYA PEKER: Whenever I see a show in the New York underground theater scene, I can easily track Foreman's influence, sometimes in stylized actions, sometimes in design approaches.

Oftentimes some of us refuse to reveal our sources of inspiration, or the lineage out of which we emerge. Some of us prefer the "I did everything instinctually" approach, that secretive standpoint. And some of us openly pay homage to the masters that help us shape our own visions.

Because there are so many weak projects out there, mere imitations that are destined to evaporate, audiences prefer to have an idea about what they will encounter before purchasing tickets to shows. Maybe that is why playbills are littered with lengthy bios and statements of purpose: just like gallery walls are crammed with placards denoting what an artwork is "about." Critics like to refer comparatively to artist's previous collaborations, maybe just to make sense of a work, or maybe to put it in a certain cluster for the audience. Sometimes it is preferable for an audience to encounter the unknown, just experience a work without expectations; sometimes it is better to have a clue about an artist's lineage so as to grasp the essence of their work. I am not sure which is better; each yields different effects. It is an everlasting, ongoing argument in the arts scene.

As a performer, having been on stage for more than twenty years, currently I am having a hard time coming across theater directors, like Foreman, whose visions I can fully trust and surrender to, and who I can learn from, who I can share a mental space with.

WILLEM DAFOE: Richard spawned a lot of, if not imitators, people who have taken aspects of his work and run with it.

RICHARD FOREMAN: *I was always a little wistful that more people who'd worked with me didn't go on to do things that, you know, [evoked the same response] like some people respond to my plays: "What the hell was that?" I didn't see too many things that I thought, "What the hell was that?" One of the most impressive things I saw, sort of at the end of the period I ran the theater, was my sound man at the time and his wife—his wife took costuming at Columbia and he was a composer—and they [Object Collection] did two pieces that I saw that I really thought, "God I don't know if that was awful or great." And that's what I would have liked to see more of.*

An amusing story about that—some people who were my interns were the people who started the Nature Theater of Oklahoma and they've been very successful in Europe especially and he said to me, because his first plays were pretty bad—he did them in my theater— he became a friend and a great supporter of my later work—he said, "Richard you know those first few plays I was trying to copy you but then I realized after a couple years that I wasn't doing a very good job of it so I took a year or two off and thought, 'What could I do if I'm not copying Richard?'" And then he started doing his own things in the theater and they've been very successful here and abroad—Pavol Liska. I met him at Dartmouth doing one of my plays.

JOHN OGLEVEE: I did a piece shortly after moving to Japan in which I utilized a number of "Foremanesque" techniques in terms of using actors as dwarfs. The Japanese theater world is most certainly not lacking in auteurs, so younger actors were very keen to work in this method of trial by error and repeat.

BRENDAN REGIMBAL: In writing shows with my wife, I brought everything that Foreman had to bear and she brought other experiences. Our handshake was something very different than what Richard would make but we were trying to bring that same sensibility—that freedom—especially to the design essence of it, and by unchaining the experience from a narrative.

DAMON KIELY: Well, I wanted to be Richard for so long that for a while I made some pretty bad experimental work before realizing that his work and my work weren't the same. There was one moment in my career where I felt I channeled him the most and that was if you can believe it in creating a production of *OKLAHOMA!* the musical. We were doing a somewhat radical thing with the show—trying to really ground it in 1900 in Oklahoma. So we only used guitars and banjos and fiddles and bass for the music and the costumes looked like real clothes and the dances were only folk dances. When we came to the dream ballet we said—what the hell does this farm girl in Oklahoma know about a ballet? She's never seen it, probably never even heard of it. She has seen vaudeville and tent shows. Let's make a vaudeville nightmare. It had a magic trick, cabaret dancing, strange dances, a demonic emcee, a knife throwing contest—it was supremely weird, original, and influenced by Richard's odd carnival theatricality. I loved it and so did audiences.

DAVID COTE: I worked a lot with Bob Cucuzza who was very influenced by Foreman. I would say Bob fused Foreman's formal rigor and gothic imagery with a more pronounced cartoon-like sensibility, one that embraced slapstick and absurdist humor, as well as a sort of accelerated 1990s punk energy.

I also worked a lot with D.J. Mendel, who I met through friends in Williamsburg and who seemed to gravitate toward Foreman around the same time as I did. I think that Foreman showed D.J., Bob, and others in our generation a way to write an

American version of [Eugène] Ionesco, [Samuel] Beckett, and others. Maybe the difference is that Bob, D.J., et al. were more eager to embrace cartoon-like comedy and pop culture, whereas Foreman was a hermetic high modernist, beyond an explicitly American or European cultural footprint.

In much of the 1990s experimental theater I saw or took part in, there were recurring devices that Foreman popularized, if he didn't outright invent them: sound loops, micro-motivations, super-fast transitions between emotions, abstract movement, incongruous dance breaks, non sequiturs, "animating" objects and environments—a table tries to seduce you, or you have a theological argument with a cantaloupe. We inherited this grab-bag of stage tactics as a kind of rigorous insanity that spanned the Marx Brothers to Ren and Stimpy. And I'm not just referring to Foreman and his "acolytes" at the Ontological; you could see it in the Wooster Group, and offshoot companies such as the Builders Association, Elevator Repair Service, Collapsable Giraffe, Radiohole continuing up to 2000 and beyond.

FRANK BOUDREAUX: It cannot be overstated how influential Foreman's total-theater approach was on everyone who worked with him. The entire Downtown experimental scene of the late twentieth and early twenty-first century grew out of his work. Of course, Tina Satter of *Half Straddle*, Richard Maxwell's New York City Players, the team of Elevator Repair Service, Eric Dyer and all of Radiohole, the entire NTUSA [National Theater of the United States of America] team, Dan Safer of Witness Relocation, Kenneth Collins's Temporary Distortion, Ryan Holsopple of 31 Down (and Shannon Sindelar who was one-half of *Down* for years and was the managing director of the Ontological and then The Incubator for years), Pavol Liska and Kelly Copper's Nature Theater of Oklahoma, to mention but a few, all had distinct artistic vision from Richard, each their personal aesthetic. But watching Richard's approach—working from an unassigned, "blank" collection of phrases and dialogues, as well as absorbing Richard's art-theory collected in books—encouraged these other artists to *find their own way* outside traditional theater-making; it helped each artistic company and individual artist *develop a series of procedures* of their own to generate Live Events intended to affect the audience beyond the conventional emotional catharsis provided by Story-with-Moral. (Liz LeCompte's *Wooster Group* was a parallel influence, of course.)

His rejection of the Story-with-Moral format of mainstream American theater does not mean Richard's work is amoral; it was deeply moral. Perhaps *only* moral. Like Brecht, Richard just did not think it was effective or meaningful to explore morality inside mimetically constructed naturalistic storytelling with conventions of character and artificial linearity.

Richard was more like a painter or sculptor whose matériaux were pure versions of Aristotelian Poetics—diction, music, spectacle, idea. His canvas and marble were language, body, posture, set. His paints were voice, sound effect, lights, props.

Despite his time period, he was not postmodern actually. Richard was deeply Modern. (The Wooster Group deconstructed. Richard constructed.) The results gave the appearance of deconstructing American theater norms. But really, Richard was not commenting, not picking apart, not even, completely, *responding*, so to speak, as was often the goal of the postmodern.

Richard was a theater-auteur, an artist who made work for the theater. And he spun his work out of whole cloth.

ROBERT CUCUZZA: All of my work reflects him and his aesthetic, sometimes very obviously. I steal from him in everything I do, and I don't feel one ounce of shame about it. I was the physical manifestation of his internal life for an entire year so I feel like I get to steal from him whenever I please. I was drawn to him for a reason—his way of looking at life is very similar to mine. He just gave me permission to let that come out on stage in its naked form. And there's no better staging tool than the "long turn," where an actor takes the long way to make a 90 degree angled turn on stage. Also, the level of precision, intensity of focus, and tension across a space. Anybody who's ever been in a rehearsal with me will tell you that these are present in everything I've ever done since I first watched him work in 1992. I work with a lot of student actors who've never performed before. Those three things—precision, intensity of focus, and tension across a space—are the three defining factors in giving them the confidence that they need to feel like they're fully engaged in a fictional world, more than any acting technique.

RYAN HOLSOPPLE: Richard's work is always on my mind when I am creating something, I am at the point where I now consciously try to put it out of my head.

Richard's sound design is bold, blown out, distorted, and demanding. This is the single influence on how I approach sound in my own work.

THERESA BUCHHEISTER: I think my attention to detail and specificity started to take shape while working on *Lumberjack Messiah*. I think the lack of adherence to linear narrative was certainly influenced by him. As well as the importance of every sound, image, and movement that makes it into the presented work. I agree with him that plays should be an hour and six minutes or less (or verrrrry long). I like spaces that are intimate while also feeling multi-dimensional. I like giving the audience more than they can possibly handle. Everything has sex and death. Everything is dark and hilarious. Repetition is very useful in live performance (used well, of course).

———

RICHARD FOREMAN: *In the very beginning I was thinking about the repetition of these ecstatic moments that I was interested in and making a structure out of the repetition of those moments. If you talk about Philip Glass and Steve Reich, it's repetition in music. I was doing that in the theater before.*

I was very lucky at Yale to have a playwriting teacher who was brilliant and very rigorous and I think I've benefitted a lot from that. This really wonderful man said, "Richard, you know you have talent and I don't say that to everybody but you have one problem. You get a moment that you think is really strong and you like it and then you don't want to let go of it. You want to repeat it or keep it there." And I went home and I said, "Oh my goodness. If Mr. Gassner was right,

I've got to figure out how to fix that." And then I thought well maybe if that's what I lust for, I should just take that failure and turn it into the center of what I do.

———

DAVID HERSKOVITS: Richard had developed a very intense way of working that was inspiring to me, like working with multiple threads and many sources at once.

By watching him I definitely learned about design and staging large groups of people.

I work with very dense layers of sound but I was already doing that before I met Richard. I could see him doing that and I could feel empowered to go on that way.

There's definitely an affinity, sensibility, values, and aesthetic that I share with Richard but I don't work in his style. I don't think anybody does really. Every individual person finds their own way to make their work and I think that's really important and I think Richard feels that too. He's not looking for people who are just mirrors of what he's doing.

WILLEM DAFOE: Elizabeth LeCompte who really was and is the central figure to the Wooster Group, loved Foreman's work. And I can't say for her but I think it was probably her favorite theater. While she's very different than him, I think he had a huge influence on her so that's had a significant effect on me.

BRENDAN REGIMBAL: Annie B. Parson and Paul Lazar [of Big Dance Theater] are probably twenty years younger than Richard Foreman so he was making his work when they were starting to make their work in the city. Obviously, being New Yorkers, they saw his work. They were confronted by it. They have similar ends and philosophical taste, but they come at it from a very different place. Although they also like sort of DIY handmade aesthetic and they like to lose track of their linearity and focus more on small things— in that, we'll find nirvana. Paul and him certainly share their love of vaudeville. So there's a lot of crossover but their route to their work is through a different practice.

I think I was a rare find for [Big Dance Theater] because most of their folks come from the dance world. They're dancers who have interesting intellectual pursuits and their designers tend to come from Oana Botez-Ban. She was Foreman's costume designer for a couple of years and is also a costume designer for Big Dance Theater. I might be the only other crossover touchpoint for them. Foreman used to go through more performers whereas Big Dance Theater is more like a traditional dance company in that they have a very small group of performers.

KEVIN HURLEY: I worked with a few Foreman people. I think the sense of just "being" on stage is somewhat the same with other companies: NYC Players, Builders Association, Wooster Group. . . . They all have different styles but the performers have a great sense of "being."

The Foreman "Family"

SHAUNA KELLY: *Theater artists who have worked with you often go on to work with each other. Are you aware of the extent to which this is true? I was lucky enough to be one of those people who went on for the next ten years to work with other Foreman alumni. And I am so grateful for having that experience and then having that core group of people to work with.*

RICHARD FOREMAN: *Yeah I'm very proud of that because I'm not terribly social—I'm not anti-social . . . . I certainly never thought that was my aim but I was extremely gratified that in spite of myself that was happening.*

FULYA PEKER: Because Foreman had been creating/constructing shows for years, and because the rehearsal process and runs were quite long by New York experimental theater standards, apparently some people (performers, designers, interns, etc.) who worked with him then share a common vocabulary, a parallel theatrical style or approach. There is undoubtedly a whole Foreman community out there. His runs had been great excuses for that community to have encounters, to discuss ongoing theatrical viewpoints, to become aware of each other's works, and to collaborate on different projects. And several of those projects currently represent the ongoing experimental theater scene in New York.

KEN NINTZEL: I worked with many performers who orbited the Ontological-Hysteric through its satellite programs like the Blueprint Series, Seven Minute Series, Downstairs Series (these took place during the months that Richard did not have a show at the theater), and main stage productions. There was more of a sense of community in the series. It was during this downtime when you could rent the theater for a few weeks. Sophie Haviland was the driving force behind these series.

CHRISTINA CAMPANELLA: I ended up working with several Foreman alumni—but even if we didn't work together, many of us found ourselves in the same circles for years to come.

BRENDAN REGIMBAL: [Collaborating with other people who had worked with Foreman] was the next six years in my life. Because we're tied to him—many people who were interns with me or after me, all made work that was influenced and driven by him.

The companies are endless—31 Down, Object Collection—almost everybody I worked with was connected to the Ontological-Hysteric and was a derivative. His grasp was so large because of the army of interns; because of the people that worked on these shows as designers, technicians, and actors. All of us were interested in similar pursuits. So he was really good at creating a family of people interested in making the next level of work—for the next generation of it, which is why the Incubator [Arts Project] was even created.

DAVID COTE: The Ontological was a huge hub for downtown theater and in the 1990s most everyone had some connection to Foreman's work. Either as performer, crew, or administrator, or because they had an opportunity to put up work when Foreman wasn't in residence (Seven Minute Series, Blueprint Series). We were (mostly) recent college graduates who wanted to make weird theater and gravitated to the Ontological at St. Marks because—as I recall—Sophie Haviland sent up a signal. Eric Dyer knew Sophie from doing tech work at the Ontological, and he told me to show up there one day in 1992, and it felt like a town hall: *We have this space, let's make stuff, I want to start a series for new work,* that sort of thing.

In the years that followed I worked with or became friends with people who would come to define experimental theater in the 1990s and 2000s: Robert Cucuzza, D.J. Mendel, Richard Maxwell, Kristin Marting at HERE, Eric Dyer, Collapsable Giraffe, Yehuda Duenyas and National Theater of the United States of America, John Collins and Elevator Repair Service, Tom Murrin, David Levine, the New York International Fringe Festival, Michael Gardner, and others. Pretty soon you figured out who was on the Mount Rushmore of experimental theater: Foreman, the Wooster Group, Robert Wilson, and Ellen Stewart of La MaMa.

You could make one of those crazy conspiracy maps with colored string connecting various people to each other: Kristin Marting worked with Robert Wilson; John Collins did sound for the Wooster Group; Yehuda Duenyas and Ryan Bronz worked (with me) on Foreman's *Pearls for Pigs* in 1997, and a few years later formed the National Theater of the United States of America (NTUSA), which I reviewed early on because the work was such a brilliant mix of Foreman-esque baroque paranoia and MTV-era pop silliness. It was a dense genealogy mapping bonds and influences.

Most everyone who worked with or around Foreman had their own company or bounced around to different directors and venues. A personal influence, although he remained marginal even in the niche of Off-Off [Broadway], was Iranian exile writer–director Assurbanipal Babilla. With his company, Purgatorio Ink, we produced work that was irreverent, ecstatic, erotic, and grotesquely comic. Didn't really fit into the Eurochic, technophile, coolly ironic vibe at the time.

FRANK BOUDREAUX: Pretty much everyone I have worked with in theater has been connected directly to Richard or to the Ontological-Hysteric and/or its successor, the Incubator Series, in some capacity. Of the *Maria del Bosco* cast and crew, I have collaborated with many of them and continued to follow their work.

Creators and performers, past and present, were all part of the same milieu—NTUSA, Witness Relocation, Half Straddle, Banana Bag and Bodice, Alec Duffy of JACK Space, Big Dance. The list goes on. And that doesn't include all of the artists that were audience members, inevitably altered by seeing his work.

STEPH SILVER: I worked almost exclusively with people from the Foreman world, or who were Foreman-world adjacent, to include The Living Theatre, Fiona Templeton, and John Jesurun. The only parallels I can draw between any of them and Foreman is that they were all contemplative experiences.

FULYA PEKER: I have collaborated with some of the people from that community over the years, and I am still in touch with some of them. We try to follow and support each other's projects as much as possible. I worked with Foreman during the last three shows he did at St. Marks Church; thereafter, some of the crewmembers of those shows continued to curate IAP [Incubator Arts Project] after Foreman left the space. So, we had the chance to continue sharing that historical stage to present our own works.

The closure of the stage at St. Marks Church affected our motivation to gather somehow, disrupted the ritual, but that community is somehow still aware of each other, even from afar. The shared language remains. And that's significant.

JULIANA FRANCIS KELLY: I've worked with and for other Foreman actors over the years, in my own plays and on others. There is a sense of recognition and camaraderie between actors who have had the inimitable experience of working for Richard Foreman.

DENISE LUCCIONI: I've remained friends with a few of them. Our professional experience [of working with Foreman] gradually merging into an almost common identity, at least roots that we can share even now, after decades.

JOHN MATTURRI: Looking through the cast lists for the three plays I was in, I was struck by the number of cast members I remained friends with, in many cases to this day. Unlike some other theater groups there was little sense of identification with the company even after being in repeated plays. Although Foreman would have opening and closing parties at his loft and performers were welcome to a Sunday salon that Kate had for a time, this was not a highly social theatrical company in any formal manner. There was no sense of having an identity with the company: one was not an "Ontological" in the same way a performer in Robert Wilson's productions of this era were "Byrds." Nevertheless, cast members frequently went out together after rehearsals and performances and close ties were formed in the plays.

Because of the relatively limited use of trained performers during a period of Foreman's work, cast members often were visual artists, filmmakers, and other artists. The relationships formed in the plays provided the basis for artistic collaboration.

JOHN OGLEVEE: Of course when one worked downtown in the 1990s one worked with just about everyone who had at some time been involved in works at the St. Mark's Church.

JAMES URBANIAK: When I did *The Universe* I was very ensconced in the downtown New York theater scene of that time, of which Foreman was a giant figure. Almost everyone I knew in that world had some connection with him, either from having seen the plays or working with him or working with people who'd worked with him.

THERESA BUCHHEISTER: I keep connecting to folks who worked for Foreman seventeen years later. As an artist, I found ways to work with various people and it keeps unfolding and overlapping. A legacy aspect of Foreman that he was not super involved in was Short Form and Incubator Arts. If I listed the people I know and love and work with, you could not fit it in the book.

Appreciation and Influence

DAVID PATRICK KELLY: I received an Obie Award in 1998 and while they called it Sustained Excellence I think it was largely because of my collaborations with Richard.

DAVID COTE: I appreciated the rigor and almost fanatical devotion to his own vision and trust that the scenographic and dramaturgical elements would eventually click. It was a lesson in patience in one's own intuition and willingness to fail over and over.

JOHN MATTURRI: The most important thing I got from the work was an extended sense of building a work gradually from the bottom up rather than realizing a preset goal. I very much appreciated the way that he would respond to the script and the performers on an ongoing basis while developing the performance. This was much more interesting to me than working with someone who knew fully in advance what the play was going to be.

WILLEM DAFOE: You try to be a sponge. When you're around strong personalities and great artists like Richard, they have an effect on you.

So much of theater is very square and very traditional and is very tied to literature and psychology. And of course Richard's

From left to right: David Cote, Yehuda Duenyas, John Oglevee, Tom Nelis, and David Patrick Kelly in *Pearls for Pigs*, 1997. Photo by Paula Court.

theater liberates us from that and lets us know that there are all kinds of ways to make events and to make these things for spectators that enliven us.

DAVID HERSKOVITS: What was exciting for me was the real artistic action—the composition of the piece. He was a great model using certain aleatory processes. Speech assignments [designating which actors would say which text] were never made and he would do them on the fly. He would bring in pages of work and swap them around. So really you just have a stack of words on pages that could be shuffled and repurposed in a number of ways. You would also get random things that would pop up in rehearsal and stay.

SOPHIA SKILES: I love the idea of gestating something for a long time as Foreman's work tends to do. One of my favorite things about the theater are the multiple levels a given piece draws from: the work or script, the length of rehearsals, and the relationship between the actors which can be exceptionally rich when the actors themselves share a history of working. And he did at one point employ some of the same people in his work.

MIKE TAYLOR: It's the idea of using what people bring with them. With stage design, he's had shows with lots of versions of classical paintings as set or props because someone on the show was a fine artist. He might put a dance in because someone can really move.

He's highly aware of architectural space, thinking about the space itself and what it has to offer, or what there is to wrestle with that is worth paying attention to.

PATRICIA YBARRA: I think that the way that he uses objects always stuck with me—as did his displacement of certain actions and moments in ways that were not representational.

DENISE LUCCIONI: I appreciate Richard's work because he focuses on one approach, one personal perspective, and builds from there.

JOHN MATTURRI: I very much appreciated his willingness to produce complex shows that made intellectual demands on the audience as well as providing extraordinary spectacles.

STEPHANIE SILVER: I always appreciated how many people came to see his work. Even if they didn't all have kind words after, people were curious.

DAVID HERSKOVITS: Maybe most importantly, the work is very mysterious and not interested in explaining itself. That has always been artistically a value that's very important to me. With Richard, here is this person putting out these weird mysteries but not trying to explain to the audience what's happening next or most importantly, how people are supposed to feel about them.

PAULA GORDON: I like that Richard would do things to interfere with the audience's total involvement in the play. And I also like that he created such intriguing worlds that he couldn't fully prevent the audience from losing themselves in his work.

FULYA PEKER: I think he has a very powerful and distinct signature as a director. But he is also able to trick his own mind. He does not give in to cheap, sentimental, or touchy ideas. He is honest because he makes the whole work for himself. There are many so-called directors who are obsessed with audience response, so much so that they end up being way too pretentious. I always trusted Foreman's vision and instincts, and such trust gave me confidence as a performer.

His directing/staging approach in general reminded me of Wagner's notion of the *Gesamtkunstwerk*. He gives directions not only to actors/performers, but to designers as well. He envisions the entire "thing": the sound loops, the light cues, the set, props, and costumes. Not to mention his recurring rope networks, letters, symbols and numbers, plexiglasses, the red-black-white striped palette, many grotesque props, lights flashing and flickering at the audience, performers never walking diagonally but always in straight lines, staring at the audience, peaking from behind walls, covering their faces, doing long turns, inclining or leaning toward objects in odd positions, constantly collapsing, some expressionist or silent-film moments. And so much more. I call all of these "Foremanoptics."

KEN NINTZEL: Richard Foreman is primarily known as a playwright and director but I would certainly make the case that you could add designer too. Essentially he designs his own sets, makes his own models, designs his own sound, and painstakingly designs his own lighting so in my mind Richard is an auteur. I personally always felt that directing and design were so integral that they were really just an extension of each other so working for Richard and experiencing that was a great influence on me and my methods of creating work.

KARL FRANKLIN ALLEN: I really learned to love working with an auteur and realized that it's great to work with someone whose decision making you implicitly trust. That actually enabled a great camaraderie among the cast since it felt like we were all aligned behind the same goal.

It was so great to see how the end product was realized.

DAVID HERSKOVITS: Aesthetically, I was very inspired by Richard's work. He obviously has a very strong and specific sense of design—with sound, lighting, scenery, and clothes. It's inspiring to see somebody work that way—in such a complete way. What was special there was that sensibility, the history, the difficulty of the work, the refusal to pander to the audience in one way or the other, that sort of thing. I just loved the challenging, polyphonic quality of the work.

DENISE LUCCIONI: In the early 2000s, I organized Bénédicte Pesle's archive; I found sound tapes of Richard's "music" for *Café Amérique* and *La Robe de chambre de Georges Bataille* [George Bataille's Bathrobe]. I asked a radio engineer to digitize them, and he was flabbergasted to hear those tapes from the early 1980s. He could recognize in Richard an early precursor of certain experimental music.

MIKE TAYLOR: I've always used sound a lot in everything; his way of using sound and light as a part of a whole to DO something rather than BE something, definitely had an impact on my work.

FULYA PEKER: It was inspiring to be in successive shows because it gave me the chance to compare how an aural (music) versus a visual (film) element affects a performer's presence and spatial awareness on stage. The way Foreman approached the ears, the way he created soundscapes by making selections between hundreds of sound loops listed on a card that looked like a "Chinese menu," stirred my interest in sound/form dynamics. Later, my explorations with such elements continued while performing in Object Collection's experimental operas.

CHRISTINA CAMPANELLA: The vocal technique I developed for myself in my own work (which was the direct result of Richard's choice to mic us) gave me the feeling that the audience could actually hear my thoughts. It felt very intimate, speaking that way, like I really only needed to *think* my lines—similar to the way actors deal with closeups in film (at least the way I do). In film, the camera does the work; in Richard's theater, the mics do. That's how I found my way into this style of [vocal and physical] performance that was totally new to me. It suddenly made so much sense. It's what led me to this entirely new vocabulary and set of rules, all distinctly non-naturalistic, without *trying* to behave in any particular way. There's no need for the usual facial expressions or gestures that go along with speaking—so then there came this great stillness in between bursts of movement.

Richard's sound world blew my mind. I loved the way he used sound to punctuate the text, and the loops he made, the incredibly musical way he'd weave them in and around the spoken text, creating a richly atmospheric sound design to support his theatrical world. I read somewhere that he said his use of sound was like creating a web of things that aren't all perceptible at the same time. My scores are threaded through with clips from found recordings, sound effects, snippets of voices, and drum loops arranged in a kind of aural landscape from which songs emerge and recede.

Working with Richard and the rigor of the whole process gave me a lot of confidence as a performer. I was in a couple films after that and became obsessed with film acting—a perfect next step, in terms of technique, after what I'd discovered in *Benita Canova*. I did an opera and a few more plays, mainly plays with music—but after the Foreman experience, I wanted to be working all the time, not just when I'd land an audition or be offered a role. Composing sound started becoming the main outlet for my creativity and the thing I could do without waiting for anyone.

DENISE LUCCIONI: I loved how his work was about building an uncanny world of beauty where he could feel safe. I've heard him describe his theater this way. And I could see that this world is not only cerebral, it encompasses a life where he is trusting his impulses and unconscious, allowing them to be structured by his amazing encyclopedic mind, while being at the same time totally and almost deliberately forgetful of this structure. Creating that world is global, I mean it's creating it from scratch, and from A to Z; I see it as a quasi-mystic undertaking really, filling up all the gaps and holes, giving them life with words and symbols, with movement and gesture, in writing and with artwork, an expression of absolute life, till there is no one minute of space that is not occupied by meaningful signs or significant meaning.

As a spectator in France even before seeing Richard's work, I was hoping for performing arts that were not pretending to be real, telling stories, being rhetorical, or larger-than-life representation, etc. I like to use my brain and senses, therefore I want to see theater and dance that open my eyes, tickle my brain, broaden my scope, and stretch my perception. As the icing on the cake, I want to be presented with dimensions and worlds that are invisible; I want to be offered access to those dimensions and worlds, whether intimate, secret, poetic, metaphysical, personal or collective, and mostly I want to see things that make me aware—politically also— of my potential to achieve a relative freedom, out of social slavery, at all levels. I want to see artforms that deal with necessity, and chance, that have a purpose and a sense of humor. I guess this description of what I am looking for applies to all aspects of life, not only art and theater. I cannot remember a specific quote, but I think all of the above might be sheer paraphrase of Richard's statements. A mix of what I obscurely fantasized before working with him, what I could perceive in his work, and what I have been interested in ever since.

BRENDAN REGIMBAL: He creates something that is unquantifiable and open and reaches human consciousness or spirit not achieved through traditional means. It's almost a spiritual practice and after you've been a part of that, you feel that every piece of art you make should be doing that at some level. You want to find ways to have the same reflectiveness or internal self-awareness while making art, focusing less on the product. It's a radical decommercialization of theater.

T. RYDER SMITH: Richard said his works were actually about mystical things, religion, spirituality, the occult. The nakedness and vulnerability I felt and found and explored during the work and the compassion I tried to express and learn from didn't seem to be anything I was projecting onto what Richard was doing, but part of it.

SOPHIA SKILES: I appreciated what first drew me to his work—the completeness and sometimes hermetically sealed sense of his own taste. I love and admire that sense of fidelity to his own artistry. In terms of "outcomes" or where that fidelity or curiosity would lead him and us, the world was so wonderfully strange and banal—the fact of a body blundering into a limit in physical space paired with a wish for something meaningful, historic, and celestial.

ROBERT CUCUZZA: I guess one of the most overarching concepts that I've taken from that time and still use today—something that I learned from Richard—was to make hermetically sealed shows, where every single moment, every single inch of the stage is mercilessly scrutinized. Where you pick your lane and then stick to it, cutting out every moment where a whiff of air can get in, allowing the audience to question the world in front of them. Everything doesn't have to make "sense," it just has to make *a* sense. If the internal logic is clear, the audience won't question the external logic.

Richard's primary focus, his mission in theater, was to manifest the naked, imperfect mind on stage. It laid bare the disordered chaos of his subconscious state, eschewing any attempt at order, logic, or rationale. He created rigorously imperfect worlds. He preferred working with actors who captured that—mentally, physically, emotionally. He actively rejected "beauty" in people and most definitely on stage. If any moment that he created was "too beautiful," or could be perceived by the majority of the audience as memorable, his "shit indicator" would go off and he'd cut it. Believe me, I saw hundreds of these moments—achingly beautiful, absolutely unforgettable stage pictures and sequences . . . in rehearsal. Then he cut them. That's not what he was interested in. His tolerance and acceptance for the imperfect—the weird, the ugly, the transgressive, the awkward, the broken and bent, the stupid and silly—was all an inspiration and why I believe so many of us returned for multiple shows. Despite the difficulty of working with him, we were welcomed and put on display in all our human dissonance.

During rehearsals for *Permanent Brain Damage* he wanted an additional performer on stage to "walk around and point at stuff with a stick." He brought in an actor who was interested, worked them into a few moments, then rejected both him and the entire idea because that actor "looked too healthy." I'm not kidding. All of us on stage were like, "What does that say about us?" Another example: for furniture and props that needed to be made, he'd scrawl rough drawings with measurements, often with a fat Sharpie, hand them to the TD and have them made according to his specs. I heard a story about how he once turned over a drawing for a table. So, the TD made a table. Richard looked at it and said, "No, no! This looks like it was made by someone who knows how to make a table! I want it to look like I made a table and I don't know how to make a table."

COLLEEN WERTHMANN: He made experiences like no other. No one can make or even approximate work like Richard's. It springs so deeply from his subconscious, so purely expressed, and he builds these hermetically sealed worlds that all feel similar, yet are distinct. The process was exhausting, and certainly more for him than the actors, but the actors were aware and eager to purely serve his vision.

I appreciate how vulgar and funny his plays are, how unexpected their id-like spurts can be, and how mournful and eerie their truths.

JAMES URBANIAK: An important element of his plays is humor. His cryptic dialogue is frequently hilarious and I loved delivering it. One line that always cracked me up was Tony's character's comment when my character ate cereal at one point: "How can you justify eating that tiny stuff?"

[I appreciate that] he knows what he wants and he gets it.

JOHN OGLEVEE: There was an incredible rigor to his method. Nothing was ever right. Everything could always be fixed, changed, made better.

WILLEM DAFOE: I appreciate him very much. There is no arriving. There is no nailing it. There is no right interpretation.

BRENDAN REGIMBAL: The most important thing is, "Nothing is precious." There's never a point of no return. Anything can be chopped up, cut up, thrown away, stamped on, turned upside down. You should never stop working something; there is no "done." There's only the state it's currently in. And you ask what else it could it be.

Those were the most important lessons and one of the reasons that I paired so well with Big Dance Theater is that they're in the same conundrum. There's never a moment of, "Oh the show's ready. The show is locked in." No. "Everything is like a piece of clay and I just left it there and I'm expecting when I come back I'm still going to push it a little bit. It was not bad before. It's just that it looks better on Tuesday if it's up there."

ROBERT CUCUZZA: The most valuable thing that I learned from him as a theater artist was the ability to not know how to solve a problem with a show for a very long time, sometimes up until the first performance. I had never worked with someone who was so willing to make so many dramatic changes so close to opening . . . and then just stop. He also made it very clear that once the show opened he would stop making changes. I think this served a dual purpose. First, it helped us to not completely freak out. Second, it supported the idea his shows are whatever they become from the moment we start rehearsal until we open, then we just perform that version of the show for an audience. At no point is it like, "Okay, this it what we've been working towards. This is the show. Good thing we found it before we opened." It was just like, "Okay, we're at this point; let's call it a show."

JOHN COLLINS: [I appreciated his] rigor, single-mindedness, and an insistence on getting things exactly as he wanted them—even if (and this was often the case) that meant making big changes at the last minute.

Foreman's aesthetic is different from mine, but his focus and commitment as well as his fearlessness were traits that I always sought to emulate, and still do.

FULYA PEKER: I think working with him, witnessing his creative process, his stance as an artist who does not concede to the commercial world, encouraged many of us to further develop our own theatrical visions, and to be insistent about that. Always unsatisfied, always unfinished, always uncertain. . . . Always experimenting. Always searching for ways to express that "thing" via theater, which is otherwise inexpressible.

A director, in my view, should be able to direct an entire piece, not just the actors/performers. I appreciate directors who can work like architects. There is a reason why we call Foreman the "maestro."

CHARLOTTA MOHLIN: [Having worked with Foreman] made it very easy for me to take direction and never take anything for granted. I loved being such an intricate part of the puzzle. It also made me want to pursue acting as a career.

STEPHANIE SILVER: It strengthened my confidence and stage presence. The experience reinforced my likes and dislikes in theater. And I gained a better sense of the roles and mediums that suited me. For example, I remember taking a cold reading for TV class not long after I stopped working with Richard and I hated it. I just couldn't bring myself to care about ordinary, slice of life reality. It all seemed so banal.

DAVID PATRICK KELLY: For me it required internalizing my personal interpretation of his SINE QUA NON (borrowed from Stanislavsky as a way to find the deeper meaning) for the four plays I was in. I was trying to apply Stanislavsky techniques to this poetic theater. I took sections of *The Cure* to my class with the great coach Mira Rostova. It was the first time she responded affirmatively to my work which had been [Anton] Chekhov and [Eugene] O'Neill scenes. I think Richard is our American Beckett. It fulfilled for me everything I'd hoped to achieve as an actor . . . such a broad range of characters and classics and styles.

Working with Richard was a continuous education in aesthetics, poetics, literature, and philosophy. I loved reading [Martin] Heidegger, [Friedrich] Nietzsche, [Gilles] Deleuze, [Pierre-Félix] Guattari, and Anatole France to get into Richard's poetics.

KEVIN HURLEY: Foreman gave me a deeper voice to help me root myself. The unknown became exciting. He created beautiful images that he would throw out the next day and leave the stage empty. That left a sense of what we experienced inside our beings even though we were in a "new" space—the kinetic energy that can come from internal conflict.

FRANK BOUDREAUX: Richard's work challenged me as an artist. It made claims on my assumptions. It makes me push myself to find the voice needed for each particular project.

JAN LESLIE HARDING: It was a time. I felt so privileged for him to keep asking me back. It was such a validation because the Public knew me as the Shakespeare person. The Ensemble Studio Theater knew me as the kitchen sink drama person but when I started to work in the avant-garde theater that's when I really found my tribe and Richard was a huge part of that for me—clicking with him.

Right around the time I worked with Richard I also started doing a lot of Mac Wellman plays so I was really fed a lot of food for thought. Deep thoughts are more interesting things than mundane human relationships. It was a really good time in my life. At the time I felt like, "These are the good old days and I know it."

I felt that the community that surrounded Richard and his art in general—oh, I felt so privileged and honored to be in that group of people at that time with the Mac Wellman people and Jeff Jones—it was a great community.

I adore Richard. From the first moment I met him he was honest and true. There was an odd humor and antagonistic banter which we both recognized as play. He expanded my understanding of theater, art, and being. I can't explain how fortunate I was to fall into his shit and come up smelling like a rose. Changed my life.

JAMES URBANIAK: I've taken the lessons I learned from working with Richard and used them in many other projects. His notes and rules are essentially a recipe for good acting, regardless of the style of the piece.

MARY EWALD: Richard came up with interesting ways of not connecting too much to the language, and throwing things away with a bemused sense of the whole endeavor. [This was helpful because] I'd often been told that I gave too much reverence to the language of a play and tended to sound too intelligent. In working on Winnie in Beckett's *Happy Days*, I found myself giving too much care to the language and needing to toss it off in a more light-handed way.

John Kazanjian adds that as a Producing Artistic Director of New City, Richard was the most humble, courteous, and sensitive visiting artist of the more than ten national artists that we invited to work with us.

Juliana Francis Kelly in *King Cowboy Rufus Rules the Universe*, 2004. Photo by T. Ryder Smith.

COLLEEN WERTHMAN: It made me more physically adventurous as a performer, and more inventive.

JULIANA FRANCIS KELLY: While Foreman's work was never a place I felt at home in (and that is one of the reasons I valued the experience) I am deeply grateful for my experience working for him. As an actor, I'm very good at crying—tears come easily to me, and I've often relied on tears as a way of testing whether I understand the play. With Foreman, I was not allowed the luxury of tears, and it made me a better performer.

Richard was one of those rare directors who make everything else seem easy. And his work has made me want to search out a particular kind of heartbreak in work—one that is not worn on one's sleeve.

SOPHIA SKILES: I still consider deeply and hope to cultivate in myself a desire to please only myself on a deep artistic level, which I connect to him.

SUSAN LATHAM: Because I worked for and with Richard for such a long time—for much of my professional life if you count being a board member—I really grew up professionally with Richard and his productions played a formative role that continues to influence my theatrical preferences.

I continue to work in theater, albeit in a different way—I'm now a fundraiser for The Actors Fund, which is a human services organization for people in performing arts and entertainment and we work primarily with Broadway types. Working with Richard opened my eyes to the realm of possibility in theater and the great variety of theatrical experiences and expression. I love Richard's theater and felt like my mind was cleansed after watching one of his productions—I feel like Richard's singular theatrical vision and experience spoiled all other theater for me, because everything else is kind of boring in comparison.

PAULA GORDON: I will say that [working with Foreman] was good training for working with people who change their mind a lot and in situations where the underlying assumption is prone to change. But the Wooster Group was also good for that, as was touring with artists who had very small production budgets. Some time ago I dubbed my business "Plan B." Flexibility is one of my selling points regardless of the service I'm providing.

JOHN MATTURRI: In a sense, I see my work with Foreman—and with Jack Smith, Ken Jacobs, and others—as a kind of apprenticeship that substituted for formal studio art training. Although I have continued to perform occasionally, I am not an actor or performance artist and my main work is as a visual artist. Participating in the Foreman plays brought me into a circle of artists who encouraged me to pursue my own work. As a spectator I had been interested in avant-garde art, film, and music since high school. When I began performing with Foreman I was training to be a cinema scholar and am not certain that I would have taken the same [career] course that I have if it were not for the accident of being in the Foreman plays.

KARL FRANKLIN ALLEN: I'm not a performer anymore. Working with Richard was one of the high watermarks of my brief career and my experiences after working with him were all deeply disappointing on an intellectual and professional level. He set too high of a bar, I guess!

MIKE TAYLOR: [Having worked with Richard] gave me a sense of how to find things and what to look for in my own presentational, stylized work—as writer/director/editor/etc.

TRAVIS JUST: Richard is without question one of the greatest artists I have been fortunate enough to work for and it shaped my work profoundly.

DENISE LUCCIONI: After working with Foreman, I think I had become a true professional, and a practical one too. I know for sure I had lost all patience for work that was petty or uselessly wordy or cute, or conventional and derivative. I went on to be a co-founder of the French dance film archive as the assistant to the director, then I became co-director of Paris experimental Théâtre de la Bastille. I was in charge of programs, so in 1985, I invited Richard to return to Paris for a French production of Kathy Acker's *My Death My Life by Pier Paolo Pasolini*, for a four-week run (after it premiered in Bordeaux, and toured in Florence and Bari, Italy). The cast and crew lived and worked in Paris. Only Kate and Richard came from the States.

As part of a recent personal project on Richard, deciding to focus on Foreman and France, I have filmed an interview of Bernard Sobel as well as a reunion of the *My Death My Life* actors and prop person, at my place. I still have to incorporate this material in my film/archive work-in-progress.

FULYA PEKER: Working with Foreman definitely heightened my aesthetic standards and expectations. Each and every work I did for him, whether in the house, backstage, on stage, or on screen, was thought provoking for me.

In 2007, I founded Katharsis Performance Project, through which I have been presenting my work as a writer and director. I went on to perform in Object Collection's experimental operas, and continued my performance research internationally with Modern Mythologies Project. My interest in philosophy, poetry, and physiology is evident in my work as a theater artist. I am compelled to link things; to create metaphors; to experiment with textual and textural materials and alternative physical–vocal approaches; to delve deeper into ecstatic states of human consciousness, such as cruelty, sexuality, and fear. A critic once referred to my work as "ritual expressionist." I can include names like [Friedrich] Nietzsche, [Carl] Jung, [Antonin] Artaud, [Jerzy] Grotowski, [John] Cage, [Alberto] Giacometti, [Samuel] Beckett, [Tatsumi] Hijikata, and many thinkers and avant-garde artists and filmmakers in my theatrical genealogy.

JOHN OGLEVEE: It gave me a very interesting counterpoint to my obsession with [Robert] Wilson's work. It was the other side of the same coin. Rather than use immense space and long stretches of time to create room for interpretation, Richard filled the room with "stuff" and created physical obstacles to disrupt meaning.

I have moved on to create contemporary works steeped in the tradition of Noh which I have been involved with intensively since my move to Japan in 1999. I feel that the movement of Noh is most certainly within the realm of Wilson's work, while the music of Noh reminds me a lot of Richard's "pings, yelps, and buzzes." Working with him most certainly gave me the courage to work in my own way.

MANNY IGREJAS: His work influenced my playwriting. I didn't think in terms of just writing plays; I aimed to make shows that were all-encompassing experiences.

DAVID HERSKOVITS: Of course, his work is very detail-oriented and that is very inspiring to me. That's always been my hope and my concern in my own work—to work in an extremely detailed way. From the start there was an affinity there about how structured and detailed.

DAMON KIELY: I appreciated Richard's level of detail—physical, aural, kinesthetic, lighting, sound, movement, character, dialogue—it's unmatched I think. That came from his insanely slow iterative process. I remember one time as a technical director I was watching an actor cross the stage and at a certain point she adjusted her hat like it didn't fit—the elastic was loose or something. I added it to my long list of things to fix. It was low on the list so I didn't get to it. I think the next day or so I happened to watch the same scene—she adjusted her hat at exactly the same place in exactly the same way—I crossed it off the list. It was one of the thousands and thousands of specific choices he made that made the work dense.

JAMES URBANIAK: What you learn as an actor in Foreman is not to take *anything* for granted. Every gesture and utterance must be deeply considered and not simply executed. Which is a lesson one can take elsewhere, outside of Foreman, to more conventional shows. An actor can never be too specific. Foreman forces this micro-specificity because on the surface, nothing makes sense.

You're forced to make sense out of the abstract. Part of what you discover in rehearsal with Richard is beats within beats. In other words, the first week, your action might be, "Cross to table and pick up mug." The second week the action becomes, "Start to cross to the table. Stop. Consider. Decide to pick up mug." Third week: "Cross. Stop. Consider table. Approach mug. Weigh benefits of picking up mug. Consider other options. Pick up mug." It's a lot of work and a lot of trial and error.

MIKE TAYLOR: Even though he's quite specific he doesn't micromanage people; he requests results and makes suggestions or asks someone to try something.

STEPHANIE SILVER: He was a benevolent dictator and incredibly savvy.

JAN LESLIE HARDING: In a Foreman piece where he's so particular you really need to rely on the specifics and the specifics of what other people are giving you too. They point this finger instead of that finger. When you're performing you've got all those micro changes in you that still resonate [from past iterations].

FULYA PEKER: Although the stage looked fragmentary, every element of it, including the performers, somehow served a whole, a "source." Hence, it felt like even when I was not under a light, even when I was in a corner staring upstage, the position of my pinky finger, or a tiny gesture I made, or the way I held a small object, was enough to alter that reality—precision, subtlety, and details amidst chaos. . . . It was intense, but it helped me to be alert, even in moments of stasis, while waiting for the expected yet untimely interruption or disruption, while waiting for the next inevitable "unbalancing act," while waiting "to fade into the past or leave into the future," while waiting to be defocused.

JOHN MATTURRI: I was struck by the way small decisions could have a dramatic effect on the play as a whole. For example, I was asked to purchase a mask during *Rhoda in Potatoland* and found what I considered an interesting one in a Times Square shop, not knowing how it would be used. I remember Richard quite liking this and noticed that it was giving a certain character to the play as a whole. I was struck by the idea that the play would have somewhat of a different character if I had made a different choice.

Similarly, because Foreman was working with his performers as found objects [using what the performers bring—physicality, vocal quality, aesthetic], there was a sense that one's own idiosyncratic ways of moving would be taken into account and have a small but definite impact on the final result. This involvement of contingency in the development of the piece had an important impact on my subsequent work.

An extraordinary example of the use of a performer as a found object was Bob Fleischner, a filmmaker who was introduced to Foreman by Ken Jacobs and who was in six plays, most notably playing Max [in *Rhoda in Potatoland*]. An extremely unassuming man, Fleischner nevertheless had an extraordinary stage presence and in his understated manner became, I think, an important counterweight to the more energetic and risky performances of Kate Manheim as Rhoda.

As in every play I've been in, I enjoyed the mutual adaptations that occur underneath the larger directorial interventions: for example, asking someone to pause for a beat so that you can get to where you needed to go or to do so in a particular manner. For all of the seeming [directorial] control, even in a small "crew role" there was room for small personal interventions.

Foreman on . . .

KEN NINTZEL: Richard is very knowledgeable and he was always sharing thoughts and opinions. Many of them went over my head and still do but he is always searching for the thing that really turns him on and gets him going. I appreciate that.

MAKING ART

DAMON KIELY: We all have a hole inside ourselves and our art should be trying to fill that hole.

BRENDAN REGIMBAL: There's something he said that we'd always laugh about. He would be watching a moment—maybe with somebody dressed as a pirate coming in backwards, smacking a bell, and saying a line. He would watch it two or three times and then say something like, "Oh making art is hell," which is obviously not true. And the fact that we could all laugh about how hard it is in many ways [means] we also know it's heaven.

MIKE TAYLOR: The only advice I recall is that someone, I think a performer, asked why he wanted to change something that they thought was really great and that he had agreed was pretty good. Richard said that Picasso said, if you're painting a painting and you have a perfect section, say only the corner of your painting is completely perfect, absolutely perfect and amazing: Paint over it. You're painting a painting, not a corner.

CHRISTINA CAMPANELLA: In my notes from rehearsal one day: "Don't be upset. Making art is a ridiculous, agonizing procedure."

DAVID PATRICK KELLY: Feeling vulnerable is a great place to be for creation . . .

FILM

BRENDAN REGIMBAL: [Richard would talk about] films and what was "worth it"—without putting it in a box of the high/low brow tastes like watching *Conan the Barbarian* is as valuable as watching *Cremaster Cycle*, The Matthew Barney films. They're both pieces of art. There's something in both of them. There's not a threshold bar because we're not looking for good art. We're looking for where does this take me? What could I experience from this?

SOPHIA SKILES: He asked a group of us what we thought movies were for. After attempts at breaking down the medium, and so on, he insisted, "because it gives people something to discuss."

RYAN HOLSOPPLE: I loved to pick Richard's brain about New York avant-garde cinema of the 1970s. Our common bond was a love for Ken Jacobs's film works and I had just seen a showing of some of Jacobs's recent films. I was entranced by Jacobs's *Nervous System*, the propeller-like motor that would run in front of two film strip projectors. I think I remember Foreman saying that many bits from *Panic! (How to be Happy!)* were based on Laurel and Hardy skits that Jacobs had deconstructed with his *Nervous System*.

I remember being on tour with *Panic! (How to be Happy!)* in Vienna. Peter Kubelka ran the cinema museum in Vienna and on a day off while on tour, I found myself at the museum going to a retrospective exhibit of Kaus Kinski, including costumes from famous films like Cobra Verde, video footage of the "I am Jesus" performances and much more. I remember running into Richard in the museum while looking at some intricate opera set designs. Richard remarked to me that he felt like we ran into each other at a peep show, and a sense of embarrassment overcame both of us. We talked a little about Kinski and how we had both read his biography that had recently been published.

Once, I remember him saying: the only reason films exist is to give people something to talk about. I agree.

MONEY

JOHN OGLEVEE: He said on a number of occasions, he was very lucky to have grown up in Scarsdale and been afforded a lifestyle that helped him establish his art at a time when New York was cheaper. His advice was to be rich if one wanted to be in the arts.

THEATER

JULIANA FRANCIS KELLY: "Don't fix it. Radicalize it." Best advice EVER. For everything, not just theater.

MANNY IGREJAS: I like Richard's line, "We live in a world where everything is interpreted for us. I'm interested in creating a different experience."

KEVIN HURLEY: Foreman spoke of going to the theater when he was younger and how everyone kind of knew what would happen in the third act and would say how great it was. He felt uncomfortable and wanted to run away as soon as possible. I felt the same way about a lot of things I saw. The familiar becomes repressive. The unknown is scary for a lot of people.

CHARLOTTA MOHLIN: When we were done with the run Richard said to me, "Go to LA. Theater in New York is dead." I still ended up performing a play directed by someone who had seen me in Richard's play. It was right after we closed and the play was called *Three Children*. It was also very experimental with no set storyline. But when that was done I took Richard's advice and moved to Los Angeles.

DAVID PATRICK KELLY: "I hate the theater." Richard would often seriously say that, then he would qualify it somewhat with some exceptions but he kind of really meant it.

JOHN MATTURRI: [Foreman conveyed that] any text could make a great play if directed in the right way.

T. RYDER SMITH: "You have to find out what the material is saying to you," Richard said a few times. "Find the *internal necessity* of it."

About *King Cowboy Rufus*, Richard said: "I want to take the bad of the world, and turn it into ecstasy. Ecstasy is made out of shit." And on another occasion: "I want to learn to syncopate *with* the tension, and turn it into a kind of jazz."

Richard said that as the director, he was therapist to the playwright. Richard the playwright lay on the couch speaking the text and Richard the director asked: Now, what do you mean by that?

JOHN COLLINS: One of my favorite quotes about the theater comes from Richard (and I'm paraphrasing since I don't have it in front of me): "A mason jar sitting on stage, being nudged with a long stick from someone off-stage—that could constitute theater." There's so much to unpack in that quote, but it seems to suggest that theater is a world of implied possibilities and magic.

I remember coming to understand what he meant when he would give me the note that my sound on a particular night was "vulgar." It was a little confusing at the time but I came to understand what he meant and it had something to do with not forcing meaning on something through sound dynamics that were too transparent. He did NOT like it vulgar. I think "vulgar" meant unsubtle and it was a kind of subtlety he was after. "Vulgar" meant that the audience would be aware of some kind of manipulation by me, rather than the sounds coming and going in an almost imperceptible way that matched the kind of magical poetry of the writing and the intense, dream-like psychology of the action. In those moments he didn't want the audience to sense my hand in things (literally, since I was running analog faders on an analog mixer) or his for that matter.

Obviously, there were other times when he wanted the sound to be aggressive and unsubtle but this note was to do with a series of cues that were meant to be almost subliminal in their effects. The two shows I worked on were much more meditative and so that was more the vibe.

He really did want to get into the subconscious of his audience and sound was an important tool for that, if properly applied.

JAY SMITH: Richard once said that he liked to opt for the perverse choice. I took that with me and have tried to make use of it in other work.

DENISE LUCCIONI: I learned a lesson from Richard about beauty and seduction. I guess it's also a [Marcel] Duchamp- and [John] Cage-ian stance. Who wants to "make" beauty? Beauty occurs, or it doesn't. Seduction, on the other hand, should be banned. Nobody needs seductive theater "pandering to the masses" (I actually learned the phrase from a play Richard produced in the 1970s).

FRANK BOUDREAUX: So much. Every one of the programs of his shows contained an artistic statement that spoke to his artistic intentions and their philosophical foundation. He always wrote about his artistic evolution and his response to the evolving world around him in those statements.

We are all lucky to have many of his ideas and methods recorded in bound books for future reference and inspiration.

LEARNING

JULIANA FRANCIS KELLY: He told me not to worry about my lack of education so much and to make work from my perspective. That meant a great deal to me.

DENISE LUCCIONI: Richard often shares a book he's read, or an author he really likes. But then a few years later he's forgotten he even mentioned it, let alone read it. I think his encyclopedic knowledge combined, oddly, with a determined trust in his unconscious mind are what structure his theater-making, and now film making. Knowledge is not really the word, it's what he makes of it: he digests and appropriates all he reads, sees, and hears. I used to feel terrible not being able to memorize things the way certain scholars do, spitting out what they read and learn. I slowly became more confident about integrating what I am interested in and letting it cook inside of me and turn into whatever use it is to me, that is, my growing and just forgetting the rest.

JAN LESLIE HARDING: At one point he gave me three books to read. He said they were his favorite books. Because it was Foreman telling me to read this stuff, they stuck with me in a different way. One of the books was about a boy who went to live in a home. While he's coming down the stairs to where his mother was picking him up, he's having all these flash backs of all the memories from the orphanage.

At some point he gave me *Madeleine is Sleeping* [by Sarah Shun-lien Bynum].

I remember the books he would suggest were books I would never have read otherwise. I needed somebody in my life to say, "Look at this." Then you're not only having this great experience of reading something that is not ordinary but it's got you thinking about stuff. It was a really lush time for me because I was surrounded by a lot of really smart people—funny, smart, and generous people. And Richard's really generous. That's what I remember about working with him the most.

———

SHAUNA KELLY: *You gifted us the David Markson book* Reader's Block *on opening night (2004). You inscribed it for me, "To Shauna: I think this is the greatest novel of our times. With thanks and gratitude, Richard." What other books/authors have you gifted over the years? What are your favorite works?*

RICHARD FOREMAN: *Oh that changes so quickly. Those days I had been reading what I didn't know was sort of a fascist, Paul Morand. I was reading him a couple months ago and got everything in English. Everything. Which, out of his vast outputs, that's maybe fifteen out of forty or forty-five and then I just started this past week reading him again and he is a great, great writer. But I'm not going to give them as gifts to anybody because they are too hard to get.*

———

FULYA PERKER: I remember Foreman mentioning thinkers, writers, or artists whenever asked about his sources of inspiration, but he would rarely, if ever, give the names of theater directors. His loft is full of books, and I am sure there were many encounters he had with other artists over the years that provoked his ways of thinking or creating, even if antagonistically. The point is how an artist receives, blends, and digests inspirational or provoking materials while developing a vision of their own. Ultimately, every work exists in a time continuum and is part of a historical lineage.

Foreman's theater definitely does not consist of stories, but, in daily life conversations, he is a great storyteller. I enjoyed listening to him talking about his memories, commenting about writers and thinkers, films and books. . . . I learned a great deal from him. Though, now that I am trying to quote him, I can only recall some highlighted words, flashing in and out of my brain, only fragments, but not contexts. Just like his shows.

This reminds me of an interview I did with him for *Hyperion: On the Future of Aesthetics* (Vol. III, No. 2, April 2008). Instead of asking questions, I picked some words and phrases he had been using frequently during the rehearsals, and I asked him to elaborate on them. I wanted readers to be able to witness his rehearsing mind, his stream of consciousness, that everlasting flow of fragments. . . . It has always been intriguing to observe Foreman contemplating, that is, communicating with his own thoughts, even when one has no idea what those thoughts truly are, or how they come to exist.

WILLEM DAFOE: Before rehearsals Richard would often come in with a reading [in order to] basically set our minds to a proper way of working. He was always interested in one philosopher or another or one aspect of pop culture and he'd be spinning off of it in a very stimulating way. I always remember he introduced the idea of "stories hide the truth," which is something that I have ruminated on a lot. I take that with me everywhere I go. To have knowledge of that ["stories hide the truth"] makes you sufficiently suspicious that you can still be all in but then once again you realize that there's not just one way. It makes you realize that things aren't black and white; things aren't good and bad. It invites you to get away from a certain kind of easy or programmed judgment or morality about what stuff means and why you make things. Richard is a fascinating mind and through the practice of rehearsing and making these plays, he gives you a little bit of that mind through the text. So you take that on and you take a little bit of Richard's brain with you and when you do that you feel very engaged and sometimes you even feel smart. [*Laughter*] No, I laugh at myself but he articulates things for you that perhaps you aren't capable of articulating but then once he gives you examples you can kind of reconstruct his thought and start to play with some of his ideas.

COLLEEN WERTHMANN: Some of the best parts of rehearsal were at the end of the day when Foreman would just talk for about a half an hour—really, just hold forth, and everyone would stretch or make notes, while he expounded. It was like a bunch of disciples sitting at the feet of a guru. The level of his erudition was just insane to me. He seemed to have read and deeply absorbed and analyzed nearly every religious and philosophical thinker in the world.

———

SHAUNA KELLY: *You're a powerful communicator as a director. You have a way with words.*

RICHARD FOREMAN: *The verbal part of the credit goes to my father who was a successful attorney, a trial lawyer and he used to provoke me at the dinner table every night. I mean he'd say something he knew I would disagree with and we'd start having these big, long, arguments and that taught me to speak, I think, to speak in a kind of way. I was trying to convince my father all the time that what he said was wrong, so I think that contributed to it.*

SHAUNA KELLY: *In order to win that fight you had to articulate your argument exactly. Cast and crew enjoyed listening to you and watching you create the show in the very unique process that it was. A director is very much in the spotlight. Our cast of ten people in* King Cowboy Rufus Rules the Universe *were attentive to you for 6.5 hours a day for rehearsal.*

RICHARD FOREMAN: *And for what—fourteen weeks, sixteen weeks?*

SHAUNA KELLY: *Yeah. And I'm not sure if you are a self-proclaimed introvert or not, but how was it being in the spotlight like that?*

RICHARD FOREMAN: *Well, I am an introvert. As a kid I was very shy. That's why I got into the theater—a chance to relate, to be social in a way that certain things were taken care of for me because I was in the theater and there was a script and what have you. But I used to enjoy it. At the same token I used to feel that it was sort of an ego trip so in a way I had mixed feelings about it. I would do it for a couple of months every year and I liked that it pulled me out of what I thought was my real self in many ways.*

———

ACTING

DAVID COTE: Stop acting. I think?

LIFE

DAVID COTE: Eric Dyer was technical director on a Foreman show, like 1993 or 1994, and he invited me to come in and volunteer to help with the set. I was so excited and thought maybe I could meet Richard. Every self-respecting downtown actor's dream was to get into a Richard Foreman show (the Wooster Group wasn't really absorbing new members at the time). So I show up and volunteer to help with the set. I think it was lunch time or something. Eric left, all the other crew were gone, and it was just me . . . and Richard. He was sitting in the house, in the back, not talking. I was supposed to take a big round disc of white foam core that had been hot glue-gunned to a stick (think a giant lollipop) and bisect it with black gaff tape. I was alone in the room with Richard and very nervous to be in the presence of the master. I was tasked with helping to construct a piece of scenic art that was going to be used in his theatrical work. I was not very handy with props or basic arts and crafts things. I had this huge roll of gaff tape and peeled off a long, unwieldy strip of it, which I tried to lay down on the large disc in a straight line. The tape formed bubbles and bad creases and wasn't straight and confident. It was not the bold Constructivist stroke I knew it needed to be. It was awful. I was getting nervous, unpeeling the tape and trying to lay it down over and over. So awkward. So pathetic. Finally, Richard walked down the steps and witnessed my struggle. He simply said, "I think it will be easier if you form the line with smaller pieces of tape. It will be more manageable that way."

There was a deep lesson there that I have never forgotten.

TRAVIS JUST: [His advice was] read, watch films. See art.

CHARLOTTA MOHLIN: So much, but mostly to trust in myself and not to listen too much to what others say or think.

DAMON KIELY: I think the main thing was always be yourself.

T. RYDER SMITH: "The psyche always speaks," Richard once said. He meant that what you desire will always find a way to express itself. It also meant to me that you can't hide who you are. And that the only useful path forward is to go beyond judgment, beyond the ego and the "self." A new philosophy and a new politics, inclusive.

THE BIGGER PICTURE

RICHARD FOREMAN: *It's interesting to think that [the work], I suppose, evokes everything I've read and seen, maybe more than I've experienced.*

JAN LESLIE HARDING: Richard believes in our cumulative experience as being part of everything that we do whether we like it or not.

Working with people like Richard means you're keyed into more philosophical questions than just going through your life. My sister used to say, "You don't need therapy, you're an actor." You're constantly going deep down into seeing why people do the things they do. If theater isn't about humanity, what is it about? All theater is about humanity so you're constantly thinking about the bigger picture *and* the details. And Richard loves lots and lots of details so you have to immerse yourself in a different realm of being which is such a breath of fresh air compared to the lives we lead in general. Those are the things I used to like to think about. I was fascinated by religion and I took mythology and humanities classes like the development of mythology with Professor Olsen at Boston University.

Richard was a good person with which to have philosophical conversations. He would always be engaged with those questions. He would always be quick to say, "I don't know," or "Yesterday I thought this, but today I think this." He was constantly moving. He didn't have a set thing. Every time I saw him, he was changed. He was still Richard as far as his optimism or lack of optimism (he's a pessimist for sure) but he would have evolved. He did not just get his set of ideas when he was twenty-four like a lot of people do and that's their thing. He's still confused by it and questioning it and giving up on it [by letting previous beliefs go and updating his worldview]. He's embracing it or not embracing it or pushing it away. He's still struggling with the big questions and the questions are changing.

I think being an actor, and an actor doing different kinds of work, is really fulfilling. And doing work with living artists, with living writers, you're not only performing their work but you're in on the process of how they are writing and why they're writing the kinds of things they are. You can read a thousand books on Shakespeare and that's fine but to have the person there to answer your most ridiculous questions and take your most ridiculous questions seriously and when you have a serious question they say, "Well that's ridiculous," you are constantly opening your eyes. They are constantly turning things inside out for you so there is a new way for you to grasp something or let it slip out of your fingers again. It changes your life because of all these existential questions and questions about art and stuff which is your life. So it's not as if then I come home and leave that storyline there. It resonates and it swills around in you and spills out into everything.

FULYA PEKER: During one of the Astronome rehearsals, Foreman told us to write "I am . . ." on our faces and to complete the phrase however we wanted, or with an invented name . . . I cannot exactly remember. But I do remember writing "I am NOT." Obviously, he immediately changed his mind. Hence, we erased the phrases. This episode relates to what I am trying to pursue in theater. On stage, I am trying to be all the things that I suppose I am not; or, I am trying to be "not." Paraphrasing Foreman, instead of re-treeing a tree, I prefer to de-tree a tree. Some sort of via negativa, or apoptosis. . . . The stage for me is an autopsy table, a laboratory, a sacred space, an alternative realm.

On Living Hell, Paradise, Death, and Rebirth

T. RYDER SMITH: He was jocular when talking of reincarnation, but also seemed to partially believe in it, or at least hope for it. Talking of it one day his face lit up: "My dream part: Leibniz!" And then said dreamily: "Monads . . . The best of all possible worlds . . ."

He said once that he keeps trying to get out of doing theater, but can't, and that in a former life he was Henrik Ibsen and before that Richard Sheridan.

JOHN COLLINS: On the first day of rehearsal, I think for *Samuel*, he was describing the play and he said, "It's about death and—well, they're ALL about death." It was said with a little bit of a smirk but I found that enlightening!

MARY EWALD: "We're all searching for paradise but living in hell. But the way we relate to hell can make it paradise. You can conquer the shit through artistic arrangement."

———

RICHARD FOREMAN: *I always used to say, my theater is really about paradise and people think, "Why do you say that?" If you make art out of lambs frolicking—yeah that's paradise but it doesn't count for anything. You've got to be able to make paradise out of all these negative things [like uncertainty and discomfort] by creating a structure—that is musical or lucid in such a way that there is a paradise in how you are able to deal with that. So yeah, that's what's interesting—to confront all the things that are problematic in life and to make paradise out of that. When you make art, you're making paradise.*

———

Contributors and Interviewees

The contributors and interviewees in this book do not comprise a company of actors who worked together for years on end. These are people who dedicated a great deal of time for a single production, or sometimes more, to work with a maestro. The biographies below make obvious their longevity in the arts, as most are multi-talented artists in it for the long haul, and their experience with Richard Foreman was only one of many.

When I started this book, I'd imagined others remembered working with Foreman as vividly and positively as I did, and I was right. I knew those individuals would have intelligent things to say about it, and they did. As I received their written content for the book and conducted interviews, I was enamored by the stories, anecdotes, and reactions about working with Foreman. I was awed by their brilliant and surprising expressions of life and work as theater professionals.

Foreman had high expectations for his art and his collaborators. He was unbending in how he got the work to where he needed it to be. Our choosing to work with Foreman was a testament to our confidence, flexibility, and grit as theater artists—and a willingness to contribute to this book underscores the importance we give that experience.

Hopefully this book has made more accessible a world of theater artists that may be unfamiliar to the average person. I feel these people have remarkable lives whose stories I am uniquely positioned to share. Thanks to the contributors for their time and articulate reflections and for helping me explain what I alone couldn't!

Most of the contributions to this book were in the form of written recollections. Transcriptions of oral interviews are marked with an asterisk. International touring locations are not included with the listings of credits for Foreman shows.

KARL FRANKLIN ALLEN is currently a theater consultant at Charcoalblue. He has worked in contemporary theater since 2002. He was the Technical Director and then Production Manager of PS 122 for several years, Technical Director and Professor of Technical Theater at Bryn Mawr College, Project Manager at Lincoln Center Out of Doors, Technical Manager at The Duke on 42nd St, and Production Manager for The Flea Theater, among others. He was the Production Manager for the world tour of Andrew Schneider's *YOUARENOWHERE* and several touring shows with Mabou Mines.

Richard Foreman Theater Credits:
Astronome: A Night at the Opera: Performer

FRANK BOUDREAUX's plays have been produced and read at The New Group, LAByrinth Theater, Hudson Valley Shakespeare Festival, 3LD, The Bushwick Starr, PS 122, Dixon Place, The Incubator, *HotInk*, and The Country Playhouse of Houston, TX. He collaborated on Reid Farrington's multimedia production *TYSON v ALI* (*NY Times, New Yorker*). While getting his MFA at Brooklyn College he studied with Mac Wellman and Erin Courtney.

Richard Foreman Theater Credits:
Maria del Bosco: Performer

THERESA BUCHHEISTER is the founder and co-director of *Title:Point*, founder and Artistic Director of The Exponential Festival, Artistic Director of the 2023 Obie Award-winning The Brick Theater from 2020 to 2024, and co-founder of Vital Joint (RIP). *Title:Point* was a member of The Silent Barn for 3.5 years. Theresa directs, produces, performs, curates, facilitates, and writes for theater and theater-adjacent performance realms. They also direct, engineer and perform for audiobooks, cartoons, podcasts, and other audio-driven content. www.theresabuchheister.com.

Richard Foreman Theater Credits:
The Gods Are Pounding My Head (AKA Lumberjack Messiah): Performer

CHRISTINA CAMPANELLA: Composer, vocalist, bandmember (keyboard), and sound artist with a deep history as a performer in theater, film, and opera (often in Joe Diebes's work) since 1997. With her "moody, driving music" (*New York Times*) and "ethereal voice" (*BUST Magazine*) she fuses songwriting and contemporary composition with aural design. She is a recipient of three NYSCA Individual Artist Commissions in Film, Media and New Technologies, a performance grant from Café Royal Cultural Foundation, commissioning from the Swedish Cultural Council, and funding from the New York State Music Fund, New Music USA, Lower Manhattan Cultural Council, and Mid-Atlantic Arts Foundation. www.christinacampanella.com.

Richard Foreman Theater Credits:
Benita Canova (Gnostic Eroticism): Performer

JOHN COLLINS: Founder and Artistic Director of the New York-based experimental theater company Elevator Repair Service (ERS) since 1991. Since then, he has directed or co-directed all of the company's productions. He worked as a designer and technician for the Wooster Group from 1993 until 2008. ERS projects include *Baldwin and Buckley at Cambridge*, Chekhov's *The Seagull*, and a project based on James Joyce's *Ulysses*. He is the recipient of a Guggenheim Fellowship, a United States Artists Fellowship, and a Doris Duke Performing Artist Award. He received a combined degree in English Literature and Theater Studies at Yale.

Richard Foreman Theater Credits:
The Mind King: Sound technician
Samuel's Major Problems: Sound technician

DAVID COTE: Librettist, playwright, and critic based in New York City. His operas have been produced in London, New York, and across the United States. They include *Lucidity* with Laura Kaminsky; *Blind Injustice* with Scott Davenport Richards; *Three Way* with Robert Paterson; and *The Scarlet Ibis* with Stefan Weisman. David's TV and theater criticism appears in *Time Out New York*, *The A.V. Club*, *Observer*, and *American Theatre*. David has written companion books to *Moulin Rouge! The Musical*, *Wicked*, *Jersey Boys*, and *Spring Awakening*. As an actor, David worked with writer–directors Robert Cucuzza, Richard Maxwell, and Assurbanipal Babilla. From 1996 to 1998, he co-edited *OFF: A Journal of Alternative Theater*.

Richard Foreman Theater Credits:
Pearls for Pigs: Performer

ROBERT CUCUZZA: Vice Chair of Arts, Media & Performance and Associate Professor of Theater Arts at Los Angeles Mission College. In Los Angeles, he directed productions at REDCAT, South Coast Rep, CalArts, and Son of Semele. He has been a member of the Obie Award-winning company Elevator Repair Service since 1997, originating the role of Tom Buchanan in *Gatz*—a staging of the entire text of *The Great Gatsby*. He performed in the *Gatz* company for over fifteen years, across the globe. As an acting and script analysis teacher, he has taught both BFA and MFA actors at CalArts, and at the legendary Lee Strasberg Theatre & Film Institute. Cucuzza has his BFA from Carnegie Mellon University and MFA in Directing from CalArts.

Richard Foreman Theater Credits:
Samuel's Major Problems: Production intern
My Head Was a Sledgehammer: Performer
Permanent Brain Damage: Performer
Panic! (How to be Happy!): Performer

WILLEM DAFOE*: One of the original members of the Wooster Group, the New York based experimental theater collective. He created and performed in all of the group's work from 1977 through 2004, both in the United States and internationally. Since then, he has performed and collaborated in the works of Robert Wilson and Romeo Castellucci. Having made over one hundred films in his legendary acting career, Dafoe is internationally respected for bringing versatility, boldness, and dare to some of the most iconic films of our time. His artistic curiosity leads him to projects all over the world, large and small, Hollywood films as well as independent cinema.

Richard Foreman Theater Credits:
Miss Universal Happiness: Performer
Idiot Savant: Performer

MARY EWALD is a founding member of New City Theater in Seattle, which has been her artistic home base since the early 1980s. There she performed in world premieres written and directed by María Irene Fornés, Len Jenkin, and John Jesurun. She has also performed at the Soho Rep and Playwrights Horizons (NYC), the Williamstown Theatre Festival, Berkeley Rep, Seattle Rep, ACT, Intiman, Theatre X (Milwaukee), and Seattle Shakespeare Co. Her collaborations with husband and artistic director John Kazanjian include the *Homebody/Kabul* (Tony Kushner) and playing Hamlet, Prospero, Timon, and Winnie (*Happy Days*).

Richard Foreman Theater Credits:
Eddie Goes to Poetry City, Part 1 (Seattle): Performer

PAULA GORDON translates fiction, non-fiction, poetry, plays, documentaries, and novels by Bosnian, Croatian, Montenegrin, and Serbian authors. Her published translations include Ljubomir Đurković's play *Refuse* (Montenegrin National Theater and a revised version by Laertes Press), and novel *Catherine the Great and the Small* by Olja Knežević (Istros Books). Previously, she worked in experimental theater and dance with artists including Mabou Mines, the Wooster Group, Jo Andres, No Theater, and Elizabeth Streb Ringside. In the 1990s she worked in Bosnia and Herzegovina with humanitarian aid and arts organizations. She was on the production team of the Sarajevo Film Festival from 1998 through 2001.

Richard Foreman Theater Credits:
Miss Universal Happiness: Props, electrician, light board operator
Symphony of Rats: Lighting designer and production manager
Samuel's Major Problems: Technical director

ETHAN GOULD creates puppetry and props for many performances in New York City. He has done visual art and scholarly work for press including Punctum Books and the (fake) anatomy textbook, *Suspicious Anatomy*, and was a curator with The Observatory in Brooklyn. He produces game art, performance sculpture, and narrative audio. His art mostly explores the ideas that objects are virtual, time is a place, and plants are fascinating. He is a graduate of The University of Rochester and has an MFA from the School of Visual Arts in Visual Narrative.

Richard Foreman Theater Credits:
The Gods Are Pounding My Head (AKA Lumberjack Messiah): Production intern

JAN LESLIE HARDING*: Last seen at the Kennedy Center in *Wilderness* with En Guard Arts, with whom she also participated in Reza Abdoh's *Father Was a Peculiar Man,* Mac Wellman's *Strange Feet* at the Smithsonian in D.C., *Crowbar* at the New Victory, and *Sincerity Forever* at BACA Downtown (Obie). She worked with many masters of the avant-garde including Theodora Skipitarus, The Talking Band at La MaMa, and in many productions with Wellman all over the country. Jan Leslie participated in The Helsinki International Theatre Festival and the Whitney Biennial. She is a member of the Ensemble Studio Theater and a founding member of the Flea.

Richard Foreman Theater Credits:
The Birth of a Poet: Performer
My Head Was a Sledgehammer: Performer
I've Got the Shakes: Performer
Pearls for Pigs: Performer

DAVID HERSKOVITS*: Founding Artistic Director of five-time Obie Award winning Target Margin Theater (TMT). He has directed a broad range of work, classics and neglected older work, new opera and music-theater, and adaptations of history and literature for TMT and other theaters, festivals, and universities all over. David has taught and lectured at The Mellon School of Theater and Performance Research at Harvard, Yale, Williams, Wesleyan, The School of Visual Art in Jerusalem, Juilliard, and other universities and drama schools. He has written for *The New York Times*, *American Theatre*, *Theater Magazine*, and *Performing Arts Journal*, among others.

Richard Foreman Theater Credits:
The Fall of the House of Usher: Assistant
City of Amateurs Directing workshop at American Repertory Theater: Directing student
What Did He See?: Assistant director
Where's Dick (Houston Grand Opera): Assistant director
Lava: Assistant director
Eddie Goes to Poetry City, Part 2: Assistant director
The Mind King: Assistant director

RYAN HOLSOPPLE develops and programs interactive systems for live performance. He is a graduate of NYU's Interactive Telecommunications Program (ITP) and has developed interactive designs for a wide range of visual, theatrical, and practical applications including 31 Down, Bill Morrison, Radiohole, Annie Dorsen, Susan Marshall, Ellie Ga, Jim Findlay, and many others. Ryan was awarded a "Best of New York 2007" by the *Village Voice* for *Canal Street Station*, an interactive telephone murder mystery set in the New York Subway system.

Richard Foreman Theater Credits:
Pearls for Pigs: Production intern
Maria del Bosco: Performer
Panic! (How to be Happy!): Performer

KEVIN HURLEY: Member of Remains Theater in Chicago, where he acted in numerous productions. In New York theater he worked with The Builders Association, NYC Players, and others. He toured widely in Europe, Australia, and Japan. His film and TV credits include *Bits & Bobs*.

Richard Foreman Theater Credits:
Bad Boy Nietzsche: Performer

MANUEL IGREJAS's fiction can be found in *Men on Men 4*, *34th Parallel*, *Chelsea Station* and Image Out/Write; and poetry in *A New Geography of Poets*. His plays include *Shrinkage* and *Kitty and Lina* (both reviewed in *The New York Times*), *Miss Mary Dugan*, *Hassan and Sylvia*, and *Margarita and Max* (Best Short Play in 2013 at the Midtown Festival). *NSA* was an O'Neill semi-finalist in 2013. He was a theatrical publicist for many years working on and off-Broadway. Clients included John Leguizamo, STREB, among many others. If you've heard of Blue Man Group, then he did his job.

Richard Foreman Theater Credits:
1997–2009: Publicist

TRAVIS JUST's work often uses text, objects, and gesture in addition to instruments, voice, and electronics. He founded Brooklyn-based performance group Object Collection in 2004 with writer/director Kara Feely, with whom he is co-director of the ensemble. He has composed five operas: *Problem Radical(s)* (2009), *Innova* (2011) and *NO HOTEL* (2013), *cheap&easy OCTOBER* (2015), *It's All True* (2016), and *You Are Under Our Space Control* (2019). He composed the music for Richard Foreman's *Suppose Beautiful Madeline Harvey* (2024). www.objectcollection.us.

Richard Foreman Theater Credits:
Deep Trance Behavior in Potatoland: Sound engineer
Astronome: A Night at the Opera: Sound engineer
Idiot Savant: Sound engineer

JULIANA FRANCIS KELLY is an Obie Award winning performer, writer, and teacher. She has originated roles for Reza Abdoh, Marie Losier, Bertrand Mandico, Young Jean Lee, Karin Coonrod and many others. julianafranciskelly.net.

Richard Foreman Theater Credits:
Paradise Hotel : Performer
Bad Boy Nietzsche: Performer
Maria del Bosco: Performer (Obie Award for acting)
King Cowboy Rufus Rules the Universe: Performer

DAVID PATRICK KELLY: Award-winning stage and film actor and musician. He has performed in every genre of film and is most known for the works of Walter Hill, David Lynch, and Spike Lee. On stage he has played leading roles on Broadway in classics, new plays, and musicals. He received an Obie Award for Sustained Excellence and created roles in Tony Award winning plays and Palm d'Or winning films.

Richard Foreman Theater Credits:
The Cure: Performer
Film is Evil/Radio Is Good: Performer

Woyzeck: Performer
The Mind King: Performer
Pearls for Pigs: Performer

SHAUNA KELLY acted in theater and independent film in New York from 1997 to 2010. As an expat in Tokyo from 2022 to 2025, she worked as an actor in TV and film. In her performance studies writing, she bridges her experience in the arts with her work in research and consulting. She has her BA from Pace University, New York City, and her MPA from the Middlebury Institute of International Studies, Monterey, California. She travels off the beaten path to places such as Sierra Leone and East Timor.

Richard Foreman Theater Credits:
King Cowboy Rufus Rules the Universe: Performer

DAMON KIELY: Chair of Performance at DePaul's Theatre School and the author of *How to Read a Play: Text Analysis for Directors* (Routledge 2016) and *How to Rehearse a Play* (Routledge 2020). He directed *Barbecue* at Steppenwolf's 1700 Space and *Boy* for TimeLine Theatre. From 2002 through 2007 he served as Artistic Director for American Theater Company. He has directed for American Blues, Strawdog, Route 66, A Red Orchid, Next and many others. In New York, he directed for the Public Theater, New York Theatre Workshop, Adobe Theater Company, PS 122, Ensemble Studio Theater, and New Dramatists.

Richard Foreman Theater Credits:
I've Got the Shakes: Assistant technical director
Benita Canova: Technical director
Paradise Hotel: Producer
Bad Boy Nietzsche: Producer

SUSAN LATHAM is a nonprofit professional with over twenty-five years of executive-level experience at New York City organizations. She is the Executive Director of the Queens Public Library Foundation. Previously, she worked at The Actors Fund, NYU Law School, and more. In the performing arts she was a fundraiser, producer, and company manager, toured throughout the United States and abroad with artist Meredith Monk and other companies, and produced shows at the Brooklyn Academy of Music's Next Wave Festival. She worked for many years at Performing Artservices as an arts administrator, raising funds and publicizing the work of avant-garde music, theater, and dance companies.

Richard Foreman Theater Credits:
1983–97: Publicist, grant writer

DENISE LUCCIONI a French translator and essayist specializing in dance and theater, had a previous career in producing, and curating, generally working closely with a number of French and American creators—for example, Trisha Brown, Steve Paxton, Merce Cunningham, Big Art Group. . . . While at Bénédicte Pesle's Artservice International in Paris, she assisted Richard Foreman on all fronts for three plays, including tours, which proved to be a most nourishing challenge in her life. Her film portraits of artists she worked with premieres at Charleroi-Danse in Brussels in 2025, Antwerp De Singel and Leuven Stuk in 2026.

Richard Foreman Theater Credits:
Café Amérique: Assistant to the director
Faust ou la Fête électrique: Assistant to the director
Three Acts of Recognition: Personal assistant to the director

JOHN MATTURRI: New York-based artist/photographer who focuses on urban environments and the interactions between images and words. He has worked with artists such as Ken Jacobs, Jack Smith, John Zorn, Stuart Sherman, Michael Kirby, Ying Liu, and Shelley Hirsch. His work has been seen at the Brooklyn Historical Society Museum, The Whitney Museum, and Collective for

Living Cinema, among other venues. He has written on visual art, film, performance, and philosophy. He's done graduate work in philosophy and cinema studies and taught these subjects at Queens College and other institutions for many years.

Richard Foreman Theater Credits:
Vertical Mobility: Performer
Pandering to the Masses: A Misrepresentation: Performer
Rhoda in Potatoland: Performer

CHARLOTTA MOHLIN: Born in Sweden and studied acting at The Lee Strasberg Theatre Institute, New York. She acted in the feature *Sweet Land* starring Alan Cumming. She met producer and writer David Milch who cast her in two of his HBO pilots. Other roles include *True Blood*, an independent film, Marvel's *Agents of SHIELD*, and Showtime's series *Kidding* (starring Jim Carrey). She played one of the leads in a full motion video game called *Immortality* for which she was nominated for a BAFTA in 2023.

Richard Foreman Theater Credits:
The Gods Are Pounding My Head (AKA Lumberjack Messiah): Performer

KEN NINTZEL's performance (creation, design, and direction) highlights include *Opera Queen, Pageant, Lapse, The Rite of Spring, 'Twas*, and *Frances Faye's Folk Song Sing-a-Long*. His installation highlights are *Spacial Gesture, Exploratory Committee*, and *You Are Here*. His work appeared at such venues as Brooklyn Academy of Music, Cal Arts, PS 122, HERE, LMAK Projects, The Whitney Museum, and St Ann's Warehouse. Grants and Fellowships include Creative Capital, The Tides Foundation, The Jim Henson Foundation, and The Lower Manhattan Cultural Council.

Richard Foreman Theater Credits:
I've Got the Shakes: Stage manager
The Universe: Stage manager
Permanent Brain Damage: Stage Manager and Prop Construction

Benita Canova: Stage Manager and Prop Construction
Paradise Hotel: Stage Manager and Prop Construction

JOHN OGLEVEE: Performing artist, researcher and educator, focusing on the art of Noh. His research explores Noh's evolution and international influence. He is a founding member of the performance collective Theatre Nohgaku. He has appeared in numerous TV commercials, music videos, radio, and promotional videos in Japan. He was a founding member of the New York performance group GAle GAtes et al. with Michael Counts and Michelle Stern in 1995. He holds a BFA in acting from New York University's Tisch School of the Arts, and an MFA in Asian Performance from the University of Hawaii.

Richard Foreman Theater Credits:
Pearls for Pigs: Performer

FULYA PEKER is a New York and Istanbul based performance/ theater artist and educator. She has performed in works by John Zorn, Robert Ashley, Katsura Kan, David Michalek, and Object Collection. She is the founder and artistic director of Katharsis Performance Project. Peker holds a BA in Theater from H.U. Ankara State Conservatory and an MA in Theater, Literature, History and Criticism from Brooklyn College/CUNY. Her literary translations, articles on experimental theater, and poems have been published both in Turkey and in the USA. Currently, she teaches at Istanbul Bilgi University as Faculty of Communication, and continues to present performances and workshops internationally. https://www.fulyapeker.com.

Richard Foreman Theater Credits:
Wake Up Mr. Sleepy! Your Unconscious Mind Is Dead!: Production intern
Deep Trance Behavior in Potatoland: Performer
Astronome: A Night at the Opera: Performer
Bridge Project film: Performer

BRENDAN REGIMBAL*: Founding member of the Incubator Arts Project that occupied the theater in St. Mark's Church after the Ontological-Hysteric Theater from 2009 until 2013. He was Director of Production and Operations at Lenfest Center for the Arts at Columbia University's School of the Arts from 2017 to 2023.

Richard Foreman Theater Credits:
The Gods Are Pounding My Head (AKA Lumberjack Messiah): Production intern
Wake Up Mr. Sleepy! Your Unconscious Mind Is Dead!: Stage manager
Deep Trance Behavior in Potatoland: Stage manager
Astronome: A Night at the Opera: Stage manager
Idiot Savant: Assistant director

STEPHANIE SILVER While living in New York City for eight years Stephanie performed extensively with poet/playwright/director Fiona Templeton, among others. She moved back to her hometown of L.A. where she got married, had two children and mostly acts in national commercials. She has a BFA from Syracuse University.

Richard Foreman Theater Credits:
The Gods Are Pounding My Head (AKA Lumberjack Messiah): Performer
Zomboid!: Performer
Wake Up Mr. Sleepy! Your Unconscious Mind Is Dead!: Performer

SOPHIA SKILES: New York City-based theater actor and teacher. She has performed in productions directed by Michael Kahn, May Adrales, Chay Yew, Ralph Peña, Andrei Serban, Mary Zimmerman, David Herskovits, among others. An experienced educator, Sophia has taught theater at Mount Holyoke College, SUNY Ulster, and SUNY Purchase. Sophia was a lead organizer for the Obie Award-winning Theaters Against War (THAW). She has a BS in Performance Studies from Northwestern University and an MFA in Acting from Columbia University. www.sophiaskiles.com.

Richard Foreman Theater Credits:
Bad Boy Nietzsche: Production intern
Now That Communism Is Dead, My Life Feels Empty: Performer

JAY SMITH: Actor based in New York City. He has worked with Richard Maxwell/New York City Players, Elevator Repair Service, The Talking Band, Clubbed Thumb, Christina Masciotti, and lots more.

Richard Foreman Theater Credits:
Paradise Hotel: Performer
Now That Communism Is Dead My Life Feels Empty: Performer
King Cowboy Rufus Rules the Universe: Performer
The Gods Are Pounding My Head (AKA Lumberjack Messiah): Performer

T. RYDER SMITH is an American actor, based in New York City. https://trydersmith.org/.

Richard Foreman Theater Credits:
King Cowboy Rufus Rules the Universe: Performer
The Gods Are Pounding My Head (AKA Lumberjack Messiah): Performer

MIKE TAYLOR writes, directs, and produces video, audio, theater, and art installations. Taylor's theater and multimedia shows in New York City include *not knowing* and *If I Were You* at The Kitchen; *The Sadness of Others* and *Not Dead Yet* at La MaMa; *no lies* at PS 122; and *Pegleg! Or, The Treacherous Journey 'Round The Horn* at Little Theatre @ TONIC. Her video work was screened at The Whitney as part of a series by and about DanceNoise. A book based on her play *not knowing* is published by Ugly Duckling Presse in their Emergency Playscripts series. Her ongoing project is a random-access dream collection at artasexperience.net.

Richard Foreman Theater Credits:
Symphony of Rats: Technical crew
Lava: Technical director
Eddie Goes to Poetry City, Part 2: Technical director
My Head Was a Sledgehammer: Technical director and Props

JAMES URBANIAK originated the title role in Will Eno's solo play *Thom Pain (based on nothing)* (Drama Desk nomination for performance). Other work at Playwrights Horizons, Manhattan Class Company, the Vineyard, Lincoln Center, and extensive work downtown with such companies as Target Margin, Elevator Repair Service, Clubbed Thumb, and Arden Party. TV credits include Hulu's *Difficult People*, Comedy Central's *Review*, AMC's *Lodge 49*, and Adult Swim's *The Venture Bros*. Films include *American Splendor*, *Wonderstruck*, *Tesla*, and *Henry Fool*. With co-writer Brie Williams he created the scripted podcasts "Getting On With James Urbaniak," "A Night Called Tomorrow," and "I Will Never Lie to You."

Richard Foreman Theater Credits:
The Universe: Performer (Obie Award for acting)

COLLEEN WERTHMANN is a grizzled veteran of New York's experimental and off-Broadway theater communities. She was a founding member of Elevator Repair Service and The Civilians, and created three solo shows downtown before working at places like Playwrights Horizons and the Public. Through a bizarre chain of life circumstances, Colleen eventually became an Emmy-nominated comedy writer, whose credits include *The Daily Show* with Trevor Noah, *The Nightly Show* with Larry Wilmore, The Academy Awards, Comedy Central Roasts, The White House Correspondents' Dinner, and the Mark Twain Prize.

Richard Foreman Theater Credits:
The Mind King: Performer

PATRICIA YBARRA: Professor of Theater Arts and Performance Studies at Brown University. She is the author of *Performing Conquest: Five Centuries of Theater, History and Identity in Tlaxcala, Mexico* (Michigan, 2009), co-editor with Lara Nielsen of *Neoliberalism and Global Theatres: Performance Permutations* (Palgrave Macmillan, 2012; paperback 2015), and *Latinx Theater in Times of Neoliberalism* (Northwestern University Press, 2018). She is working on a digital project about queer Iranian American director Reza Abdoh's *Father Was a Peculiar Man* and a monograph, *Theatrical Retrospeculation: Reza Abdoh's Queer Theory* (University of Michigan Press).

Richard Foreman Theater Credits:
The Universe: Production intern
Maria del Bosco: Administrator

Appendix A
Richard Foreman Plays Featuring Contributors and Interviewees

(Original works are by Richard Foreman unless otherwise noted.)

Vertical Mobility (1974)
Pandering to the Masses: A Misrepresentation (1975)
Rhoda in Potatoland (1975–6)
I've Got the Shakes (1977)
Café Amérique (Paris 1981)
Faust ou la Fête électrique by Gertrude Stein (Paris 1982)
Three Acts of Recognition by Botho Strauss ("Trilogy") (1982)
Miss Universal Happiness (1985)
The Birth of a Poet by Kathy Acker (1985)
The Cure (1986)
Film Is Evil/Radio Is Good (1987)
Symphony of Rats (1988)
City of Amateurs (American Repertory Theater, 1988)
What Did He See? (1988)
Where's Dick (Houston Grand Opera, 1989) Composed by
    Steward Wallace, libretto by Michael Korie
Lava (1990)
Woyzeck by Georg Buchner (1990)
Eddie Goes to Poetry City, Part 1 (1990)
Eddie Goes to Poetry City, Part 2 (1991)
The Mind King (1992)

Samuel's Major Problems (1993)
My Head Was a Sledgehammer (1994)
I've Got the Shakes (1995)
The Universe (1995–6)
Pearls for Pigs (1997)
Permanent Brain Damage (1996–7)
Benita Canova (Gnostic Eroticism) (1998)
Paradise Hotel (AKA Hotel Fuck) (1999)
Bad Boy Nietzsche (2000)
Now That Communism Is Dead My Life Feels Empty (2001)
Maria del Bosco (2002)
Panic! (How to be Happy!) (2003)
King Cowboy Rufus Rules the Universe (2004)
The Gods Are Pounding My Head (AKA Lumberjack Messiah)
    (2005)
Zomboid! (2006)
Wake Up Mr. Sleepy! Your Unconscious Mind Is Dead! (2007)
Deep Trance Behavior in Potatoland (2008)
Idiot Savant (2009)
Astronome: A Night at the Opera (2009)

OTHER RICHARD FOREMAN PLAYS NOTED IN THE BOOK

Angel Face (1968)
Dr. Selavy's Magic Theater (1972)
Hotel for Criminals (1974)
Pain(t) (1974)
Penguin Touquet (1981)
Dr. Selavy's Magic Theater (1984)
Supreme Beings (2002)
Old-Fashioned Prostitutes (A True-Romance) (2013)

VARIOUS ABBREVIATIONS OF PLAY TITLES

Dr. Selavy (1972 and 1984)

Pandering to the Masses (1975)

Potatoland (1975-6)
Rhoda (1975-6)

Samuel (1993)

Sledgehammer (1994)

Benita Canova (1998)

Maria (2002)

Panic! (2003)

King Cowboy Rufus (2004)
Rufus (2004)
Cowboy Rufus (2004)

Gods (2005)
Lumberjack Messiah (2005)
The Gods are Pounding My Head (2005)

Deep Trance Behavior (2008)
Behavior (2008)

Astronome (2009)

Old-Fashioned Prostitutes (2013)

Acknowledgments

Thanks to Shannon Sindelar for conceptualizing the project with me and connecting me to the right people. Ryan Holsopple, Patricia Ybarra, and Robert Cucuzza directed me to works of oral history to study for content and structure. Heather Flaherty had the lit. industry expertise and gave me the invaluable help of writing a query letter and book proposal. My agents Ewan and Philip Turner and editor Chris Chappell were outstanding to work with for so many reasons but especially thanks to their superb edits and familiarity with New York theater. I greatly appreciated the many creative teams at Bloomsbury and those I interfaced with most: Chris Chappell, Emily Burr, and Barbara Claire. T. Ryder Smith, Evan Cabnet, Walter Raubicheck, Damon Kiely, Frank Boudreaux, David Cote, Danuta Lipinska, Karen Cahillane, Jay Sanders, Charles Bernstein, Lance Scott Walker, and Tony Torn allowed me to consult them about publishing and their ideas for improving the book. Thanks to Robert Cucuzza for reading an early draft in its entirety and inviting his contacts to contribute to the book. Thanks to Theresa Buchheister for sharing their impressive network to include the marvelous Oriana Leckert. I am indebted to Maura Adams for her detailed edits and guidance in shaping thematic sections over the course of a year! Thanks to Julie Squires for astute and candid feedback about the writing. Esa Nickle and

Jay Sanders went above and beyond to help me access Paula Court's photography. Mimi Johnson at Performing Artservices Inc. was a huge help in obtaining additional photos. The visual art in this book adds so much thanks to Paula Court, Tina Barney, T. Ryder Smith, and John Kazanjian. It is an honor to have prefatory material in the book from Helen Shaw and Jay Sanders. Endorsers generously took the time to read and comment: F. Murray Abraham, Charles Bernstein, Eric Bogosian, Willem Dafoe, Sara Farrington, Marie Losier, Mark Russell, Tina Satter, and Neal Swettenham. Thanks to Helen Shaw for the opportunity to announce the publication of the book and moderate the actors' panel at the October 6, 2024, Richard Foreman reunion at NYU Skirball. Thanks to Margaret Champagne and Mahalia Cohen for always making it feel like NY is one of my homes while I'm doing this work. I am so lucky to have found Foreman community in Tokyo with the talented theater professionals Mei Usui and John Oglevee. I owe nearly all of my New York theater and film acting opportunities, and the lasting contentment that comes with that, to my mentor D.J. Mendel. Thanks to all of my family for championing me in my pursuits. I'm grateful to my husband, Drew, for believing in this endeavor, supporting me, reading sections (and laughing out loud), and smartly suggesting major structural shifts. Thanks to Richard Foreman for supporting this project, doing four interviews with me, and providing the artistic experience I/we value so much.

Notes

Foreword

1 Richard Foreman, "The Carrot and the Stick," *October*, 1 (Spring 1976): 22–31.

2 Kate Davy, "Kate Manheim as Foreman's Rhoda," *TDR: The Drama Review* 20, no. 3 (September 1976): 37–50.

3 Richard Foreman, "A Conversation with Richard Foreman," by Charles Bernstein. *TDR: The Drama Review* 36, no. 3 (Fall 1992): 103–30.

Foreman 101

1 "About Us," Ontological-Hysteric Theater (R. Foreman), http://www .ontological.com/history.html (accessed August 15, 2024).

2 David Savran, *Breaking the Rules: The Wooster Group* (New York: Theatre Communications Group; Reprint ed., January 1, 1993), 33–5.

3 Ten Obie awards for sustained excellence, directing, and best play of the year; a MacArthur "Genius Grant" Fellowship; literature award from the American Academy and Institute of Arts and Letters; a "Lifetime Achievement in the Theater" award from the National Endowment

for the Arts; the PEN Club Master American Dramatist Award; and Officer of the Order of Arts and Letters of France. Richard Foreman, "Ontological-Hysteric Theater (R. Foreman)," http://www.ontological.com/biography.html (accessed August 15, 2024).

4 I use "our" and "we" throughout the book to help describe the experience because I was a performer in his show in 2004 (see my bio on page 284).

5 The recording project was performed with Willem Dafoe and recorded by Andrew Lampert and Jennifer Krasinski (also see Foreman's 2025 book *No Title* edited by Lampert and Christine Burgin, with an introduction by Krasinski).

6 Richard Foreman, "Penn Sound: Center for Programs in Contemporary Writing at the University of Pennsylvania," writing.upenn.edu/pennsound/x/Foreman.php (accessed August 15, 2024); "Writings, Sounds, & Film," Richard Foreman, writing.upenn.edu/epc/authors/foreman (accessed August 15, 2024).

7 Steven Simmons, "Rhoda in Potatoland," The online edition of *Artforum International Magazine*, March 1, 1976, https://www.artforum.com/print/197603/rhoda-in-potatoland-38012.

8 David Sterritt, "'I've Got the Shakes' Is Richard Foreman at His Best," *The Christian Science Monitor*, January 23, 1994, https://www.csmonitor.com/1994/0123/23132.html.

9 Mel Gussow, "Stage: 'Miss Universal'," *The New York Times*, May 30, 1985, https://www.nytimes.com/1985/05/30/theater/stage-miss-universal.html.

10 Mel Gussow, "Stage: 'Film Is Evil: Radio Is Good'," *The New York Times*, May 5, 1987, https://www.nytimes.com/1987/05/05/theater/stage-film-is-evil-radio-is-good.html.

11 Diane Solway, "Richard Foreman: 'I Want People to Have Fun'," *The New York Times*, January 3, 1988, https://www.nytimes.com/1988/01/03/arts/richard-foreman-i-want-people-to-have-fun.html.

12 Hilton Als, "The Big Roundup: Richard Foreman Takes on the Ghosts of Imperialism," *The New Yorker*, January 19, 2004, https://www.newyorker.com/magazine/2004/01/26/the-big-roundup-2.

13 Ben Brantley, "The Difference between Sex and Sexy," *The New York Times*, January 27, 1999, https://www.nytimes.com/1999/01/27/theater/ theater-review-the-difference-between-sex-and-sexy.html.

14 Robert Simonson, "Richard Foreman's Bad Boy Nietzsche Emerges, Jan. 27-April 30," *Playbill*, January 27, 2000, https://www.playbill.com/article/ richard-foremans-bad-boy-nietzsche-emerges-jan-27-april-30-com-86721.

15 Jonathan Kalb, "The Maddness of King Rufus," *Hot Reviews* (Hunter Department of Theater Online Reviews), 2004, http://www.hotreview.org /articles/madnessofking.htm.

16 Stella Gorlin, "Richard Foreman's Bittersweet Prophecy," *The Village Voice's University Wits* (The Village Voice), May 10, 2017, https://www .villagevoice.com/2005/02/08/university-wits/.

17 Les Gutman, "Zomboid! (Film/Performance Project #1), a CurtainUp Review," *CurtainUp*, 2006, http://www.curtainup.com/zomboid.html.

18 *Unbalancing Acts: Foundations for a Theater* was published in 1993 by Theatre Communications Group and is by Richard Foreman and edited by Ken Jordan. It includes more than fifty pages of essays on Foreman's theater process and aesthetic, followed by five of his plays. This book, as well as Neal Swettenham's *Richard Foreman: An American (Partly) in Paris* (London and New York: Routledge 2017) provides excellent descriptions of Foreman's theater-making and philosophy.

Interviews with Foreman

1 Only a tentative title at the time.

Working with the Ontological-Hysteric Theater

1 Bruce Weber, "Jonas Mekas, 'Godfather' of American Avant-Garde Film, Is Dead at 96," *The New York Times*, January 23, 2019, https://www .nytimes.com/2019/01/23/obituaries/jonas-mekas-dead.html

FINDING FOREMAN

1   The Wooster Group produced Symphony of Rats again in 2024.

ROLES

1   Michael Feingold, "Shanghaied Gestures: Two New Shows Explore the Fun of What's Been Seen Before," *The Village Voice*, January 21, 2003, Theater.

Index